11⁴⁰

We've Got

The Life and Times of America's Greatest Cheerleading Team

James T. McElroy

Simon & Schuster

Simon & Schuster
Rockefeller Center
1230 Avenue of the Americas
New York, NY 10020

Designed by Sam Potts

Manufactured in the United States of America

1 3 5 7 9 10 8 6 4 2

Library of Congress
Cataloging-in-Publication Data

McElroy, James T.
We've got spirit: the life and times of
America's greatest cheerleading team/James T. McElroy.
p.   cm.
1. Cheerleading—United States.
2. Greenup County High School (Greenup, Ky.) I. Title.
LB3635.M334 1999
791.6'4'09769293—dc21   98-37655 CIP

ISBN 0-684-84967-4

Contents

Kings Island

Regionals

Nationals 'Ninety-Eight

For Peyton

Nationals

'Ninety-Seven

Chapter One

Cheer to Win

Shawnda Bates sprints down the parking lot outside Disney/MGM Studios. With arms raised, her palms scraping the cloudy Orlando sky, Shawnda leaps headlong into the air. She shoves off the pavement with her hands and lands on her feet, facing in the opposite direction. Then she hurls herself backward, uses her hands to bounce off the blacktop, flips over, springs off her feet, tucks her knees into her chest while spinning upside down in the air, and finishes with a *clack* of sneakers against blacktop.

Hands on hips, deeply breathing the morning air, Shawnda, a lanky seventeen-year-old high school senior, walks back across the parking lot to the end of the line of Greenup County High School cheerleaders. There she stands, slightly hunched, her head cocked forward, her hands still on her hips, her knees locked, her feet shoulder width apart, and watches her teammates whip their bodies across the asphalt.

Shawnda's tall for a cheerleader, about five feet, nine inches. With her long arms and broad shoulders, she stands out from the other girls with their compact, Kerri Strug–like bodies. She's got brown, shoulder-length hair and, like the other Greenup County girls, she holds it up and out of her face with a white bow clip. Her face is covered with a heavy cream foundation, accented by blush, bright red lipstick, eyeliner, and a thick coat of mascara. Over a white nylon turtleneck, Shawnda wears a yellow halter top with the letters "GCHS" inscribed in green. To complete the outfit, she has on white jogging shorts, white socks, and white tennis shoes. Her tennis shoes are not sufficiently white, however, for Greenup's upcoming competition performance, nor are her shorts sufficiently femi-nine. Inside her green monogrammed gym bag, Shawnda, like all of her teammates, has a new pair of white shoes, which she will change into just before it's time to take the cheerleading stage. Also in her gym bag, Shawnda keeps her yellow-and-green cheerleading skirt, carefully folded, with masking tape holding the pleats perfectly in place.

When Shawnda and the rest of the Greenup County cheerleaders com-pete, they will run and tumble on a special foam mat. But Greenup County High School back in northeastern Kentucky doesn't own any such mat. Shawnda's used to tumbling on hard surfaces like this Disney World park-ing lot because she does most of her tumbling on her school's hardwood gym floor and on the paved track that winds around the football field.

I ask Shawnda if she ever falls when flipping across asphalt like this, without a mat, without pads. Realizing that I've been watching her, Shawnda rocks her shoulders back, arches her chest forward, and tilts her head sideways, flipping her hair across her shoulder.

"Oh sure," she says, flashing a coy smile and batting her eyelashes. "You aren't perfect all the time."

Greenup County cheerleading coach Candy Berry tells her girls to halt their warm-ups. It's picture time.

The Greenup girls take their skirts out of their gym bags and gingerly pull off the masking tape holding the pleats. Then they slide the skirts up their legs and over their shorts. After that, they demurely slide their shorts down from under their skirts, not bending over any more than they have to.

Soon they're properly dressed. The photographer assembles them in front of a big sky-blue Disney World sign, peers at them from behind his camera, and shifts them about till they're posed just right.

He never has to say, "Smile!" The cheerleaders have that taken care of. They can smile sweetly and naturally whenever the need arises.

Before the photographer can snap the team picture, however, the cheerleaders from Boyd County, Kentucky, walk by. At once, the Greenup girls stop smiling, turn, and look.

Greenup County sprawls across the northeastern corner of Kentucky, amid the rolling Appalachian Mountains, beside the muddy Ohio River. To the north sits Portsmouth, Ohio. To the east, Ironton, Ohio, and Huntington, West Virginia. And to the south, Boyd County, Kentucky.

Boyd is Greenup's rival in everything: football, basketball, steel production, and cheerleading. Boyd County High School won last year's national cheerleading championship, while Greenup settled for third.

The Boyd cheerleaders have noticed the Greenup cheerleaders now, and they watch the Greenup team pose for their photograph. Afterward, the Greenup and Boyd girls mingle. They smile and chitchat. Then they hug good-bye and wish one another good luck in the upcoming preliminary round.

Once the Boyd girls move on, the Greenup cheerleaders go back to their worrying and pacing, worrying and stretching, worrying and hair-fiddling. The team's three male assistant coaches worry along with them. Randy Peffer, a trim, dark-haired, slightly balding math teacher at Greenup High—and a former cheerleader from the University of Kentucky—walks back and forth, looking down at the ground, his hands clasped behind his back. Tom Pack, Greenup's short, stocky, dark-complected gymnastics expert, works with the girl with the weakest back tuck, Amanda Pennington, a senior.

Then there's Hank Light, Greenup's tall, muscular choreographer. He stands, knees locked, arms folded, and asks five girls to perform a particular stunt again and again. Light began working with Greenup cheerleading when he was nineteen. Now, at twenty-six years old, he's still the youngest of the Greenup coaches, but has more coaching experience than all but head coach Candy Berry.

Coach Berry, looser than her assistants, leans back on a bench and needles her girls for "stressing" so much.

"Look at Aubrey," she says, pointing out Aubrey Warnock, a sophomore with short blond hair and wide shoulders. "She's stressing." Berry pauses. "I've had two of her aunts in the program."

Short, stout, and in her mid-forties, with close-cropped hair dyed black, Berry talks—on the few occasions when she does talk—in loud, choppy sentences, much like the chants she teaches her cheerleaders to perform.

I sit down beside Berry and ask her how many teams she's coached to a national championship during her twenty years with Greenup High cheerleading. "Eight," she says immediately, then begins to laugh. "Did I just tell you eight?" she says. "I just told him we've won eight championships," she bellows at Coach Peffer. "That's so funny." Berry lowers her voice. "We've won seven national championships. We'll have won eight after [the championship finals] tomorrow night."

An amazing motivator, Berry is feared and loved and worshiped, like a god. Her girls will do anything for her, and they seem to gain strength and resolve by being near her, following her commands. As Berry has shown year after year, she's the queen of a cheerleading dynasty who can take almost any group of girls and mold them into national champions. She's a female incarnation of Vince Lombardi.

Just a month after Greenup's disappointing third-place finish at the 1996 nationals came the Kentucky state cheerleading championships. Ten seconds into the team's performance, Kristi Click, then a Greenup senior, was finishing a tumbling run when she tore the anterior cruciate ligament in her left knee and crumpled to the floor. Grimacing, Kristi started to get up, but the ruined knee couldn't support the weight. Kristi then tried to crawl off the court. She wanted to get out of the way of her teammates, and she didn't want the judges to see her cry.

Berry jumped up from her courtside seat, ran to Kristi, and, like a medic in a war movie, dragged the girl off the court. At the same time, Berry hollered at Charon Hamilton, another senior on the Greenup varsity, to abandon her usual duties as a tumbler and dancer, and play Kristi's role as a base during the stunts, lifting and throwing Greenup's flyers into the air. Shawnda Bates, also a base, whispered to Charon where to go, what to do, and how to do it, and the Greenup team somehow finished the routine without missing a beat. Afterward, the packed Lexington crowd gave them a standing ovation.

The judges took pity on the Greenup squad and decided not to judge them on the injury-marred performance. Instead, they gave the Greenup cheerleaders five minutes to catch their breath and figure out how to redo the routine without Kristi. In those five minutes, Berry told the team what to change, and how. She praised Charon for stepping in and performing so well—then told her to get out there and do it again. Greenup took second place at the '96 Kentucky state championships, but, as at the '96 nationals, Boyd County again came out on top.

Berry's got everything a good male coach has, but as a woman, she's got something more. She shows tenderness toward her athletes. She compliments them on their hair, on their jewelry. She shows absolute confidence in their abilities. And she never, ever gives up on them. She heaps praise on them when they work hard and make progress. She insists that they can do anything, especially the tumbling runs and stunts that give them trouble. She tells them to ditch their "loser" boyfriends if those boys don't treat her girls right. She cracks the whip when the girls goof off. Her love and support are unconditional. And the Greenup cheerleaders feel it.

After cheering for Greenup County's Russell High School in the late 1960s, Berry learned she was pregnant and quit cheerleading to get married. Berry's boy was born in 1970, and after she graduated from high school that same year, Berry became a full-time mom at eighteen.

In 1973, her former cheerleading coach at Russell High asked Berry if she'd like to return as an assistant coach. And after a couple of years at Russell, she got the job coaching the team at Greenup High. The sort of cheerleading Berry did in high school was much less athletic than what she coaches now. Cheerleading in the sixties consisted of pom-poms, cutesy chants, big smiles, and revealing uniforms. There were no gymnastic tumbling runs. No complicated stunting. Never any injuries. About the most athletic thing sixties cheerleaders ever did was a cartwheel followed by the splits.

Since then, Berry has become an expert on back tucks, whip-backs, full-twist flips, and X-outs. Learning from other high school teams at first, then small-time college teams, and now Division I college teams, Berry has devoured all there is to know about cheerleading: the stunts, the chants, the gymnastics, and the dances. And she passes on what she learns. Every year, high school cheerleading teams throughout the country learn a new cheerleading move—a new flip, a new tumbling run, a more complicated stunt—by watching the Greenup team perform at nationals.

A couple of years ago, Berry taught her girls partner stunts, a more difficult and precarious way to hold girls aloft and display them to the crowd. During a partner stunt, a squad divides into three or more groups of four (three bases and a flyer). Each group of bases lifts their flyer up into the air. The flyers have no one to hold on to for balance. They must simply stand with one foot upon the hands of their three teammates, and stiffen their bodies to keep from wobbling to the side and crashing to the ground.

Group mounts have been around much longer. During a group mount, the team's bases lift up three or more flyers side by side, and the flyers hold on to one another as they rise and hold their poses, making a fall much less likely. Berry learned of partner stunts when top college programs began using them ten years ago. Other high school coaches had never thought of such a thing. But then Berry began putting partner stunts into

Greenup County's routines, and the other coaches had to follow suit to keep their teams competitive.

Ever since she led Greenup County High School to its first four national cheerleading championships, in 1981, '82, '83, and '84, Berry has set the example that the rest of the cheerleading world follows. Every competitive cheerleading coach in the country teaches her girls to emulate the cheerleaders from Greenup County, Kentucky. Like Lombardi, she's become legendary.

Berry has never received much pay for the work she does for Greenup cheerleading. In fact, for the past twelve years, she's received no pay at all. And she has turned down numerous offers, complete with extensive compensation packages, to coach college programs throughout Kentucky and the United States. She does not seek out recognition—in the form of money, awards, or anything else—nor does she enjoy recognition when it is thrust upon her. Berry simply follows her nose, teaching fragile Greenup girls to be tough Greenup women by winning cheerleading championships year after year.

Shawnda Bates is watching her friend and teammate Kasey Dillow lose her mind. Moments ago, Kasey caught her reflection in a turned-off television monitor beside the warm-up tent. Now, she's running her hands through her thick brown hair. But it's tangled.

Frantic, Kasey asks Berry for the Greenup team hairbrush, then kneels down on the asphalt, nervously rubbing her hands together while Shawnda tries to brush her hair.

When Shawnda's done, Kasey stands up, takes the brush, and starts picking at her head.

"Does it look terrible?"

"No, no, it's fine," says Shawnda, using her fingernail to scrape some dried skin off Kasey's upper lip. "It's just fine."

Amanda Pennington takes a break from her back tuck practice to announce that she's too fat for her skirt. That's why she's having trouble with her standing back tuck.

"Gosh, Amanda," Shawnda says, "I wish I was as fat as you."

Sophomore Jessica Newell sits quietly on the blacktop. For the past day and a half, Jessica has had a bad stomach virus and has been unable to keep any food down. She's vomited four times in thirty-six hours.

"The maids came to the hotel and cleaned the room three times with disinfectant," says Berry. The Greenup coaches don't know what Jessica will be able to do today without any calories to burn. They will wait and see how she holds up when the girls run through their routine inside the warm-up tent.

Taking Jessica out of the competition and making do without her is never discussed.

The girls clump together now, near the entrance to the warm-up tent. It's almost their turn to go inside. Four teams are allowed in the tent at once, to use one mat each for exactly four minutes, enough time to run through a routine, then focus on trouble spots.

It's dark, humid, and loud in the tent. As the girls crowd inside, an amplified voice announces through the din of pounding dance music and shrieking cheerleaders, "Greenup County. Mat Two. You have four minutes." The Greenup girls don't respond at first. Lulled by the languid Orlando morning, they blink and stand on their heels.

"Come on, girls! C'mon now!" Berry hollers, herding the girls to their mat. "Get going! C'mon!"

The girls hustle over as Peffer cues a tape in the Greenup team boom box. When the girls settle into position, Peffer hits Play and a generic, mind-numbing dance song bleats out of the speakers.

The recently vomiting Jessica Newell seems okay during her tumbling run.

Then all nineteen members of the Greenup squad do a standing back tuck simultaneously. Even Amanda Pennington hits it.

Cheerleaders from other teams gasp. Berry requires every member of her varsity to learn to do a standing back tuck, an extremely difficult gymnastic move. You start from a standing position, then jump, tuck your knees into your chest, flip over backward, and land on your feet. Many competitive teams have a few girls who can do a standing. But very few have a squad of Greenup's size in which every girl can hit it.

The most difficult move of the routine comes next. Shawnda and two teammates stand side by side and face forward. They jump backward, shove off the mat with their hands, flip over, land on their feet, jump backward, shove off with their hands, flip over, land on their feet, jump, shove, flip once more, then jump backward, really high, and flip over, while spinning 360 degrees. Then they land on their feet, facing forward.

The onlookers gape.

Peffer shuts off the music now, and the Greenup chants begin. On the hands of their bases, four flyers rise up into the air. Each flyer balances on her teammates' hands with one foot and holds her other foot above her head, all the while chanting, "G! C! H! S! GREENUP! IS! THE! BEST!"

The Greenup girls have prepared for this all year. In practice, they would lie on their backs and, with knees locked, lift their legs about six inches off the ground, straining their stomach muscles. Then, while keeping their legs up, they hollered the Greenup chants as loudly as possible.

Shawnda is one of the bases holding up Aubrey Warnock, who loses hold of her foot and doesn't pull it over her head.

Last comes the dance. The girls broaden their smiles as they stomp to the throbbing techno-funk. At one point, the girls stand, spread their legs, slowly move their hands down over their breasts to their crotches to their thighs, then gyrate their hips backward and thrust forward.

Jessica Newell collapses at the end of the routine, and the amplified voice announces, "Two minutes. Two minutes remaining."

As the Greenup coaches gather around her, Jessica lies on her back with her hands over her face. She is very pale. Pack coaxes her off the mat with a water bottle and an ice pack.

"One minute, thirty seconds. One minute, thirty seconds."

Berry barks orders at Shawnda, who rounds up Aubrey and the other bases. They lift Aubrey up over their heads, where Aubrey balances on one foot and tries again to pull her other foot over her head. She can't do it. Shawnda and the others drop her down to the ground.

"Thirty seconds. Thirty seconds please."

Berry directs Shawnda and her partners in the triple back hand-spring–plus–back flip with full twist to give it one more go. With Berry five feet in front of them, the three girls lurch backward. Berry follows, clapping her hands and yelling, "C'mon! C'mon!"

After Shawnda lands safely on her feet, Berry pats her on the back. "All right," the coach says. "You're ready. All right."

The Greenup squad exits the tent and heads over to the Indiana Jones Super Stunt Spectacular theater, where they will perform in this morning's preliminary round. There are thirty-one other high school teams from around the country competing against Greenup. Ten will be chosen for to-morrow night's finals.

Berry pulls the sick Jessica Newell aside and tells her to water down her tumbling run. Normally, Jessica would do a round-off with two whip-backs. A whip-back is a straight-legged back flip, like a back handspring except you don't use your hands to push off midway through. Berry wants Jessica to do a round-off to a back handspring to a back tuck instead.

As the girls come closer to the theater, they grow quiet. They can hear the crowd now, and that thumping dance music. Then they hear the often sampled cheerleading tag line booming from the theater's speakers: "It ain't over till the fat lady sings."

Berry lets out a wail—"AAAAAAHHH!"—and laughs. Her tense cheerleaders manage to smile; a few giggle.

Near the line of cheer squads waiting to perform, a dusty mat lies on the asphalt, to be used for last-minute practice. Berry tells Aubrey to try her heel stretch. So Shawnda and company hoist her up, but again, Aubrey fails to hold the foot above her head.

"You've got to hold it," says Berry. "You're not stretched. You're not stretched, see? Girls, get her stretched."

Berry walks away. Aubrey starts to cry.

"You're okay," Shawnda says. Shawnda uses the broad side of her finger to catch Aubrey's tears before they run down her face and streak her makeup.

Aubrey takes a deep breath and sucks back her tears. Then she lies down with her back on the asphalt while Shawnda and the other bases stretch, rub down, and pound both sides of her left thigh.

Aubrey tries the heel stretch again. This time, she holds it, but looks shaky. Her teammates go to work on her again, stretching, rubbing, pounding.

The rest of the Greenup team unpacks their competition shoes.

Berry watches as Aubrey tries the heel stretch once more. Again she holds it, and looks less shaky.

"Okay," Berry says, "put on your shoes."

Once all the cheerleaders are in their new white shoes, Berry tells the girls to sit down together on the blacktop and close their eyes.

"Visualize, girls, visualize," Berry says while standing over them. "One, two, three, four, five, six, seven, eight. One, two, three . . ."

Berry counts to eight again and again. The girls, heads bowed, eyes closed, envision each moment of their routine. When the chant portion comes up, Berry stops counting, and in whispers, their heads still bowed, their eyes still closed, the girls chant. "Funkytown" ("Won't you take me to funkytown?") blasts behind them.

"g. c. h. s. greenup. is. the. best."

Afterward, many of the girls hug, hold hands.

"It was perfect," Shawnda says, smiling. Then she directs Aubrey to lie back on the pavement and stretch her thigh some more.

"No stressing here," says Berry. "No stressing here."

Most of the Greenup girls get in line behind three other teams. It shouldn't be long now.

Amanda Pennington tries her standing back tuck again. Aubrey practices her heel stretch while Berry watches.

"Don't bend your leg," says Berry. "Don't even think about it."

Aubrey's foot slips out of her hand; she falls.

Jess Madden, a senior, squats down, propping her head up with her hands. Coach Light walks behind her and whacks her on the butt with a rolled-up competition program.

"Whuuuut?" Jess drawls as she stands up.

"What's wrong?" asks Light.

"I'm nervous."

"Here," Light says, "bite my arm."

Jess looks up at Light's face. Then she takes his forearm in her hands and chomps down.

"Feel better?"

"Yeah," Jess says, momentarily relaxed.

Light kisses Jess on the cheek, and whacks her on the butt again.

With one more team to go before the Greenup girls perform, Shawnda gets the team lipstick from Berry. A handful of girls crowd around Shawnda and pucker up. The crowd roars as the team ahead of Greenup enters the theater.

All nineteen cheerleaders get in a circle, put their arms around each other, and chant the Lord's Prayer while dance music blares, cheerleaders shriek, and the audience whoops. With her wide wing span, Shawnda holds nearly half the Greenup huddle in her arms.

"Our Father—"

"WhoooOOOO!"

"One, two, three, four, get your booty on the floor!"

"—hallowed be Thy name. Thy kingdom come, Thy will be done, on earth—"

"Gotta gotta get up a' get down, gotta gotta get up—"

"—this day, our daily bread, and forgive us—"

"WHEN WE SAY GO! YOU SAY FIGHT!"
"—as we forgive those who trespass—"
"GO!"
"FIGHT!"
"—us not into temptation, but deliver us from—"
"R-E-S-P-E-C-T, find out what it means to—"
"—for You are the—"
"Sock it to me, sock it to me, sock it to me, sock it to me—"
"Amen."

Chapter Two

She's a Cheerleader at Greenup!

When she began high school, Shawnda Bates, already an accomplished gymnast, earned one of only two freshmen spots on Greenup High's varsity cheerleading team. In that year, 1994, Greenup last won the varsity national championship in Orlando. A week before traveling down to Orlando for the '97 nationals, Shawnda tries to remember winning the national cheerleading championship as a freshman. She took that '94 title for granted, she says. She didn't feel as if she'd won it, so much as Greenup County High School cheerleading had won it—again. Shawnda had heard so much about Greenup High's cheerleading success that, as far as she knew, Greenup won the national cheerleading championship every year. Of course they would win it her freshman year. With or without young Shawnda Bates.

Then came sophomore year. That January, with less than three weeks before the '95 nationals, Shawnda and the rest of the varsity were practicing in the Greenup High gym. One stunt called for Shawnda, along with two other teammates, to lift sophomore Jess Madden high into the air. Jess would balance her right foot on her teammates' hands and pull her left foot over her head, pressing her left knee against her cheek. As Jess pulled that foot above her head, there was a pop. Shawnda and the others let Jess down, and she collapsed to the hardwood floor. She'd torn the anterior cruciate ligament in her left knee.

A torn ACL is one of the most dreaded casualties in sports. It's the

same injury that hobbled New York Knicks swingman Bernard King in the early eighties and Philadelphia Eagles quarterback Randall Cunningham in the early nineties.

To repair the ligament, Jess had to undergo extensive surgery. After that, she'd put in six hours of rehab exercise every week for over six months before she could rejoin the cheerleading team. And in the meantime, someone had to replace Jess to keep Greenup's national title hopes alive. Two weeks before the scheduled trip to Orlando, Jerri Floyd, a hard-nosed sophomore with light brown shoulder-length hair, who had been cheering with the Greenup JV, was asked to come to a varsity practice and perform Jess's role during run-throughs of the varsity routine. Jerri did what she was told. Afterward, the Greenup coaches told Jerri that she would now be cheering for the varsity at nationals.

According to Shawnda, it was very difficult for Jerri to make the jump from JV to varsity in just two weeks. And it was also difficult for Shawnda to relearn the routine with a new flyer. The Universal Cheerleading Association dictates that a competitive cheerleading routine can run no longer than two minutes, fifteen seconds. It's a whirlwind of flipping, dancing, tumbling, chanting, and stunting. There's no time to think about what comes next. Normally, the Greenup varsity has practiced its nationals routine so much, for so long, that when nationals rolls around, each girl can perform her part blindfolded. Even after the Greenup team arrived in Orlando, just three days before the '95 championship, Shawnda was still teaching Jerri which moves came when.

There was no preliminary round at nationals that year, so the Greenup cheerleaders had to go out and do it once, may the best girls win.

At the beginning of the routine, Shawnda, the team's marquee tumbler, would turn a round-off, to a back handspring, to a back flip with a full twist, to a back flip with a tuck. In practices back in Kentucky, Shawnda had never so much as stumbled while completing this tortuous tumbling pass. But during the team's warm-up before the '95 nationals, she tripped herself up and fell at the end of the run. She tried again and hit it during that warm-up, but she kept seeing that first fall running in slow motion through her head.

"I was scared," Shawnda remembers. "Every time you compete after you fall like that, every time you get ready to go on, that's in the back of your mind, like, 'I hope that doesn't happen again.' I'd done that so many times too. The thing that you think is not going to mess up: it is."

During the competition, in front of 2,000 screaming Disney World tourists, ESPN cameras, and the twelve UCA judges, Shawnda got a little too high in the air during the back flip with the full twist, and her balance was slightly off when she started the back flip with the tuck. She landed on her head.

"I kinda had a fall on my face," says Shawnda, smiling down at her hands.

Later, Shawnda lifted Jerri during the same stunt in which Jess had shattered her knee. Shawnda still felt dizzy and disoriented from the blow to her head. She doesn't remember exactly how Jerri fell.

Greenup finished twenty-first at the '95 nationals, the only national cheerleading competition in which a Greenup team finished worse than fifth.

Shawnda has wanted to be a cheerleader since she was four years old. And not just any cheerleader: a cheerleader for Greenup County High School. She grew up in a one-story, blue-nylon-sided house along a winding mountain road, and she didn't have much to do—except to play with her *Wizard of Oz* dolls in her room, or ride her bike in circles on her family's front lawn. The nearest kids, other than her two brothers, lived miles away.

The year Shawnda celebrated her fourth birthday, the cheerleaders from Greenup County High School won their fourth consecutive national title, and Charles Kuralt featured them on his nightly "On the Road" segment for CBS News. Shawnda worshiped the girls on those Greenup cheer squads of the early 1980s. They were pretty, polite, sweet, sexy, and strong. They were adored throughout the county. They were everything Shawnda wanted to be.

That year, Shawnda began her gymnastic training. Three days a week, either her mom (a teacher's assistant and cheerleading coach at Greenup's Wurtland Middle School) or her dad (a diesel mechanic working at a Walker Machinery plant out in Huntington, West Virginia) would drive their little girl through the mountains, over the Ohio River, to a private gym in Ironton, Ohio. Those gymnastics lessons were expensive, $10 to $20 an hour. But Shawnda loved them, and her parents made do.

When Shawnda was five, she performed as a cheerleader for the first time, turning cartwheels and round-offs as an honorary member of the

Wurtland Middle cheerleading team. When she was six, she began competing as an individual gymnast and as a member of her gym's tumbling
team. Soon after that, she started tap and modern dance lessons.

When Shawnda was eight, her life got complicated. She grew.

"I really got really tall," Shawnda says, "and I felt kind of weird. Because
all the other ones were on the little bars and I was on the adult bars and
things. It's just harder for the taller girls."

Shawnda might have enjoyed other, traditionally male sports, like basketball or soccer, where her size would have been an asset, but no soccer or
basketball leagues existed for girls in Greenup County. For boys, there was
pee-wee and middle school basketball, pee-wee and middle school football, Little League and pony league baseball. In the 1980s, in a county and
a state obsessed with scholastic sports, no team sports were available for
girls below the high school level. Except cheerleading.

"Ever since I was little," she explains, "I always wanted to cheer at the
high school. I always wanted to be a varsity cheerleader at Greenup.
'Cause that's just the people that you look up to. That's why I like it so
much. 'Cause all the little kids are like, 'She's a cheerleader at Greenup!'
That's the best feeling in the whole world, to have all these little kids look
up to you."

During Shawnda's fifth-grade year, her first at Wurtland Middle
School, she won a spot on a real, organized cheerleading team. In
Greenup County, each of the five middle schools has a cheerleading team
for every grade—from fifth through eighth, with ten to fifteen girls on
each squad. Shawnda continued to compete as a gymnast and tumbler,
and to perform at dance recitals, but she never drew as much attention and
praise from her family, friends, and community as when she put on a short
skirt and a halter top, held pom-poms, wore a brightly colored ribbon in
her hair, and cheered for the boys at Wurtland's basketball and football
games.

Shawnda lives just outside the Greenup High school district, which
sprawls across the northern, mostly unincorporated end of the county.
Technically, she should have attended Russell High, a school drawing
from the county's more developed southern section. However, so that their
daughter could live out her dream, Shawnda's parents requested and received special permission from the Kentucky State Board of Education to
allow Shawnda to go to Greenup High.

Greenup High, traditionally, does not produce the top-quality students that Russell High is known for. And Shawnda might have received a better education at Russell High, but that didn't concern her.

Shawnda and her mother sit across from one another in their living room and explain why Shawnda chose her high school on the basis of its cheerleading excellence. It's a small, neat room with wall-to-wall carpeting, one couch, and one chair. On a wooden bookshelf beside the chair where Shawnda's mother sits, there are six different pictures of Shawnda in her Greenup cheerleading uniform, posing with trophies that are almost as tall as she is. Beyond the living room, there is a small kitchen—big enough for one cook—across from a miniature foyer. Past the kitchen, at the end of the narrow, carpeted hallway, an end table sits outside the door to Shawnda's bedroom. On the end table stands the trophy Shawnda received as a member of Greenup's 1994 national championship team.

Shawnda has a small shrine to *The Wizard of Oz* in her bedroom, underneath a hammock full of stuffed animals that friends and family members have given her for luck before gymnastics and cheerleading competitions. Medals and ribbons and certificates of merit cover the top half of the far wall. Below are two shelves filled to overflowing with trophies.

I ask Shawnda, "According to Coach Berry and the other Greenup coaches, you're the best tumbler on the team, right?"

"Yes," her mom interjects.

"Well . . . not the best," says Shawnda.

"Yes, she is," says her mom.

"Who do you think is the best?" I ask.

Shawnda hedges. "Um . . . I don't know."

"She is," Mrs. Bates says again.

Shawnda smiles and shrugs.

Truth be told, Shawnda knows what a great cheerleader she is, what a great athlete she is.

"I'm not the best," she says, after a moment. "But I'm up there."

When Shawnda walks, she struts like a runway model, holding her head high, moving fast, purposefully swinging her arms, swiveling her hips so that each step falls perfectly in line with the next, terribly aware of the eyes upon her.

She thinks it's "great" that cheerleading has become a sport in its own right, separate from basketball and football. Cheerleaders, she says, have become less concerned with boosting boys' egos, so now they can focus on winning acclaim all for themselves. At competitions, she points out, no other athletes are present, only cheerleaders. Competitive cheerleaders cheer for themselves.

"You can't cheer for other things if you don't have enthusiasm for yourself," Shawnda says, still trying to maintain her modesty.

Does Shawnda mind cheering for the boys at football and basketball games?

"When the crowd is into the ball games, it's fun. If they're not, it's still fun because we have fun with each other on the sidelines. But it's a whole lot more fun when the crowd's yelling with you. I like to cheer at competitions better, though. When you cheer at ball games, there's not the pressure that you feel at competitions. And I think the stress is what helps me.

"A lot of people don't realize how hard we work. I mean, they know that football players have practice, that basketball players have practice. But what they don't realize is that those sports are only a season thing, and we practice all year round. For both seasons. It's just as hard. We work just as hard as they do.

"People sort of think that we think we're better than everybody else. But then when they get to know us, they know that we're just, you know . . . I think they kind of think that we're snobs. Because we don't have time to really, you know, to go out with other people. We don't really have a lot of time. We spend so much time practicing that we don't have time to go out to parties and things like everybody else. They kind of think we're snobs because we're always with each other. But then when they get to know us, they seem to like us, I guess."

As she runs through all this in her head, Shawnda begins to get angry. Her voice rises.

"I mean, we work really hard, and when you have your mind set on things, it's hard to be with other people who aren't in your activity or sport or whatever. I think it's that way with a lot of things. Like when boys play football, during football season they hang out with their football friends. If they play baseball, during baseball season they hang out with their baseball friends."

The boys who play football and basketball at Greenup High often act like overprotective husbands, upset that their wifely cheerleaders are going out and making a name for themselves apart from football, basketball, and boys. Over the years, Greenup's football team has generally performed dismally; Shawnda can remember one year—when her older brother Jason was on the squad—in which Greenup High didn't win a game during the entire season.

As for the basketball team, it has enjoyed some limited success, advancing to the state tournament just twice in the past twenty years.

Meanwhile, the Greenup High cheerleaders keep rolling along winning national championship after national championship. The girls are routinely featured in the *Greenup News-Times* and the *Ashland Independent*, and ESPN broadcasts their performances at nationals every year. All the accolades won by the cheerleaders sometimes get on the nerves of Greenup's boys.

Two years ago, Greenup hired a new head football coach, who's worked hard to turn around Greenup's lousy gridiron tradition. This past season, the football team won its district championship for the first time in nearly fifteen years. But the Greenup cheerleaders didn't cheer for the boys that night. They had a prior engagement in Lexington, Kentucky: their own regional competition. The Greenup girls won first place and easily qualified for 1997's nationals.

Shawnda and the rest of the varsity planned to leave for Lexington early in the morning. In spite of that, she and her teammates stayed up late the night before decorating the football players' individual lockers and their entire locker room, hanging a large, handmade banner over one wall, and posting little notes, cards, and crepe-paper decorations that encouraged the boys with slogans like, "Beat 'em!" "Stomp 'em!" "You're the best!"

Many football players were still miffed at the cheerleaders' absence during their big game. Some footballers were heard saying that their team won the district championship game only because the cheerleaders weren't there to bring them down.

Those slaps at her squad don't much bother Shawnda. She doesn't need the football players—or the basketball players—to cheer for her. She'll do fine cheering for herself.

Shawnda's a good student, and in the future she sees herself as a dentist. ("I just have this fixation with teeth. I don't know why.") She's done her research and found that the University of Louisville has a good predental program. So she plans to go there next year. She hopes to cheer there as well.

Because of her height and accompanying weight, Shawnda can't cheer for most top college cheerleading programs—for instance, the University of Kentucky, the best college cheerleading team in the nation, winner of seven national championships. UK has a coed cheerleading team. The girls in the program are all tiny—no taller than five foot two, no heavier than 110 pounds—and the boys are all enormous. Many are former football linemen, weight lifters, or heavyweight wrestlers. A girl like Shawnda, no matter how strong her cheerleading skills, is too big to be a flyer.

"I don't think it's fair to have the height requirement and the weight requirement and all that," Shawnda laments. "But I know it'd be hard for the guys to throw up the bigger girls. And it would be hard to do what the guys do, 'cause they're stronger and they can hold girls—I know I can't hold girls like they can. It makes me sad. But I can see their reasoning."

The University of Louisville, unlike UK and most Division I college cheerleading teams, sets aside a handful of slots on its team for exceptional tumblers. Shawnda hopes to prove her gymnastic ability to the U of L coaches and earn one of those positions.

It takes three hours to drive west from Greenup to Louisville, Kentucky's biggest city, so Shawnda won't be too far from home if she enrolls there. But most Greenup High kids prefer to stay even closer; they attend Ashland Community College, Marshall University, Morehead State University, or Sewanee, all less than an hour away.

"I kind of want to go somewhere that my friends go. But it doesn't really bother me because I know I'll be able to make friends somehow. That's always a big issue. Everybody's like, 'Where you gonna go to school?' because they all want to go together. But none of my friends are going where I'm going.

"I think it'll be hard to move from this sort of secluded area to Louisville. I mean it's not really a big city, you know, but it's more than I've ever experienced 'cause it's a big place. I think that'll be the biggest difference that I'll experience. Culture shock, probably."

Shawnda has plenty to keep her busy in the meantime. Besides cheerleading, Shawnda has a rather serious relationship going with her boyfriend, Nick Warnock, a sophomore at Ashland Community College and the older brother of cheerleader Aubrey Warnock. Shawnda also has a role in the high school's upcoming production of *Grease,* playing one of the Pink Ladies. And, like any other teenager, Shawnda likes to stay up on weekends with her friends and watch *Saturday Night Live.*

In particular, Shawnda loves the *SNL* cheerleaders, played by Will Ferrell and Cheri Oteri. She thinks they're hilarious. Which is surprising. In their biting parodies of high school cheerleading, Ferrell and Oteri make cheerleaders look like pathetic hangers-on, blithely performing a silly, useless task.

"No, no, they're not making fun of cheerleaders," Shawnda insists. "Remember? They're supposed to've *not* made the *real* cheerleading team. So they're not real cheerleaders, and they want to be cheerleaders so bad, so they go around and cheer like that."

"So they're making fun of wanna-be cheerleaders?"

"Right."

"Not real cheerleaders."

"Right."

Asked if she can imagine her life the past four years without cheerleading, Shawnda thinks a moment, then says, "I can't see myself just sitting at home every day. I'm not that type of person. I've got a really competitive edge." Shawnda thinks some more. "That's a hard question to answer. I may have been a totally different person. Cheerleading sort of helped me build my character. It's kinda helped tell me who I am."

Asked if there might be an aspect of cheerleading that is sexist—the cheering for the boys from the sidelines, the sexually provocative dance moves, the tight, short uniforms—Shawnda wrinkles up her nose, and says "No."

Shawnda's mom says that four years on the Greenup varsity cheerleading team have molded her daughter into a strong young woman, a killer competitor, so how can the sport be sexist? To illustrate her point, Mrs. Bates recalls a time during her daughter's junior year when Shawnda lost her balance while finishing a tumbling pass at the beginning of a competition run-through. Shawnda's hands reached out for the hardwood to break her fall, and her left pinkie got smashed.

"Shawnda finished the whole routine," Mrs. Bates says, struggling to contain her pride. "Crying the whole time, but she finished the whole routine."

Falling on her face at the '95 nationals has been hard to live down. For the past two years, Shawnda has tried to shake the memory, tried to focus on the '94 nationals, when she and the rest of the Greenup varsity won. But

Shawnda says she won't be able to let that fall in '95 go till she wins another championship.

During the '96 nationals, she got her first chance. She had broken her pinkie only a week before, but a doctor put a splint on it and wrapped it with a cloth bandage, and she performed her part of the routine very well, as did the rest of the Greenup team.

Still, Greenup lost. First place went to local rival Boyd County. Shawnda and the others took third.

Shawnda believes the judges favored Boyd because Greenup had won nationals so many times in the past. Shawnda thinks the UCA judges won't give Greenup another championship unless she and her teammates perform perfectly.

"I think they [the judges] expect things of us," Shawnda says. "I think they expect us to be better than really good. Last year, we thought we did really good. And then, we got third. You know, we *were* really good. But we weren't perfect."

Failing to win for two years in a row was hard. In Greenup County, people expect the cheerleaders to finish first. Also, if they're going to lose to anyone, they'd better not lose to Boyd.

Since the recession of the early nineties, when Greenup County's CSX rail yard laid off over 1,600 of its 2,000 workers, and AK Steel bought out the Armco steel mill on the Greenup-Boyd border, eliminating more than 3,500 jobs, it's been hard to find work in either county. That bad situation was made even worse in the past year by layoffs at the Ashland Oil refinery down in Boyd. Amid the poverty and scarcity of good jobs, high school sports give Greenup and Boyd residents something to look forward to and something to be proud of.

"After you win so many times, the whole community just sort of takes it for granted," says Shawnda. "If we don't win, we get, sort of, a hard time. When Boyd County won, we took a lot of flak for that. People said things to us. I don't know. They just say things, you know, like little comments about how Boyd County beat us. We got a hard time."

This year, the Greenup cheerleaders eked out wins over Boyd at two lesser competitions leading up to nationals. And two weeks ago, Greenup hosted Boyd in an interdivisional basketball game. Both cheerleading teams were there, and there was as much tension between cheer teams as between basketball teams. The overflowing Greenup crowd even stayed behind after the game to see their county's cheerleaders perform their nationals routine. To the glee of the Greenup crowd, the Boyd cheerleaders had to stick around, too, and get their noses rubbed in "Go Greenup!" cheers.

Shawnda can't help smiling as she describes the scene. All those Greenup folks yelling and screaming, holding up posters, waving green-and-yellow pennants and pom-poms, the feel of the Boyd team watching them, knowing the Boyd girls were scared, knowing she was a member of the great Greenup County Musketeers cheerleading team—as always, the squad to beat come nationals.

It's good to be the favorite, says Shawnda. It'd be better to be the champion.

Shawnda looks up at the small sitting room's ceiling. With her legs crossed, her mind racing, she leans forward, grasping the air in her hands, and tries to explain the importance of winning this national title.

"People tell you how, you know, how good you are and everything," she says. "But you really want to prove how great you are. And you want to make everyone know that you're the best."

Chapter Three

Perfection

The Greenup High cheerleaders did well enough during the preliminary round to qualify for tonight's finals. Amanda Pennington missed the landing on her standing back tuck, but because of where Berry had put her—in the back left corner of the formation—that was hard for the judges to see. Aubrey Warnock managed to hold her heel-stretch, although Berry criticized her for not smiling a broad cheerleader smile while doing so. "You looked scared to death!" Berry told her.

Shawnda nailed her three handsprings with the full twist–back flip.

Jessica Newell made it through despite her illness, then stumbled off the mat and collapsed. But the judges didn't see that.

It's a bit before seven P.M. now, and the Orlando sun has set. As a cold February wind sweeps over the MGM parking lot, the Greenup cheerleaders practice their tumbling runs on the asphalt, this time in the dark.

The nine other finalists are here too. Boyd County is here. From Memphis, Houston High School is here. They took second place last year, ahead of third-place Greenup. Paul Lawrence Dunbar High School, another Kentucky rival, is here from Lexington. Dunbar won nationals two years ago, the year Shawnda fell on her face and dropped Jerri Floyd. Germantown High School is here, also from Memphis. The Germantown varsity has never won at nationals, but consistently places in the top five. Germantown's JV, however, has taken the champions' trophy three times, including last year, and its feeder school's cheerleaders have won the junior high title four times.

The Greenup girls stand with arms folded, cold in their short shorts.

Looking for something to do, Shawnda takes out her skirt, and peels off the masking tape. Some of her teammates scold her.

"You don't have to put on your skirt," Shawnda tells them. "I'm just putting on mine."

Pretty soon, the rest of the team follows Shawnda's lead. These are brand-new skirts, and the girls have never worn them before. Holly Gillum, a blond, blue-eyed senior, classically pretty, walks up to Candy Berry and turns around so her coach can see her rear.

"Is this too short?" Holly asks. "Does it cover?"

Berry laughs. "No, honey. It's short, all right, but it covers."

The coach checks her watch. "Hey, you girls've got an hour and twenty minutes. You don't need to get those on."

Coach Peffer smiles.

"Candy told them they weren't going to leave the hotel till around six-thirty, six-forty-five," he says. "They were ready at four."

The girls spent part of the day practicing their routine on the grass in front of their Disney World hotel, and waited out the rest sitting in their rooms. If they win tonight's championship, their coaches have promised to let them spend tomorrow at nearby Daytona Beach, rather than flying immediately back to Greenup.

Brooke Meenach, a Greenup sophomore, stands, arms folded. Then she turns.

"Oh, GOD!" she blurts, to no one in particular. "I hate to wait. That's the only thing I hate. I HATE waiting."

Berry has gotten permission to move the team into the heated warm-up tent. In from the cold, the girls will the time to fly. Many cling to stuffed animals brought in their gym bags. Shawnda has a small Big Bird doll. Kasey Dillow holds a little rabbit that wears a tiny Greenup sweater. Jerri Floyd has a large gray elephant. Jess Madden clutches her right leg, then her left leg, then her right leg, and stretches over and over.

Jessica Newell feels much better today. After the prelims, she managed to keep some food down. Now she helps Aubrey loosen up her thigh. Amanda practices her back tuck with assistant coach Pack. Holly asks her teammates if they can see her butt.

"Seriously," she begs, "is it too short?"

Of the ten finalists, Greenup will be the fifth team to compete tonight. Houston High and Germantown High will perform before, Boyd County and Dunbar after. Right now, Houston and Germantown are taking four minutes on the warm-up mats. Once they're done, Greenup and Boyd will get their four minutes.

Berry doesn't want the Greenup girls to watch their rivals, so she gathers them into a huddle.

"It's an easy routine for you guys to do. Just do it. Now's the time. Show 'em. Show 'em the excitement. All right? All right. 'Fear not' on three. One, two, three . . ."

"FEAR NOT!"

When Greenup takes its four minutes on the mat, the girls lack focus and commit a number of sloppy mistakes. Hank Light gets angry. "All right, do it again," he says, interrupting the routine after another missed stunt. "Do it aGAIN!"

The girls try the stunt once more, but are unsettled by Light's anger. Shawnda, scared and confused, inexplicably stops in the middle, and fails to lift Aubrey Warnock.

Light glares at her.

"What are you doing? Keep going. What are you doing?"

Shawnda says nothing.

The amplified voice announces, "Time's up, Greenup and Boyd."

As the Greenup team walks stiffly out of the tent toward the theater, Light seethes.

"What was she doing?" he demands, to no one in particular.

Berry walks in front of Light, then turns to face him and points her finger.

"Shut your mouth," she says.

Light halts. "Who?"

"YOU," Berry growls, and walks away.

For a moment, Light stands where Berry stopped him, watching the Greenup team move away in the dark. Then he catches up with Shawnda and puts his arm around her.

"I'm sorry," he says. "I'm sorry." Shawnda is crying. Light pulls her into him as they walk. "I'm sorry. Never mind me. I'm sorry."

Suddenly, a Disney usher steps out of a shadow and asks, "Which one of you is Shawnda Bates?"

"I am," says Shawnda, carefully wiping the tears away so as not to smudge her eyeliner.

The young man hands her an envelope. "Can I at least see what it says?" he asks. "I've been holding it for an hour."

Shawnda opens the envelope as the rest of the team crowds around. There's a card in the shape of Dorothy's ruby slippers from *The Wizard of Oz*. Shawnda opens it and reads, "Good luck. Love, Mom, Dad, and Shane."

Shane, Shawnda's eight-year-old brother, also made the trip down to Florida with Shawnda's parents.

"My favorite thing in the world is, like, *Wizard of Oz* stuff," Shawnda says, sniffling. "This was just what I needed."

Before the girls join the line of teams waiting to perform, Berry has them get in a circle. Then she takes a tiny felt bag out of her purse. Berry tells each girl to make a silent wish, then jiggle the bag. Inside, there's a small bell.

"When you hear the bell ring," says Berry, "it means an angel has granted your wish."

Berry hands the bag to the girls. Each member of the team closes her eyes, furrows her brow, shakes the bag next to her ear, then hands it to the teammate beside her. What with techno music, cheering, and the crowd's whooping nearby, the girls have a hard time hearing the bell. Some shake the bag over and over again until they're sure they've heard a jingle.

After Aubrey makes her wish, she starts stretching out her thigh.

Light, still riled up, can't help talking to the girls while they make their wishes.

"We're the premier squad that everyone's here to beat," he says. "It's not up to the other six, seven, eight squads. It's up to you. It's all about you."

As in the prelims, the girls press into the line of teams waiting to perform. There are two teams ahead of them now, and one has already begun to perform.

The Greenup girls huddle together, their arms clasped around each other's backs, and chant the Lord's Prayer. After the girls say "Amen," they stomp their feet and grunt.

Light decides he has to kiss everyone for luck. Frantically, he darts around the Greenup team, kissing each girl on the cheek.

"Nobody deserves this more," he says. "Nobody."

The team before Greenup is performing now.

"Perfect!" Light proclaims, thrusting his fist into the air.

"Perfect," Aubrey echoes. "No mistakes."

"And now, from Greenup County High School, in Greenup County, Kentucky . . . the Musketeers!"

In an instant, the dark, worried faces of the Greenup cheerleaders brighten. As they skip out in front of the crowd, the girls' 120 friends and relatives, who made the trip from Greenup County to witness these next two minutes, stand and hold up their glossy green-and-yellow "Greenup County" posters. They yell and clap and yell some more.

With the dance music beating, the girls zigzag across the mat, flipping and tumbling.

Amanda hits her standing back tuck. Nobody notices except her.

Shawnda nails her back flip–full twist, throws her fist in the air, and yells:

"YEAH!"

The stunts and chants begin. Aubrey is lifted up by her teammates; she balances her right foot on their hands, lifts up her left leg, grabs it with her left hand, and pulls it above her head, but her body begins to tilt to the right.

"C'mon Aubrey, c'mon Aubrey!" hollers Pack. Light grows pale. Peffer has hidden his face in his hands. Berry chants loudly with her cheerleaders.

Still tilting, Aubrey stiffens her right thigh. Then she jumps down, and the routine continues.

"Yeah, yeah," Pack hollers. Light jumps out of his seat and pumps his fist. "Yes," he says under his breath while sitting back down. Peffer looks up from his hands. Berry keeps screaming the Greenup chants.

Next comes the basket toss. Shawnda and Kasey hold out their arms for Jerri to step onto so they can throw her up into the air. Jerri's foot slips, and rather than standing on her teammates' arms, she ends up kneeling. Shawnda and Kasey throw her anyway, but Jerri doesn't fly nearly as high as she's supposed to. When she does the splits in the air, she almost kicks Shawnda and Kasey in their heads, and she comes back down so quickly that Shawnda and Kasey barely catch her before she hits the ground.

The dancing comes last. The girls go through these sexy motions almost unconsciously. They are so drained, so beat. As they struggle to breathe, their faces form huge, grotesque smiles. All the while they count in their heads: One-two-three-four-five-six-seven-eight-one-two-three-four-five-six-seven-eight-one-two . . .

Afterward, the Greenup cheerleaders bound off the mat, showing the crowd nothing but high, perky energy. In the driveway leading back to the parking lot, many of the girls bend over at the waist, rest their elbows on their thighs, and try to catch their breath. Shawnda is breathing so hard she can barely cry. That missed basket toss ruined the routine. It wasn't perfect.

"Man, and I watched, too," Light says to Peffer.

"I did, too."

At most competitions, neither of the two men can bear to watch the girls compete. Light often leaves the performance area. Peffer stays, but buries his face in his hands.

Not all the girls saw that low basket toss. When they hear what happened, they start to cry.

Brooke Meenach, who still hates to wait, stands stone-faced, tears streaming down her cheeks, and watches Boyd County perform on a TV monitor near the warm-up tent.

"A girl just fell on her face," she says, pointing at the screen. "That girl fell on her fool face. Big time."

Most of the Greenup girls have their stuffed animals with them. They pace the dark parking lot, sniffling, each silently calculating the team's chances. Shawnda has separated herself from the others. She sits on the asphalt with her back against a chain-link fence, holding the ruby-red slippers in one hand, the little Big Bird doll in the other, and she cries and cries. Of all the things to mess up, it had to be that basket toss. That was the first stunt Shawnda learned with Kasey and Jerri way back in July, during their cheerleading summer camp in Morehead, Kentucky. Not once in all those months did they have trouble with that basket toss. Not at the Kings Island competition in Cincinnati, not at the football games, not at the regional competition, not at the basketball games. Not once.

Meanwhile, the last of the cheerleading teams finish their routines. The Greenup squad must return to the theater for the awards ceremony. As the Greenup girls head back, they come across the Boyd cheerleaders, all bent over, all crying. Brooke saw it on that monitor outside: one of the Boyd girls had a bad fall, taking her team out of the running.

The Greenup girls hug the Boyd girls and rub their backs. Then they move on into the theater.

Susan Ray, Light's half sister and an assistant coach who works mostly with the Greenup JV, has seen all the teams compete tonight. She's got the lowdown: Boyd had that fall, so they're out of it. Houston High also had a fall. They're out of it, too. Dunbar had a couple of bad stumbles. They don't have much of a chance. Ray thinks it will come down to Greenup and Germantown.

Greenup had that odd basket toss, which maybe the judges noticed, maybe they didn't. If they did notice it, how much would they take off? Germantown had a couple of out-of-bounds violations. In competitive cheerleading, you lose points if one of your cheerleaders steps out of a designated area on the mat.

There are twelve judges, Coach Ray continues. Each judge has to take off one point for an out-of-bounds. The highest and lowest judges' scores are dropped. Germantown definitely had one out-of-bounds. So that means Germantown will lose 10 points. But Coach Ray thinks she saw another out-of-bounds. If every judge caught that second out-of-bounds, then Germantown would lose 20 points. Of course, every judge probably *didn't* catch that second out-of-bounds. And it's hard to say how many judges caught Greenup's fumbled basket toss, or how many points they would take off if they did. And Henry Clay High School looked pretty good. Yep, Henry Clay didn't look bad. So there's no way to know who'll win. But it'll probably be Germantown or Greenup. Or maybe Henry Clay.

The championship organizers gather the finalists together. ESPN is taping the championships, so everything has to look right. A producer arranges the teams in a semicircle facing the audience, with the table full of trophies placed in the middle. Nine big trophies, and one gigantic one.

ESPN's cheerleading commentators, Jeff Webb—the founder and owner of UCA (as well as "a recognized expert in the spirit industry," as the competition program puts it)—and Julianne McNamara, a former Olympic gymnast, greet the crowd and talk about how great an event this has been, and blah, and blah, and blah.

With their faces downturned, the Greenup girls hold on to each other's hands and shoulders and thighs.

"It's a lot of pressure we put on these teenagers," Peffer says quietly.

Jeff and Julianne announce the tenth-place finisher. It's not Greenup. They announce the ninth-, eighth-, seventh-place finishers. They're not Greenup. Jeff and Julianne announce the sixth-, fifth-, fourth-place finishers. Still not Greenup.

Then Jeff asks the crowd for a big applause. The crowd cheers as Jeff speaks into a camera, but gets tongue-tied trying to say, "We're back, at the national cheerleading championships, and it's time to announce the winners."

"Wait a second. Let's do it again," Jeff says. "Can you give us another applause, folks?"

More applause, and Jeff nails his lead-in. Then he announces the third-place finisher. It's not Greenup. Julianne announces the second-place finisher. It's not Greenup.

The Greenup girls grab each other as broad smiles split their faces.

"And now, the 1997 national cheerleading champions . . ."

Shawnda leaps across the mat and takes the huge championship trophy in her arms as the rest of the Greenup cheerleaders jump around her. For a few moments, the girls face the crowd and hop up and down. Then most of them run to their parents and friends in the gallery.

Shawnda stays and hugs that trophy. As she presses her cheek against the gold-painted metal tubing, her makeup mixes with her tears and gets smeared all over her face.

Tryouts

Chapter Four

To Leave
Greenup County

It's not easy to leave Greenup County, especially if you're starting from its hilly northern half, where all the children eventually attend Greenup County High School. You might have to drive as much as forty-five minutes over cracked, torn-up asphalt, often gravel, sometimes dirt, before reaching an honest-to-goodness highway. Hillside roads like Route 1043 lead up, down, and around, past gray trees, trailer homes, run-down houses covered with splintered wood or rusted tin, redbrick houses with gleaming white columns, and the twisted bodies of dead animals—possums, skunks, rabbits, cats, dogs.

Route 1043 is dark from the cover of trees even in the midday sun. At times, you must slow to ten miles an hour to negotiate a steep hill or a treacherous curve.

Along the way, you'll pass what used to be Latimer's Garage—an old two-story wooden house. The front balcony and porch, blackened by rot and fire, now lie crumpled in front of the structure's remains. Decaying cars lie among the leafless trees in the lot next door.

Many people who live along these hillside roads sell whatever will bring in extra money. Not far from Latimer's, a hand-painted sign reading "Firewood for Sale" stands in front of a small wooden shack. Farther down the road, another sign, hung tidily beneath the newspaper tube of a brick house, advertises "Handmade Quilts for Sale."

Everyone has a bulbous gas-storage unit somewhere on the property.

The units look like smooth capsules stretching out ten feet parallel to the ground. Some residents try to hide theirs with flowers or carefully pruned bushes.

There are many farms, with silos to store feed and barns to store small tractors. In the low, flat areas along 1043, you pass wide fields strewn with tightly wound balls of hay, cows grazing here and there, horses preening inside oval paddocks.

Kids looking for fun can't leave their isolated homes without their parents and a car, so many houses and trailers have wooden jungle gyms or brightly colored metal swing sets in the accompanying yards.

You come upon a creek, eventually, that follows the road north. And when you pass the small lake on your right, the highway isn't much farther. You pass Jim & Joe's Car Repair—where run-down cars, not cattle, graze in the field—then take a steep uphill turn to the left. As you climb out of the shadow of the trees, the sun reflects brightly off a grassy knob studded with headstones. Watching over this garden of marble and slate is the Mount Zion Baptist Church, organized, according to the sign out front, in 1820. The whitewashed church glitters in the sunlight. You continue past the big red-and-black K.D.'s Auto Sales sign and finally reach U.S. Route 23.

Greenup County is a rough circle, bordered to the north and east by the Ohio River; Route 23—also known as "Country Music Highway," in honor of the various recording artists who grew up near its four lanes: Billy Ray Cyrus, the Judds, Ricky Skaggs, Keith Whitley, Patty Loveless, Tom T. Hall—winds parallel to the Ohio around the county's outer rim. The road runs from the northwestern corner over to the northeastern corner, then bears around to the right and heads south down Greenup's eastern edge till it crosses the county line into the city of Ashland in Boyd County.

From the 1043 junction, you can turn left on Route 23, head west through the Greenup town of South Shore, then turn right and head north, crossing over the Ohio River into Portsmouth, Ohio. Or you can turn right and follow Country Music Highway east, then south, toward Ashland. Portsmouth and Ashland are cities similarly small in size, but Ashland boasts the area's only Amtrak station and is on the way to the airport in Huntington, West Virginia. Portsmouth is on the way to nowhere.

Before turning right off 1043 and taking 23 toward Ashland, you can't miss the Markwest Hydrocarbon plant looming on the other side of the highway. The smooth white tanks and silver smokestacks don't seem at home among the gray-brown trees, the straw-colored grass, and the black river beyond.

Driving down Route 23, you pass the Old Country Store, which houses both the Christmas Room and Adkins Horse Supply; you pass Hardin's Greenhouse and Coontuckee Sportsman's Supply. You follow the road as it bends to the right along the river, and then, for the next twenty minutes or so, you head south at fifty-five miles an hour with almost nothing new to see. Just the railroad tracks and the river on your left, and on your right, jagged mountain cliffs littered with a brownish-gray tangle of trees, bushes, and rocks.

A big blue warehouse on the right-hand side of the road interrupts the visual tedium. On a sign outside, someone has scrawled in red letters, "Fireworks." As you come closer, you notice an array of junky little knick-knacks—teapots, dishes, figurines—displayed upon card tables, with the mountains rising behind.

Then there's the Star of Bethlehem Baptist Church, a white, one-room wooden building set among the brush at the base of the mountains. It has a triangular roof; a yellow five-pointed star is nailed above the front—and only—door. Two outhouses stand in the lot beside it, one marked "Women" and one marked "Men."

Not far beyond, there sprawls a cluster of long-abandoned trailer homes, their once-shiny chrome now severely corroded by rust. This trailer graveyard marks the approach of your first stoplight. Here, you could turn right and follow Route 1, a new road that carves its way through the hills of northern Greenup County. Route 1 will lead you southwest to other rural counties—Carter, Mason—in eastern Kentucky. Or you could turn left onto the Jesse Stuart Bridge, cross over the Ohio River, and drive on to Ironton, Ohio.

Jesse Stuart, who died in 1984, was Greenup's great literary hero, a man who lived out his seventy-seven years in the county, writing hundreds of poems, short stories, and novels about life here in the Kentucky hills. Robert Penn Warren once wrote that in Stuart's work one could sense Greenup County's "primitive brutality," which "can be transformed [by people who live here] into stoicism, courage, endurance, fidelity, and even love."

Past Stuart's Bridge, you'll see the local Ace Hardware—Sweet Feed 50 lbs for $5.99, Black Powder .50, Rifle $97.99, Barbed Wire $19.99—a number of farms preparing for the coming spring harvest of tobacco, and then the town of Lloyd, home to Greenup County High School. The lights standing four stories tall over the school's football field appear first, then the dark green bleachers. The wide, three-story brick box that is Greenup High sits beside those bleachers, as does the school's large asphalt parking lot.

Soon the faded but still colorful "Greenup County Musketeer News" marquee and billboard with a cartoonish drawing of three musketeers will come into view. Each musketeer wears an Erroll Flynn–style, nineteenth-century French costume—complete with plumed hat—and holds an epee. Below, five lines of chipped plastic letters have been wedged onto a slotted board. It's April 1997, two months since Shawnda Bates and the rest of the varsity Greenup cheerleaders won their school's eighth national championship in Orlando. The "Musketeer News" is this:

STATE SWEET 16 B-BALL
REGION 12 B-BALL CHAMPS
DISTRICT 64 B-BALL CHAMPS
DISTRICT 64 FOOTBALL CHAMPS
CHEERLEADING CHAMPS

After passing the high school, you pass the rest of Lloyd—small houses mostly, and fields with cows. On the right, there's Wireman's Greenhouse and a brown, windowless building with a sign announcing Vanhoose Furniture and Appliances. On the left, there's the Elsea Home Center, selling "Mobile Modular Homes," and Hobart's Pizzeria. Then there's a number of new brick houses with expansive lawns. One family has dug out a thirty-by-twenty-foot rectangle of earth from their yard, creating a river-water pool for children to swim in.

Once Lloyd fades from your periphery, the road threads between the brownish-black hills on the right above and the brownish-black river on the left below. As you come over a rise, you can see the river winding off in the direction of the tree-covered mountains of Ohio and West Virginia, slumping toward the horizon. Long coal barges, their decks piled high, slowly make their way downstream.

Descending now, you pass Dangerous Dan's Fireworks & Discount Furniture, then cross over the Little Sandy River, which cuts through northern Greenup. When you see the Town Hall Plaza on the right and Wright's Motel on the left, you know you're approaching the town of

Greenup, county seat, population 1,200. The Town Hall Plaza, a strip mall, contains Gerber's Family Restaurant (the only nonchain restaurant in the county), a Dollar General Store, the Little Sandy Tire store, and Tammy Jo's Studio, a wide three-story building covered in nylon siding where the Greenup cheerleaders go once a week for gymnastics lessons. Next to Gerber's, a wooden sign in the shape of a church with a steeple points the way to the Raccoon Baptist Church. Wright's Motel across the street is the only place in the county where an outsider can spend the night. It has just ten rooms, but there's always a vacancy.

Downtown Greenup lies two short blocks behind the motel, between Route 23 and the Ohio River.

In the early 1800s, many folks called Greenup (then Greenupsburg) Hangtown because the small riverside burg held many grand public hangings. The last one took place in 1852. Nearly a hundred years later, in 1951, two elderly Greenup women named Nina Mitchell Biggs and Mabel Lee Mackey wrote a 247-page book called *The History of Greenup County, Kentucky*. Biggs and Mackey have since died, but in 1990, the county historical society reprinted a new hardcover edition with an olive-green dust jacket, and sells copies for $10 each at the county library on Main Street, a block from the county courthouse and half a block from the river.

Biggs and Mackey's history describes that final hanging of 1852. Basing their story upon newspaper reports of the public reprisal for "the most terrible murder in the annals of Greenup County," the two women depicted the scene downtown when two men were put to death for the murder of a man and his wife at their hillside home near the area called Argillite in south-central Greenup County, not far from where Shawnda Bates and her family live today:

> Instead of hanging these men on the tree where the hangings originally took place, a scaffold was built on west Main Street near the Little Sandy River. A cart carrying the condemned men, who were sitting on their coffins, passed slowly under the scaffold, the black caps were placed in position, the nooses in the ropes were adjusted, the fife and drum played the death march, the oxen and cart moved on, and the bodies were left hanging in the air.
>
> On the day of this execution, Greenupsburg was filled to overflowing with people, women as well as men. They came

for miles on horseback, on mules, in wagons, and on foot.
The women wore dresses with very full skirts and were
dressed in costly attire of that time. Men with great mustaches were present wearing bleached muslin pleated shirts,
blue jean trousers, and nail-keg hats.

These days, downtown Greenup rarely fills to overflowing. There is not
one restaurant in town and there are no bars, only a handful of stores selling cars, car parts, farming and gardening supplies, and clothes—including Team One, directly across the street from the courthouse, which
advertises a "Wide Selection of Cheerleading Apparel." There's also a
number of law offices, a dentist's office, a doctor's office.

The old courthouse still stands in the middle of Main Street, its rear
abutting the Ohio River. Greenup has never had a flood wall in town, and
the courthouse, which was built over 150 years ago, has survived numerous
floods. It houses the county judge executive's offices, the school board
meeting room, and the four-man sheriff's office.

Then there are the three in-town churches: the Living Word Victory
Center, a white brick structure with turquoise doors and windows; the
United Methodist Church ("Come Be a Part of a Family, Since 1846");
and the Greenup Christian Church.

The Greenup County Fairgrounds, a few blocks south of the courthouse, also calls the town of Greenup home. For over fifty years, this riverside field with its four barns and showring has hosted the Greenup
County Fair at the end of the summer. And for the past twenty-six years,
the fairgrounds have served as the starting point of Greenup County High
School's homecoming parade.

As you pass by the town of Greenup on Route 23, you'll see a McDonald's, WorldWide Video, the Greenup Church of God, Gary's Carpet &
More, an Ashland Gas Mart and Taco Bell, a Hardee's, Kinner Lumber,
Harvey's Auto Parts & Things, a Subway sandwich shop, and Super
Quick gas station; the Full Service Pride Oil, which sells regular unleaded
for 99 cents per gallon and premium unleaded for 99 cents per gallon; the
small Applegate Shopping Center with its FoodLand market; Radio
Shack, Stultz Pharmacy, Musketeer Beauty Shop, Country Garden Wedding Chapel, Video Express; then the Greenup County Industrial Com-
plex, built at the expense of the local government and woefully short of
tenants, advertising "34,000 Square Feet, For Sale or Lease."

You'll drive by the tiny town of Wurtland, whose welcome sign reads "Home of Ernest 'Ernie' West, Recipient of Medal of Honor, Korean War, 1953." Wurtland was named for the Wurts family, German immigrant farmers who owned the town's land in the first half of the nineteenth century. Besides the small houses dotting the land on either side of 23, you pass a sign pointing left to the Wurtland First Missionary Baptist Church, and a sign pointing right to the Wurtland Freewill Baptist Church.

Next comes the town of Raceland, first built around a horse track that a local entrepreneur named J. O. Keene spent a million dollars to erect in the 1920s. Keene planned to turn Raceland into a thriving resort town with hotels and restaurants built along the river, which is within walking distance from the track. Rich horse enthusiasts would have come from all over Kentucky—and the country—to watch the Thoroughbreds run and to vacation on the river. Only four years after the track opened, however, the stock market crash of 1929 ushered in the Great Depression, and wealthy America stopped caring about which horses ran the fastest in the eastern Kentucky mountains. The fancy restaurants and hotels never came to be, and Keene dismantled the grandstand, selling the steel as scrap. The oval was later sold to real estate developers, who built modest one-story houses on the land. The town's name is the only reminder of the racetrack's existence.

Continuing south, you come to Russell, the most populous—with over 3,000 residents—and most developed town in Greenup County. On the side of the road stands a once-colorful sign showing a black locomotive chugging along under a clear, blue sky. The sign has become so decrepit— the paint faded, peeling—that it's hard to make out exactly what it says. In big red script on top of that perfect sky, you can still read "Welcome to Russell, KY, Former Home of Rail City, USA Railworks, America's Largest Locally Owned Rail Yard," then there is something more, smaller, illegible.

The condition of the sign indicates that it's been some time since Russell housed the largest locally owned rail yard in America. In fact, CSX Transportation, Inc., a conglomerate based in Jacksonville, Florida, bought the yard in the 1950s and took over its production of rail cars for hauling coal and steel. By 1982, CSX employed over 2,000 Greenup residents. Now, in 1997, after a series of layoffs, just 400 people work at the Russell yard, which, after climbing a slight rise in the road, appears before you: sixty-some pitch-black rail cars sitting side by side and lined up one after another along ten rows of track.

Beyond, there is a Uniroyal Tire Shop, the Water Bed Store, and a white one-story building one hundred yards long called the Hill Billy Country Store—"Your Complete Bible Outlet." On the right, there are two strip malls, one old and one new. The newer one thrives these days. It looks sleek and bright with white storefronts and a long red roof, and it houses hip new stores like Petland and Universal Computers. The older strip mall, which lies farther from the road, past a sprawling stretch of black parking lot, teeters on its last legs. An Ames sign still stretches high above the asphalt, even though the Ames store sits empty. One of the larger buildings, which probably housed a supermarket or department store, is boarded up.

Greenup County's most popular restaurant, the Golden Corrale Steak and Buffet, stands about a block away. On weekend nights and Sunday afternoons, packs of teenagers, young couples, older couples, and families of four line up in the parking lot. Together, they wait their turn to pay $6.75 and have at the Corrale's all-you-can-eat buffet with its sliced ham, sliced turkey, roast beef, baked potatoes, French fried potatoes, scalloped potatoes, fried potato wedges, greasy rolls, and, tucked over in the far right-hand corner, its salad bar.

Inside, the bright fluorescent lighting and maroon-and-brown plastic furniture create a cafeteria-like atmosphere, which, for adults of a certain age, seems to re-create high school. As Greenup residents get second helpings of butter-baked string beans and carrots, or stand in line for a soft-serve ice-cream sundae, they can greet their friends and neighbors and gossip about the local goings-on. When not laughing, talking, or ingesting the heavy food, Corrale patrons can look out through the floor-to-ceiling windows and marvel at the sprawling hundred-foot-tall crimson sprouts of metal tubing, twisting upward, spewing fire and smoke, on the opposite side of Route 23. The AK Steel works is all that's left of Greenup's 200-year dependence on iron.

Small-time farmers traveled west from Virginia in the 1760s, crossed the Ohio River, and became the first settlers in the Greenup County area. They grew tobacco and raised cattle on the few flat, arable pieces of land. But the need for axes, plowshares, picks, crowbars, shovels, and other tools soon led those farmers to discover the region's most abundant natural resource, iron ore. By the early 1800s, men trained in pig iron production in western Pennsylvania and southern Ohio journeyed to Greenup, mined the county's iron ore deposits, and built small brick furnaces, which boiled down tons of iron a day. As Greenup's iron industry grew, furnace owners bought large tracts of land throughout the county and stripped the mountains of their trees, using the wood to make charcoal for the melting of ore.

In the 1850s, Greenup's first railroad lines took the iron to market, and Greenup residents have depended upon iron production and iron transportation to keep money flowing into the county ever since. By the 1960s, Armco Steel, then the world's largest producer of iron, had assumed control of the county's iron production. All the individually owned furnaces had long since shut down. But a few of the old brick furnaces still stand among Greenup's trees. They look like chimneys without houses—rectangular brick columns two stories high, alone in the woods.

Armco opened up a new plant on the Greenup County–Boyd County border in 1963, the same plant that sits across from the Golden Corrale now. Back then, it was the largest, most productive steel plant in the world. It was something Greenup County and Boyd County residents were very proud of. When the furnace was lit for the first time, dignitaries from Boyd and Greenup attended the ceremony. The plant whistles blew, fireworks shot into the air, and a Boyd County high school band played "My Old Kentucky Home."

Now, white smoke hovers in the air over the seemingly random turns of blood-red pipes beside the road. Once you pass the plant—since acquired by AK Steel and drastically downsized—you have left Greenup County and entered Boyd. And after coming around a steep downhill bend, you'll finally make your way into the city of Ashland, Kentucky, population 27,000. The Ashland Town Center Mall will appear on the right, the Movies 10 theater on the left.

This is the only place to go "out" if you're a teenager from Greenup County. The Ashland Mall has much of what every mall in America has—a food court, three large department stores, scores of novelty gift shops, a few trendy upscale clothing shops, the requisite video arcade, and the only movie theater in the area, a ten-screen multiplex, across the street.

Still, the kids who attend Greenup High don't come down here much. They hardly go out at all. Growing up in the Kentucky hills, Greenup kids get used to entertaining themselves at home, alone or with one or two friends. They don't obsess over what to do or where to go on the weekends. Generally, they are content to hang out at home, maybe get some take-out pizza and watch TV or a video. Sometimes, Greenup teenagers will throw a party, but rarely. Kids who are old enough to drive and have access to a car might go cruising down in Ashland or up in Portsmouth, but not often. According to Greenup High principal Jim Thoroughman, about the most risky thing that local teenagers do is smoke cigarettes. Occasionally, they'll drink a little beer, and some have been known to get their hands on marijuana.

Mostly, the county's kids entertain themselves with school sports. In the fall, they go to football games; in the winter, basketball games; in the spring, baseball; and in the summer, summer basketball. Greenup High often holds dances after the games, charging $2 for admission.

Parents are very strict with their girls when it comes to dating. According to one Greenup High cheerleader, there's an unwritten rule in the county stipulating that a girl may not go out alone with a boy until she's sixteen. "Every girl I talk to," she says, "it's like, 'I'm not allowed to go out till I'm sixteen.'" But that doesn't stop nearly every teenager with a modicum of self-confidence—including the majority of Greenup cheerleaders—from diving into steady, somewhat serious attachments with members of the opposite sex.

At school ball games, the boys and girls all couple up. They flirt while applauding their school's team and coo over one another as they sit in the stands, occasionally stealing a peck on the cheek. The girlfriends of team members dutifully sit together and clap for their sportsman mates. The boyfriends of the Greenup cheerleaders also clump together, always down in the front row so they can be close to their cheerleading significant others.

Like all kids their age, Greenup teenagers want to grow up as fast as they can. When a boy in Greenup County turns sixteen, he often gains access to a sports car or a pickup truck, definitely American made. Then, he and his girlfriend—so long as she has reached her sixteenth birthday—can officially go out all by themselves. And they can park somewhere along one of Greenup's dark mountain roads and do what they please.

Now that you've made it to Ashland, you can catch a Greyhound bus or an Amtrak train. Or you can keep driving south to I-64 and take it east about twenty miles, past the huge, smoke-spewing Ashland Oil petroleum plant (currently the largest employer in the area but the subject of persistent layoff rumors) to Huntington, West Virginia. There, you can buy a ticket at the small Huntington airport, where planes take off over an Appalachian cliff.

* * *

It's early evening on a Tuesday, and the Greenup varsity's triumph in Orlando two months ago has lost much of its luster. In late February and early March, the county was declared a disaster area when heavy rains poured down and the Ohio, the Big Sandy, and the Little Sandy all overflowed their banks, drenching much of the county, killing crops and cattle, ruining homes and businesses. Greenup High was closed for a week. None of the Greenup cheerleaders or their families lost much during the flood. But the widespread destruction of property and land has cast a pall over the county.

The month of April is more than half over, but spring is not in the air. Clouds rest heavily upon the mountains. The air hangs cool and gray, and the trees have yet to bloom. Yesterday, for about an hour, snow flurries drifted down from the dark midday sky. The ground, meanwhile, still squishes underfoot because of the lingering floodwater. Walking on the shifting earth through the cold, bitter wind, you can feel the "primitive brutality" that Robert Penn Warren found in Jesse Stuart's writing.

Tonight, the members of Greenup High's JV cheerleading squad will try to transcend that brutality. Their parents will drive them over the Jesse Stuart Bridge, about a mile north of Greenup High, then ten miles west along Route 52 to Wheelersburg, Ohio, and down a side road to a pizza joint called Fred's. There, they will celebrate the end of another year of Greenup County JV cheerleading.

Fred's is a dimly lit, old-style pizza restaurant with cut-glass lamps hanging low, a video rental store in the back, outdated video games near the front door, and newer video games lining the empty patches of the dining room walls. Fred's doesn't get much business on Tuesdays. An old couple eats quietly in one corner of the dining room, and a family of five chitchat in another.

Greenup's JV coaches, the serious Randy Peffer and the talkative Susan Ray, arrive first and tell a young waiter that they have reserved the back room for their big end-of-the-year team banquet. The waiter doesn't know about it, so he leaves to get his manager, who doesn't appear much older than the waiter. The manager doesn't seem to know what's going on, either. In a restrained panic, he asks the Greenup coaches to wait, and disappears behind a door marked "Employees Only." Eventually, the manager returns, sweat glistening on his forehead, and asks Peffer and Ray to follow him. He leads them through the lonely dining room, to the back of the restaurant, then through the video rental store, and up three narrow stairs to a cramped room where two rows of booths sit barely four feet apart. On a raised shelf in the corner of the room are a TV and a VCR. The Greenup coaches plan to show videos—some made by parents with shaky camcorders, one pirated from ESPN—of the JV performing in competitions throughout the year.

The girls arrive in twos and threes, shepherded by their parents. Peffer and Ray sit in a booth at the back of the room and talk about how awful next year will be for cheerleading at Greenup High. Tryouts start tomorrow, and this year's crop of graduating eighth-graders from McKell and Wurtland middle schools can't cheerlead. They can't tumble. Their motions are sloppy. They certainly can't stunt. Worse, because of the tremendous reputation of Greenup High cheerleading, none of the school's rising freshmen even feel qualified to try out for Greenup's JV. To top it all off, many of the girls on this year's JV refuse to try out for the varsity squad because they don't think they can make it, or they simply don't want to endure the rigors of cheering another year. Shawnda Bates and seven other seniors on the varsity will graduate in a couple of months, so at least eight girls from the JV need to step up and replace them. As things stand now, only six of the fifteen JV cheerleaders are even trying out, and two of them can't do a standing back tuck, *the* varsity requirement. Peffer estimates that at least seven members of this past season's junior varsity easily possess the skills to cheer on the varsity next year, but they simply don't feel like participating. After cheering one year for the Greenup JV, they're burnt out.

Rachel Brown, a freshman on the JV, isn't burnt out, although she has reason to be. In the past year, Rachel has dealt with a rash of physical problems that have inhibited her cheerleading progress, notably the development of her standing back tuck. Rachel has also made some enemies on the varsity squad by having a romantic encounter with a varsity girl's boyfriend. Still, she's all smiles now as she talks with friends, her soft, pretty face animated, her thick brownish-blond hair swishing back and forth across her shoulders.

Even if Rachel manages to land her standing back tuck and Coach Berry places her on the varsity, next year's squad will have only sixteen girls within its ranks, not enough to qualify for the Universal Cheerleading Association's all-girls large varsity division. Instead, Greenup would compete in UCA's all-girls medium varsity division, which, as Berry knows, is not as big a deal. The competition would still be rigorous—maybe even more so, because there are more medium varsity teams competing through UCA—but the level of prestige would plummet. ESPN doesn't broadcast the medium varsity finals as often as they broadcast the large varsity finals.

Those who know, know that the best large varsity squad is the best all-around squad, the best of the best. The best medium varsity squad is merely the best among squads designated medium varsity. So two months after celebrating yet another national title and reestablishing the Greenup program as the country's top producer of competitive cheerleading teams, Candy Berry and her Musketeers face a big step down in cheerleading status.

Three accomplished competitive cheerleaders from two nearby high schools may save the program. Two hail from Russell High School, the academic powerhouse in southern Greenup County, and have already transferred into Greenup High for the sole purpose of cheering for the varsity team. They first made the hour-long commute up north for school last week, after spring break.

The Kentucky state schools superintendent, however, has barred the Russell girls from cheering for Greenup because he wants to discourage the recruitment of cheerleaders—or any other student athletes—by public high school coaches. Another girl, who lives in Boyd County and attends Boyd County High School, Greenup's bitter cheerleading rival, has considered moving up to northern Greenup County—with her whole family—so she can cheer for Greenup High. Since the ruling against the two Russell girls, however, she's reconsidering.

Coach Berry plans to help the Russell girls appeal the ruling against them, on the grounds that in Kentucky, cheerleading is not officially considered a sport. If the state is to regulate cheerleading as a sport, Berry says, then cheerleading should receive the perks that official sports like football and basketball receive: more money for the program, more money for the team sponsors, more money for transportation; basically, more money.

Berry expects to get those three outsiders onto the Greenup varsity. Keeping them off wouldn't be right, and she'll be darned if she's going to let the state schools office do what's not right. Still, even if she manages to get those girls onto the team—and assuming Rachel Brown learns to throw her standing back tuck—Berry must depend upon a corps of young, relatively inexperienced cheerleaders to lead Greenup to another championship. The way things are shaping up, there will be eight sophomores on next year's varsity, five who've never cheered varsity before. There will also be one junior who's never cheered on varsity.

That junior would be Rachel Wills, called Wills by the Greenup coaches to distinguish her from Rachel Brown. Wills, a sophomore, laughs stiffly in a booth with a gaggle of fellow JV cheerleaders. She can smile when she wants, but not effortlessly like the other girls. She must force her wide mouth with its long, thin lips to curve up, revealing her slightly buck teeth. Wills has shoulder-length dark brown hair that she always wears up and back, away from her rigid, pale face, away from her large black eyes. Wills joined Greenup cheerleading late, during this, her sophomore year. Her freshman year, she was busy moving into a foster home after having difficulties with her father.

The final wild card of this year's tryouts is Linda Goble, a feisty, freckly, red-haired freshman finishing her first season on the Greenup JV. Peffer says that if Linda tries out for the varsity she'll make the team, "No questions asked." But he doesn't think Linda's going to try out.

Moments ago, Linda arrived here at Fred's with Melissa Morris—another freshman JV cheerleader—and Melissa's mom, Linda Morris. Linda Goble and Melissa Morris are much more reserved tonight than Rachel Brown, Rachel Wills, and the other JV girls. As the two newcomers scoot into a booth seat together amid their giggling, gossiping teammates, they seem close to tears. Stone still, Linda and Melissa look down at the table and let their straight hair hang down, as if they want to hide their faces. Mrs. Morris, a hefty, outgoing woman, plops down beside Peffer and Ray, sighs melodramatically, then grins. The two coaches chuckle.

One of the parents has started a video and Linda tilts her chin up so that her big green eyes can see the TV through her bangs. There's the Greenup mascot on the gym floor, shot by a parent at a basketball game. Trying to break out of her bad mood, Linda says, a little too loudly, "Hey, it's the Musketeer!"

Silence follows. Linda, her shoulders hunched, looks around at her teammates, searching for a response. The other girls give in eventually, saying, "Yeah! Look! Hey!"

Only Melissa refuses to join the party. She avoids watching the videos. Mostly, she looks down at the pizzeria table, keeping her dour face behind a curtain of dirty-blond hair.

*　*　*

For the past school year, Linda Goble has lived with Melissa and the rest of the Morris family at their home in northeast Greenup on the Ohio River side of the railroad tracks. She doesn't see much of her own family. Her dad has spent most of Linda's fourteen years in trouble with the law. He has served time for disorderly conduct, resisting arrest, driving while intoxicated, assault, and burglary. One of her older sisters, Rachel, aged seventeen, still lives at home, but she's got a car to free her up and often sleeps over with their other sister, Connie, who's twenty-six. Linda's two older brothers, Rickie and Darrell, aged twenty-one and twenty-seven, don't have much time for Linda either, what with caring for their young children and trying to pay their rent. Linda's mom gets in touch with her occasionally, but only when she wants her little girl to make her feel loved.

Since the fourth grade, cheerleading has given Linda's life its only structure, its flip-by-flip progress, its few moments of joy. Over the years, the coaches and parents of Linda's various cheerleading teams have made sure that Linda has continued to lead cheers. Often they discuss Linda in whispers, as Mrs. Morris, Coach Peffer, and Coach Ray do now at Fred's over a hot pepperoni-and-mushroom pizza.

Linda has needed money, a heap of money, to cheer—money she could never have raised without the community's help. Greenup High cheerleading spends $3,000 on every cheerleader every year. The middle school programs cost far less, but they still approach $500 per girl per year. But Linda has also needed help keeping her many cheerleading uniforms pressed and washed and with transportation to and from practice and ball games.

Linda appreciates the help she is given, but it heightens her insecurity. Growing up as she has, she feels entitled to nothing. With every thank you she utters, a smile pressed onto her lips, Linda gains more guilt and loses more confidence. She can tell when the help she receives is given reluctantly. She knows she's a burden. So she talks a little too loudly. She makes biting jokes. And she feels as though she's very demanding.

Her JV teammates all love Linda, but, they say, she can wear on them. When Linda visits a friend's house, she wants to see and use and touch everything. For the friend, the visit can be more like baby-sitting than hanging out.

Still, Linda was harder to get along with when she was at Wurtland Middle, before she met Melissa and before the Morrises took her in. Wurtland's cheer squad, like the Greenup JV, didn't start practice until five-thirty P.M. every day after school. (The boys' sports teams used the gym till then.) To travel to and from practice, the girls needed parents with cars. Linda's mom has never had a car and has never had time for her youngest daughter, so throughout middle school, Linda mooched rides from her teammates' parents. Picking up Linda from her mom's house before practice and then returning her there afterward added an extra two hours of twisty-turny driving. To lighten the burden on her teammates' parents, Linda stopped going home. She would go to a cheerleading friend's house after school, catch a ride with the friend to practice, then grab a ride back to the friend's house and spend the night.

In middle school, that cheerleading friend, more often than not, was Shiritta Schaffer. Shiritta's parents did a great deal for Linda through her four years at Wurtland Middle. Besides giving her rides, they often fed her, bought her school supplies, and helped pay her cheerleading expenses. But the Schaffers were not in the market for another teenage daughter. If Linda could stay with another cheerleading family or with one of her sisters, the Schaffers encouraged her to give them a break.

Last spring, Linda and Shiritta both made Greenup High's JV team. The following summer, Linda took her first trip outside the Greenup area when she and the rest of the JV squad traveled ninety miles southwest to Morehead, Kentucky, for a four-day UCA summer camp at Morehead State University. There, Linda roomed with Melissa Morris, another new member of the Greenup JV and a recent graduate of McKell Middle.

Melissa and Linda hit it off right away.

"They're exactly alike," says Mrs. Morris, lounging in her sunny sitting room. "They're two peas in a pod. Just exactly alike. They're not only the same size, they're the same temperament, the same everything. Everything about them is identical. They mesh so well."

Linda spent the rest of the summer with the Schaffers. But when school started, Linda began to spend more and more time with Melissa. On occasion, Linda spent the night at the Morrises'.

Then Shiritta quit cheerleading. For Linda's sake, Shiritta's parents kept making the arduous nightly drives to and from cheerleading practice. A few weeks into the school year, however, they got sick of it. One Monday morning, after Linda had spent a weekend with Melissa and the Morrises, Mrs. Morris carted Melissa and Linda to school. She drove by the Schaffers' house so that Linda could pick up a book she needed that day. Linda hopped out of the car, and Mrs. Morris watched as she skipped up the steps only to stop short at the top, still a ways from the front door. Linda then turned around and slowly started back. She was carrying a basket, looking down at it as she walked.

Mrs. Morris felt a pang. She got out of the car to find out what was going on, and Linda handed her the basket. Inside sat all of Linda's belongings in a clump—some clothes, a few books, cheerleading uniforms, a pair of shoes. On top, pinned to a piece of clothing, was a note that said the Schaffers no longer wanted Linda to live with them.

That afternoon, after talking it over with Melissa, her husband, Jimmy, and her younger daughter, twelve-year-old Amber, Mrs. Morris made Linda an offer.

"When Linda moved in here," Mrs. Morris says, "she moved in on the same basis as the girls. She's never been treated any different. We love her just as much as if she'd been born into this family."

Mrs. Morris didn't want Linda to think that the Morrises felt even the slightest reluctance. She wanted to give Linda a home.

Leaning in and whispering, Mrs. Morris continues:

"She didn't have any more than she could hold in her two arms." Mrs. Morris extends her arms. "She'd never had her own jewelry, makeup, bras, hairbrush, *tooth*brush, hardly any clothes, shoes, nothing. She didn't know how to clean house, do chores. She'd never done that before. Like I said, we treat her equal. She has to do chores."

Mrs. Morris leans back in her little wooden rocking chair.

"Johnny, my husband, he loves her. He's as close to her as he is to any of the other girls. He's a cutup. My husband's a cutup. He likes that. And Linda cuts up with him. We always wanted more children and couldn't have them. We always wanted a little boy and couldn't. My littlest one is as rough as a little boy. And Linda's rough too."

Mrs. Morris says she's watched the girl blossom over the past year. Linda's less diffident than she used to be around adults. Her grades have improved "tremendously." And her sense of humor has lost its bitter edge. Linda's just happy.

Once in a while, however, her family will come back into her life, and Linda will slip into a funk. Linda's father phoned this past Christmas, asking to speak to Linda. He'd gotten the number from his wife. Mrs. Morris answered the phone first, but didn't say anything to the man. She just told Linda who it was and handed her the receiver. "Nobody wants to come between a family unit," she explains. "At all."

Linda is still fourteen. She isn't old enough to hate her parents, no matter what they've done. When her dad asked her to visit him, Linda said yes.

Mr. Morris drove Linda down to the state prison in Boyd County on Christmas Day, and Linda spent time with her dad in the jailhouse meeting room. "After that," says Mrs. Morris, "Linda moped around the house for a few days."

The same thing happens when Linda's mom invites her daughter over for a visit. Linda can't say no, so she goes. And for the next few days, she mopes.

"The cheerleading keeps her going," Mrs. Morris says. "It gives her something to do every day. The structure that gives you, it also teaches you even as everything is falling around you, there's always something to focus on."

Mrs. Morris believes Linda has gained a resilience from cheerleading that her parents never possessed and could never teach their daughter. Linda's parents never face troubles head-on. Neither has held a good job in years. Linda's mother has never sued for a divorce from her husband. More often than not during the past four years he's been in jail, but when he gets out, she always welcomes him back. Rather than confronting her husband, she becomes more like him. These days, Mrs. Goble receives welfare because, as she told Mrs. Morris, she needs extra money to take care of Linda.

"Psychologically, she can't cope," Mrs. Morris says of Linda's mom. "With some people, when something bad happens, they fold. And some people grow and get stronger. My married life has not always been perfect. No. You don't always have everything you need. But you take the weaknesses and you try to make them stronger."

Linda has learned to do that through cheerleading and, since the Morrises took her in, she's also learned about family and love.

Recently, Jimmy Morris got a great job offer. He'd been working as a salesman at the State Electric store in New Boston, Ohio, a half-hour north of Greenup. Now, he's going to manage a State Electric store of his own in Mason County, Kentucky, an hour and a half to the west, closer to Louisville and Lexington.

"It's something we had to do to make [the children's] lives better in the long run," says Mrs. Morris, sitting up, her arms crossed over her chest, resting on her stomach. "They're closer to colleges down there. There's just so many more things there than in this little rural area. And in the long run, it's going to be better for them. You know, the economy's better. Everything's better."

As she speaks those last words, she raises her arms up over her head, imploringly.

"It's a regular farm community just like this, but it has grown by leaps and bounds. And there'll be pay raises, a new company car. All kids want and want and want. This way, when they want, they might get a few things."

Mrs. Morris has offered to take Linda, too, but Linda doesn't want to go. She wants to stay with the Morrises, for sure, but she also wants to keep cheering for Greenup County. Mason County High School has a cheerleading team, and it's not bad. But it doesn't compete outside the state. It doesn't have Greenup's rich cheerleading tradition.

Meanwhile, Linda's mom has yet to give her blessing to the move.

"We can't be Linda's mommy or daddy," Mrs. Morris says. "It's a decision Linda will have to make." She thinks a moment. "Or, being a minor, she'll probably have to go along with what her parents have decided for her."

Mrs. Morris looks down at the backs of her hands and picks at her nail polish.

"I know that she wants to do whatever makes her parents happy. I know that's part of it. At her age, even though they haven't made all the decisions for her up till this point, she's still going to try to do whatever her parents want."

Still, Mrs. Morris pushed hard for Linda to move to Mason County. She's managed to convince Linda that it's for the best, which wasn't easy—Linda still cries at the thought of never cheering for the Greenup varsity. Mrs. Morris has also had a lawyer draw up papers that will make the Morrises Linda's legal guardians—once Linda's mother signs them.

Linda's mother has those papers now.

At Fred's, while the JV girls giggle, eat pizza, and watch themselves in the parent-produced videos, Mrs. Morris tells Randy Peffer and Susan Ray why Linda and Melissa are so sulky tonight. The two girls just finished their first day of classes at Mason County High School. They had to enroll now, before the beginning of the next school year, so that they will be eligible to try out for the Mason High cheerleading team. Mason's tryouts start in a couple of weeks.

"They hate it," Mrs. Morris confides.

"Oh, they'll get used to it," Ray says. "You'll see. It'll take a little while, that's all."

"I know. They just want a place, like every other child," says Mrs. Morris. "They just want to belong. Once they've got a spot on the squad, they'll belong."

Mason County schools have consolidated with Mason City schools, so many Mason High students come from the city. Linda and Melissa, reserved country types that they are, feel like visitors on another planet. The Mason City kids wear weird clothes, they talk weird, and they think they're so great. Also, the girls at Mason High know that Linda and Melissa have enrolled now simply to try out for the cheerleading team. They know that Linda and Melissa are from Greenup County, that Linda and Melissa used to cheer for world-famous Greenup County High School.

Mrs. Morris whispers, "They think Linda and Melissa are going to come in there and take over."

On top of all that, the Kentucky state superintendent of schools is giving Mrs. Morris a hard time about letting Linda and Melissa try out for the cheerleading team, for much the same reason that he is barring the two Russell girls from the Greenup tryouts—to prevent high school recruitment of cheerleaders.

Mrs. Morris saw that coming. Months ago, she sent a state school official documents showing that her husband recently became the manager of that State Electric store in Mason—proof that her family's move to Mason has nothing to do with cheerleading. But that damn bureaucrat told her this afternoon that he never received any such documents.

"He was an absolute butt today," Mrs. Morris spits.

Coach Ray, concerned, asks whether the girls will be able to try out.

"Oh, they'll be at tryouts," Mrs. Morris says, peering over her shoulder at Linda and Melissa. "They'll do cheerleading. If I have to go to Lexington and see this man myself, they'll do cheerleading."

The pizza and soda are almost gone now, and Ray decides it's time to make a speech. She stands up. The girls quiet down, wipe the smiles off their faces, and turn toward her.

"I just want to thank you guys for a great season," Ray says flatly. "You girls trying out for the varsity: good luck. Remember, you can always come see me if you need anything. You know my phone number. You know where I am. Anyway, thanks. That's all."

Peffer and Ray hand out plaques to the girls. Each plaque has the name of its recipient engraved on a faux bronze plate set on a shiny block of faux wood. The plaque lists the year and the JV team's accomplishments—it took second place at nationals in Orlando—and bears two glossy color photos, one of the team and one of the recipient.

The girls study their plaques, comparing their portraits, whining about how awful they look.

"Linda, Melissa, it's time to go, girls," Mrs. Morris says. "You've got tumbling."

The two girls look up from their plaques; then, quietly, they shuffle out from their booth. The rest of the team grows quiet.

Shiritta Schaffer, who rejoined the JV not long after her parents dismissed Linda from their household, has tears in her eyes. Despite everything, Shiritta and Linda have remained close friends. Shiritta hugs Linda first, then Melissa.

The rest of the JV girls take turns hugging the two departing girls.

"You come back if you don't like it," says Rachel Brown, sniffling.

"Yeah, don't be a stranger," Wills says, putting a hand on Linda's shoulder and trying to make eye contact.

Melissa can't take it any longer. She tries to hold her breath and keep the crying back, but she can't. With a loud hiccupping sob, she starts into it, and hard.

The sound startles the younger sister of another cheerleader.

"Why's she crying?" the small girl asks. "Why's she crying?"

No one answers. Mrs. Morris ushers Linda and Melissa toward the hallway leading out of the restaurant.

"Why's she crying?" the little girl asks, louder this time, sensing she's being ignored. "Why's SHE CRYING?"

Mrs. Morris turns around, faces the child, and forces a smile.

"She's testing her makeup, honey."

Chapter Five

An Appendectomy, a Car Wreck, a Back Tuck

Tryouts begin today without Linda Goble, without Melissa Morris, without the two girls from Russell, without the girl from Boyd. But Rachel Brown's here, and she hopes she's brought a standing back tuck with her.

It's a cold April Wednesday, not long after three P.M. School has just let out. Prospective Greenup High cheerleaders quietly report to the school's gym, with its big, goofy Musketeer, dressed in the school's green and gold, smiling up from the basketball court, holding an epee in one hand and dribbling a basketball with the other. The two decks of wooden bleachers on either side of the hardwood floor are pushed back now, and look like glossy, blond-wood walls. Above them, gray concrete stands slope up to the roof.

On the far side of the gym, behind another raised section of concrete bleachers, an American flag clings to the yellow brick wall. Seven green-and-yellow banners hang from the gym's rafters in front of Old Glory. They commemorate Greenup High's various accomplishments in boys' basketball:

SWEET SIXTEEN FINAL FOUR 1974
KHSAA #1 DEFENSE 1993
OKAC CO-CHAMPS 1993
16TH REGION CHAMPS 1974 1983 1985 1991
63RD DISTRICT CHAMPS 1981 1983 1984 1985 1987 1990
63RD DISTRICT CHAMPS 1995
KHSAA FINAL EIGHT 1991

On the wall above the concrete bleachers on the left, in big black, yellow, and green letters, are the words "WELCOME TO THE GREENHOUSE." On the near side wall above the stands, "GREENUP CO MUSKETEERS" is painted in green and yellow letters with dramatic, tapered shadowing, like the Superman comic book font. Four banners hang in front, three in honor of the boys' baseball team, one for the girls' basketball team:

GIRLS 63RD DISTRICT CHAMPS 1984 1988 1995
63RD DISTRICT CHAMPS 1980–81
1996 MUSKETEER BASEBALL KENTUCKY MR. BASEBALL AARON MCGLONE
1996 MUSKETEER BASEBALL STATE RUNNER-UP RECORD 36–2

As assorted high school kids in jeans and T-shirts, with backpacks fashionably slung over only one shoulder, filter through the gym on their way out of school, varsity cheerleading hopefuls gather near a single bleacher.

These girls are the same freshmen and sophomores who celebrated the end of their JV season the evening before. This afternoon, they are not nearly so chatty. A couple sit on the lone bleacher and pull on their ponytails. Others start to stretch out. They sit on the gym floor and turn their lithe bodies into pretzels.

A few boys shoot hoops at one end of the court. Behind them, the girls' fast-pitch softball coach puts together a nylon mesh batting cage, hanging the netting from a wire stretched the width of the court and anchoring the ends to hooks in the floor. She leaves the gym, then returns a few minutes later pushing a pitching machine on wheels.

The boys playing basketball get in the softball coach's way, their basketball slamming into the nylon cage again and again. Some of these boys can really play. Others appear slack and awkward. The varsity basketball coach, Randy Ward, walks down the side of the court to his office in the corner of the gym and makes a joke at one of the boys' expense. The boy, who plays for Ward, smiles without showing his teeth, and doesn't look at him.

Ward, a short, rotund man with sloped shoulders, pasty white skin, and thin blond hair, halts with his hands on his hips and has a good laugh. The boy ignores him, and keeps shooting his hoops. Ward's laughter slowly peters out. Half smiling, he peers around the court, as if worried that someone is watching him. His face has become less animated now, almost sullen. As he walks off to his office, he looks at his toes.

It's been a hard couple of weeks for Randy Ward, who has coached Greenup High basketball for over twenty years. Back in March 1997, he experienced one of his career's greatest triumphs. He took a team no one thought particularly strong all the way to the state tournament in Lexington, where they won their first-round game and a spot in Kentucky's Elite Eight. Then, in the second round, his boys came from over 20 points back in the second half, and barely lost to a powerful squad from Louisville.

Sitting in his little, windowless office behind the gym, black-and-white pictures of his former players mounted in dusty black frames from floor to ceiling on all four walls, Ward described that heroic defeat. That gritty loss, he said, was just another victory for him and this year's team.

Not long after the state tournament, however, the setbacks began rolling in. The mother of one of his players found out from her son that during the Lexington trip Ward had taken the team out to dinner at a Hooters restaurant. That mother, for reasons that Ward says have more to do with her son's playing time than with his sexual purity, complained to the school board, publicly assailing Ward for exposing his players to the famous Hooters waitresses—who dress not unlike cheerleaders, with their tight tank tops and super-small shorts.

A county-wide controversy erupted. Those in Greenup who'd never liked Ward used the Hooters visit to vilify him. Those who'd always supported the coach dismissed the charges as holier-than-thou hogwash. Kentucky, Ohio, and West Virginia news stations mentioned the dispute in their broadcasts. The *Ashland Independent* ran a story on the front page. The *Lexington Herald* picked it up. And then, a week before these cheerleading tryouts, Jay Leno got into the act, making a joke during his *Tonight Show* monologue that ridiculed Ward and the county.

Like any good politician, the superintendent of the Greenup County schools carefully balanced himself on the fence, thus angering everyone and satisfying no one. A couple of days after the Jay Leno joke, he fired Ward as basketball coach, but allowed him to remain in his phys. ed teaching job and also decided to let him reapply for the coaching spot. If Ward does reapply, the superintendent is off the hook, because according to Kentucky state law, the Greenup High principal has the authority to hire his school's varsity basketball coach no matter what the superintendent has to say. According to everyone in Greenup—from assistant cheer-

leading coach Randy Peffer to *Greenup News-Times* editor Mason Branham, to County Judge Executive Bobby Carpenter—Greenup High principal Jim Thoroughman will probably give Ward his job back.

As Ward walks out of the gym, Shawnda leads a pack of Greenup cheerleading veterans in. On this day and the next, the senior cheerleaders will teach the younger girls the chants, dances, and stunts they must perform, one at a time, in front of a panel of tryout judges. As recent national champions, and soon-to-be high school graduates, the seniors take the opportunity to swagger. They talk among themselves and giggle. Shawnda and Jerri Floyd flirt with the boys playing basketball, making fun of them whenever they miss a shot or make a bad pass. Kasey Dillow, her long, thick brown hair hanging unrestrained down the middle of her back, demands the ball from the boys, who chivalrously consent. Kasey drains a foul shot, then coyly walks away, denying the boys so much as a backward glance.

Rachel Brown sits on the gym floor, stretches out her thighs, and watches the senior cheerleaders with a pained expression on her face. She is thinking, as she is wont to do, about her standing back tuck, and hoping that the older girls can let bygones be bygones about her mix-up with that other girl's boyfriend.

The standing has eluded Rachel for almost a year now, and she still can't land it without someone behind her, spotting her, bracing her with a hand on her lower back, so she won't hit the floor with her face. She's afraid, that's all. It's some sort of mental block. A curse, really.

A few days before, on a gray Saturday afternoon, Rachel explained this curse. She was sitting on a plush brown leather couch in her family's expansive brick house, which stands three stories tall in northern Greenup County, not far from the river and Portsmouth, Ohio. Rachel's father is a dentist, and his thriving practice provides the Browns with one of the most opulent lifestyles in all of Greenup County. But nothing comes easily here. While their beautiful house was under construction in 1995, the Browns, who had already sold their previous house to finance the project, had to live in a barn next door to their new property. Now the Browns use that barn as a garage for their two new cars, a minivan and a sedan.

Rachel looks past her parents, who sit quietly on an adjacent couch. She's peering out the glass doors of the den at the brown-and-yellow valley that snakes off to the west below the Browns' ten acres of land. A pretty blue lake once shimmered in that valley, but the recent flood caused a dam to burst, and the lake scuttled off into the Ohio River.

"My bad luck started at the beginning of the year when we first had physicals," says Rachel. "I found out that I had two extra bones in my knee. I just have really bad knees and ankles anyway. So that's always been a problem for tumbling and stuff. Since we found that out, like a month later, I fell on the track at a football game, and I like, chipped my elbow, or something. And I did something to my tailbone. I was out for a couple of weeks then. And then, after that, I don't know what I did after that. I hurt my back or something, because of basin', it was hard on me. And then I had my appendectomy. Two weeks later, I was in the car accident, you know, got a concussion."

Despite Rachel's tendency to fret over everything, she usually manages to appear calm. Her legs are carefully crossed now, her hands held serenely in her lap. But her darting eyes and fast-talking mouth betray her. Rachel's words tumble out of her mouth, unrestrained. She loves to talk. Her lungs and tongue strain to keep up with her churning thoughts. As she talks, she glances up, down, out at the empty lake, at her mom, at her dad, at her hands. Rachel has trouble controlling her thoughts. She thinks about her weight, she thinks about her appearance, she thinks about whether she's nice enough, she thinks about the older cheerleaders, who don't seem to like her, she thinks and thinks and thinks about her standing back tuck. Coach Berry calls her Psycho Child.

Rachel isn't big and strong like Shawnda Bates, nor is she tiny. She's short, about five feet tall. And she's slim, but not skinny. She's got a softness about her that she exaggerates by calling "chubby." At times, she's been a flyer, but in recent years, she's become a bit too heavy, so she's been basin'. Lifting girls up into the air who aren't much lighter than she is has strained her back and made mastering her standing that much more difficult. To complete a back flip from a standing position, Rachel must have good muscle flexibility in her back.

Then there are all the other, unlikely ailments that make Rachel feel cursed. Those two extra bones floating around beside her kneecap may have been chipped off it at some point during her cheerleading career, as a result of hundreds of landings on asphalt and hardwood. (Rachel has cheered seriously since the fifth grade, and she began her gymnastics training when she was old enough to walk.) Or she may have been born with them. Either way, her knee hurts now, and the pain makes her leg muscles constrict when she tries certain gymnastics flips, namely the standing back tuck. Rachel worries that she may shatter one of those bones somehow. Then she would need surgery to remove the bits of bone gumming up her knee's works. So Rachel worries about surgery, because with surgery comes rehab and a prolonged absence from cheerleading.

While cheering at a JV football game this past fall, Rachel fell on the concrete Greenup High track. Her tailbone still hurts from that one. Then, in February, she noticed a weird pain in her side just before the national JV competition at Disney World. She'd first felt a twinge a couple of weeks before, during some of the last few practices in Greenup, before the trip to Florida. She thought her body was just cramping, so she loaded up on Advil. The day of the JV team's performance in the Indiana Jones theater, the pain got worse. This time, despite the painkiller, it wouldn't go away. Rachel gritted her teeth and let adrenaline soothe the pain; she and the rest of the Greenup JV won second place in the country.

The day Rachel returned home from Orlando, she went to her private tumbling class at a gym in Ohio. She'd already put nationals behind her and wanted to figure out the standing back so she could make the varsity at the April tryouts. But when she warmed up with some simple flips, she nearly passed out.

"I just did a back handspring," she recalls, "and I was going to do two. And it had always hurt, you know. But I didn't think nothing about it. I just thought that I'd pulled a muscle or something. You know, that's what [the Greenup coaches] told me. They were all, 'You probably just pulled a muscle. You'll be all right. Just tough it out.' So I did. I mean, you know, I didn't think anything about it being my appendix. And you don't have time to complain, you just have to do it. The more you complain, the more you set the squad back. But after those two [back handsprings], I felt like something was just killing me, something was jabbing in my sides."

That day, she was admitted to the hospital. The surgery went well, but the doctor expected Rachel to take it easy for at least two months afterward. No tumbling, no stunting, no cheering. But tryouts were set to begin in two months, and Rachel had to get her standing under control before then.

"I tumbled about four weeks after the surgery," Rachel says." I wasn't really supposed to. But I wanted to do it. I wanted to prepare myself."

Two days after she resumed her training, her sister Sara, who at seventeen years old had recently acquired her driver's license, gave Rachel a ride home from the gym. Along the way, Sara misjudged a tight turn, and the car slid off the narrow mountain road and into a tree. Rachel and Sara were both wearing their seat belts, luckily, but Rachel's head slammed into the passenger-side dashboard. She got a concussion and had to be hospitalized that night. Again, her doctor told her to take it easy, but the next day Rachel was back tumbling.

Rachel knows that the Wednesday and Thursday tryouts are only practice sessions for Friday, when a panel of two judges picked by Coach Berry will rate Rachel's stunting, dancing, chanting, and tumbling. Rachel also knows that, when all is said and done, Berry will pick the team. So she hopes to impress the coach these first two days with her work ethic, her seriousness, and her desire to land the dang standing.

Rachel has already been through the stress of cheerleading tryouts five times—during all four years of middle school, and last spring, when she made the Greenup JV—but, she says, "This year will probably be the worst ever. I know I'm just one trick away. And if I don't do it, I'm gonna be so mad at myself. I just, I don't know. I mean it's really not that nerve-racking, because you have fun when you do it. Hopefully, tomorrow, I'll throw it. Just as long as I attempt it. As long as I try it, they'll know I'm close."

And just how close is she?

"For me, the reason I haven't been able to do my standing yet is I'm slow with my knees in going up. When you go up, you've got to go up to a certain height. And when you go up, everything's supposed to all go together. Your knees are supposed to go with your hands. And I just can't get that. You're supposed to be like a puppet, that's what Candy always tells me. And when you get to the highest point that you think you're supposed to go, you do like a back roll, and you just pull your knees over." Rachel claps her hands. "And land. But I just can't get that puppet action going. You see, you have this muscle right here in the back of your leg." Rachel grabs the base of her right calf. "And it's especially for jumping. It's the muscle you have to use. But it just hasn't helped me yet. So what I do is I go straight back, and I just kind of crash. I land it sometimes, and sometimes I can't."

The cheer coaches have arrived at the Greenup County gym. Hank Light has rounded up the seniors and led them over to the school's cafeteria, where he will teach them a dance he choreographed for these tryouts. Once the seniors learn it, they'll teach it to the younger girls. Berry and

Peffer sit together on the lone bleacher near the stretching cheerleaders, talking in hushed tones about who has shown up for today's tryouts and who hasn't. These are slim pickings.

At first, Rachel watches them and tries to make out what they're saying. But their whispering and pointing only stress her out more, so she turns her attention elsewhere, choosing to stare very intently at the glossy wood on which she sits and stretches. At times like these, when Rachel worries so much over herself, she tries to calm down by thinking how lucky she is. She thinks of Linda Goble.

Linda and Melissa Morris probably got into Mrs. Morris's boxy Buick at Mason County High School a few minutes ago and began the hour-long drive back to Greenup County. This coming Saturday, the day after tryouts end, Linda and the Morris family plan to go house-hunting in Mason County, in preparation for the June move.

Rachel became good friends with Linda over the past year, and she cried last night when Linda and Melissa left the pizza party at Fred's. A few months ago, she even entertained the idea of asking her parents to put Linda up in their big new house so that Linda could stay—and cheer—in Greenup.

"Linda's different, you know," says Rachel. "She's had a really tough life. She's really mean. She's really two-faced, you know. She just don't know how to act. And she thinks she can go back and live with her mom and dad, but she can't. Sometimes, she says, 'I would love to live with you. You have such a nice life. I'd love to live with you.' But, I mean, I couldn't put up with her. I mean I'm pretty nice, but somebody grabbing at me all the time, taking my clothes, using my makeup, that would just about get on my last nerve. We had an exchange student last year, and that just about got me."

According to Rachel, some girls from the JV squad may not miss Linda as much as others.

"Linda talks about some of the girls really bad," Rachel says, squinting upward then looking me square in the eye then looking down then looking at a lamp to her right. "She's caused a lot of fights on the squad. I don't think she thinks about what she says. But it hurts people. She has a lot of power in her, and I think she tumbles from within, with her anger. I think she's trying to make her mom and dad proud. She's just got to understand that she can't live with them. She says people treat her bad here, they treat her different because she doesn't live with her mom and dad. She thinks people want her to leave, that no one here likes her."

Rachel pauses, maybe for breath.

"At least she can do her standing."

Rachel finishes stretching, then practices her tumbling runs across the basketball court. Before and after each dash, jump, shove, flip, and whirl, Rachel glances furtively at Berry and Peffer to see if they are watching her.

Soon, Hank Light and the seven senior cheerleaders return from the cafeteria and set up the team's stereo underneath one of the basketball hoops. On the other side of the court, those boys keep playing their pickup basketball. Occasionally, they let the game spread to the middle of the court and Berry barks at them to rein it in.

"Watch it, boys. If Coach Ward had the gym, he wouldn't give my girls a foot of the floor. I'm doing you a favor. Brooke!" Berry says, calling to sophomore Brooke Meenach, who is practicing her tumbling at center court. "You tell me if those boys get in your way."

Brooke nods, embarrassed. The boys mumble something among themselves and laugh, but they move their game away from the cheerleaders.

"They better not give me no attitude," Berry mutters.

Light has turned on the stereo now and is playing the song accompanying his new dance. With a pumping techno beat in the background, a soulful female voice screeches, "Can you feel the groove? Can you feel the groove? Can you feel the groove?"

Shawnda, making sure she knows the dance, swings to the rhythm filling the air and bouncing off the concrete bleachers up above. Rachel and the rest of the younger girls join in and try to imitate her.

It's a tricky little dance, and the younger girls get frustrated.

"I don't know about you," says freshman Amanda Kitchen to Rachel, speaking in a low voice so as not to be heard by the coaches, "but I can't feel the groove."

Peffer and Berry, meanwhile, continue their own hushed conversation, landing on the topic of the seniors' postgraduation plans.

Jess Madden, the girl who tore up her knee just weeks before nationals two years ago, came back so strongly this season after a long, difficult rehab that the University of Kentucky recruited her for their squad, offering a partial scholarship. But Jess says she's going to attend nearby Ashland Community College, live at home, and help out at her parents' two family-owned day care centers.

"That girl has so much ability," says Berry, shaking her head. "But she's immature, *very* immature. Her parents give her no drive."

Certainly, Jess has drive. And Berry knows it. Jess never would have recovered from her torn knee ligament if she didn't have drive. Berry's just frustrated by Jess's fear of the unknown, her inability to strike out on her own.

When Jess first came out of surgery, she had to stay off the injured leg and let the reconstructed knee heal for almost a month. She wore a cast from her ankle to the top of her thigh, so she could walk only with crutches, and she could not sit down. About all she could do was lie on her back—which she did, most of the time.

Then the cast came off, and Jess began her rehab. At first, she could hardly straighten her leg in front of her from a seated position. Her leg muscles were so feeble that she could barely lift three pounds. After four weeks of exercise, three two-hour workouts each week, full of leg extensions done again and again, like drip-torture, Jess could lift eight pounds. Four weeks later, after another twelve workouts, she could lift fifteen pounds. She got used to the bruises under her arms and on her rib cage that came from having to lean on crutches every time she stood or walked. Still, she drove on.

When asked if she ever thought about letting her rehab work go, letting cheerleading go, Jess has said, "Yeah, I thought about that, but I was willing to work at it, because, I mean, cheerleading is, you know, my life."

Yet Jess is now prepared to give up cheerleading rather than move away from her family and her cozy Greenup womb. As it is for Linda Goble and Melissa Morris, Greenup County is a part of Jess's being that she can't bear to let go.

Jess practices an elite mount directly in front of Berry. Two girls pop her up over their heads, holding only her right foot and ankle. With grace and ease, Jess flies straight up into the air, lifting her left foot up over her head as she goes. When she reaches the top of the mount, Jess's left hand meets her left foot above her head, and for a few moments, she balances there, her body perfectly still.

"Oh, my word," says Berry, her voice low, "that was beautiful. Just beautiful. Oh, that breaks my heart. Jess!" she says, her voice rising, "you better come with me and Shawnda and try out at Louisville. You better. Shawnda, you tell her."

Upon dismounting, Jess smiles, shakes her head stiffly, and looks away from Berry.

Shawnda, confused, looks at Berry, then at Jess.

Shawnda will try out two weekends hence for the tumbling contingent of Louisville's cheer squad, and Berry feels confident that she will win a spot on the team. Berry's more worried that those tryouts will come and go with Jess still stuck at home with her parents, doing nothing.

Watching Jess nail that heel stretch so beautifully reminds Berry of another of her worries regarding next year's team. The Greenup varsity has only two flyers returning from last season: Aubrey Warnock, whose shaky performance at nationals nearly gave Berry a heart attack, and Kelena McClurg, a steady, graceful flyer, who'll be a senior next year. Berry will need one, maybe two, new flyers for next year's team. Rachel Brown might do, but she'll have to lose some weight. And the fact that she doesn't yet have a solid standing back doesn't inspire much confidence.

Rachel Wills may have to do. She's the skinniest of all the prospective members of the varsity, so weight will not be a problem. (Coach Peffer calls her Olive Oyl.) Berry knows of Wills's run-in with her father, so she also knows Wills is tough, something she can't say about Rachel Brown and most of the other young girls coming from the JV. But Wills's edgy style and wooden facial expressions make her a mediocre flying candidate as well.

From the far corner of the gym, Rachel Brown's mother walks in and takes a seat on a plastic chair across the court from the coaches. Mrs. Brown tried to stay away, but she's concerned about her daughter's desperate desire to make the Greenup team. "If she doesn't make it," Mrs. Brown said at the JV pizza party, "I don't know what she'll do. She'll be devastated."

Rachel's parents didn't want her to get involved with Greenup High cheerleading in the first place. Sitting on a loveseat in their large brick house, they explained their mixed feelings.

"It's a lot of time," Mrs. Brown begins. In fact, the Browns felt it was a lot of everything—a lot of time, a lot of money, a lot of traveling, a lot of stress.

Then Dr. Brown, the only father to attend the JV pizza party, takes over. Slouched back in a couch, wearing a pricey white nylon sweat suit, he props himself up onto his elbow so he can be heard. "It's a very demanding program," he says. "Our whole life, instead of us just scheduling our life, we have to schedule it around the cheerleading. Everything."

"We're very involved with our church," adds Rachel's mom, "and Rachel can't come when we go on Wednesdays."

"We're at a place where we can't have people buy stuff from us. There's no way," says Dr. Brown, referring to the extensive fund-raising in which every Greenup cheerleader must participate. As well off as the Browns are, it wouldn't feel right hitting up their poorer neighbors for money. "So I'm writing checks for a hundred dollars to Avon, or if she doesn't sell any, I just make it for sixty dollars because that's the profit they're supposed to make. There's a lot of things like that. I mean I'm not a wealthy dentist, but I've got a good practice and everything. So we can finance it and do that kind of thing. But everybody can't do that. So the moms are out trying to sell all this stuff for their daughters. Somebody used to be at my office every day. Now that I've got a daughter who's a cheerleader, at least I don't have to hear it no more, for right now."

Dr. Brown knows that once Rachel leaves cheerleading, either when she graduates from high school, or if she fails to make the team this year—he'll keep giving money to Greenup High cheerleading, just as he's always done.

"I've been here seventeen years, and every year I'd help send them to Florida," he says. "I've always helped sponsor the team and stuff because they are the proudest thing we've got in Greenup County, as far as notoriety. You know, people will say, 'Hey, you're from that school that's got that cheerleading squad.'"

It was only this past winter, however, when he traveled to Florida to see his daughter compete for the national JV championship, that Dr. Brown saw what all the fuss was about.

"I mean, I didn't realize the level of competition," he says. "And it really brought a sense of pride and stuff that you do have when you see the team win."

Rachel's father smiles; the corners of his blond mustache dance. "We're enjoying it for her. We're glad that she's happy. It takes a whole family's commitment."

Rachel laughs at her dad's apparent graciousness.

"I begged, and I cried, and I threw the biggest fit till I got to cheer," she says, smiling at her father and setting the record straight. "And I'm glad they let me, because I don't regret a bit of it."

Unlike Jess Madden, Rachel wants desperately to cheerlead at the University of Kentucky. Ever since she was five years old, it has been her dream of dreams.

"I just love the publicity," she says, her eyes momentarily still as she imagines herself amid the hype that swirls about the UK cheer team. "I just want to be . . ." For once, Rachel can't find the words. "You know?" She laughs. "I just seen 'em cheer, and that's what I want to do. I'm not gonna be going up there to be Miss Kentucky or nothin'. I just want to cheer."

To get to UK, Rachel must not only make the Greenup squad, but she must become a top flyer for the Musketeers. Otherwise, the UK coaches won't notice her. To be a Greenup flyer, she's going to have to lose some of her "chubbiness." She weighs 115 pounds right now. By next fall, she hopes to get down to 95.

Rachel worships the cheerleading world and its ideals with a nearly religious faith. For her, cheerleading is about more than publicity, flying high on her teammates' shoulders, hitting back tucks, and getting skinny. Cheerleading is such a great, honorable endeavor, she says, because it requires its participants to maintain a constant state of grace, to aspire to the height of idealized female virtue.

"You have a certain image," Rachel says. "And you really need to keep that image to be liked. You have to really watch what you do, watch what you say. Because no matter what, people're gonna say, 'She cheers on the varsity for Greenup County. Can you believe what she just said?' You know, it gets around. When I was little, I always saw Greenup cheerleaders as pretty and nice. And I just wanted to be one. Because they were cheerleaders."

Trying to explain the Greenup cheerleader image, Rachel brings up Staci Bates, Shawnda's cousin and a sophomore on the recent national champion Greenup team. Rachel likes Staci a lot, but unfortunately, Staci won't be able to be on the varsity next year because her father couldn't find work in Greenup. A few weeks ago, Staci's family moved an hour north to Ohio, where Staci's father got a job operating a forklift at a plastics plant.

"Staci is probably one of the best cheerleaders that I've ever met," says Rachel. "She's so sweet and kind. You never hear her say anything bad about anybody. She really is a model cheerleader. That's what Greenup County wants. They want somebody like her. It was really tough for everybody to see her leave. It's hard on everybody."

Rachel thinks she's fairly sweet and nice, but, she says, some of the older cheerleaders don't agree.

"A lot of the girls on varsity—well not a lot of them, but a few of them—don't like me," says Rachel. "They think I've tried to steal their boyfriends, stuff like that, stupid stuff like that. You know Kelena Mc-Clurg? She doesn't like me because she thinks I like her boyfriend, and I don't even like her boyfriend. But she just doesn't understand . . . I understand how she feels with some of the rumors people say. I would get mad, too. But she talks with people about it on varsity, and it gets more people turned against me, and it's just like, *I don't like him.* I think next year will be better if I make it. Because she'll get to know me, and get to understand that I'm not like that."

The rumor among the cheerleaders is that Rachel had a tryst with Kelena's boyfriend. Despite Rachel's denials of this and her earnest desire to get along with everybody—especially the varsity veterans—many of the girls won't let the issue drop. All of the cheerleaders going out for the Greenup varsity are plenty attractive, but Rachel might be the one who turns the most heads. That doesn't help her standing with Kelena and some of the other girls on the squad, some of whom have jumped to the conclusion that Rachel has a habit of stealing other girls' boyfriends. As one cheerleader puts it, "Rachel does have a way of doing that to people."

Rachel tries to demonstrate her sweetness, her niceness, even as she describes how she's been victimized by the other girls' jealousy. She refuses to say anything bad about Kelena or anyone else. For Rachel, talking diplomatically about all this is an exercise, another cheerleading exercise.

"When you have differences, and you perform, you have to put those aside," Rachel says. "Because those differences can make somebody fall. And if I was a base next year, and I had to base her, if we were still mad at each other, I mean maybe I would drop her. I wouldn't, you know, because I know I'd get in a lot of trouble. Some people just handle their anger in different ways. I don't hold a grudge against her. Because I understand. She's in love, and she's hurt."

Wearing white shorts with the words "I'm Behind the Musketeers" emblazoned in hot pink across the seat, Kelena watches Rachel practice her standing back tuck. Coach Light is spotting Rachel, placing his hand on her lower back and bracing her while she flips around. With Light there, Rachel lands the flip, once, twice, three times, four times.

"That was all you," Light says. "I'm not doing anything."

Light backs away. Rachel stares straight ahead, her eyes open wide. Rachel claps, claps again, lowers her hands to her sides, and makes two fists. She sucks in her breath, holds it, and jumps up and backward, but she puts her hands down on the floor and turns the back tuck into a back handspring.

It's nearing the end of today's tryout practice. Many of the girls have already left the gym and have begun their trek home. Those still here have ended their workouts, and like Kelena, turn their attention to Rachel and her standing back tuck.

"Just do it, Rachel," Coach Peffer shouts.

Beside him, Berry sits silently with her legs crossed and her arms folded, watching.

"Trust me, just throw it. It doesn't hurt to fall," says Amanda Pennington, the girl who had the most trouble with her standing at nationals last February, and fell during the preliminary round.

Rachel has straightened herself up, trying to forget her failed last attempt. She brushes a wisp of hair out of her eyes that escaped from her frayed ponytail, and gets ready to go for it again.

Rachel's mother is leaning forward in her chair. Her hands hold her cheeks.

"Pull, Rachel, pull," Wills hollers. "You can do it."

Rachel, wide-eyed, claps twice, makes her fists, and lunges back. She turns a disappointing back handspring.

"I'm just scared," she says, breathing hard, her face red and sweaty. "I'm scared of the floor right now."

Kelena and the last remaining cheerleaders talk and giggle as they walk out of the gym.

Rachel's mother hasn't moved. She's still gripping her cheeks.

Coach Peffer looks at Berry. Berry meets his eyes with her own, raises her eyebrows, and lets out a small sigh.

At Rachel's request, Light steps back up and spots her some more. Berry, meanwhile, has seen enough. She pushes herself up from the bleacher and starts walking away. Rachel tries to stay focused, turning her back tuck with the help of Light's comforting hand as Berry walks past her and out of the Greenup gym.

C h a p t e r   S i x

Olive Oyl

Rachel Wills is mentally the most impervious but physically the most fragile of all the girls going out for the Greenup varsity. When she cheers, the taut muscles in her arms and legs cling to the bones under her skin. When she dances, she doesn't project a coy vulnerability. She doesn't radiate eroticism. Her motions, like her body, are hard, rough, brittle. Not full, not soft, not sensuous.

"Olive Oyl," Coach Peffer's nickname for her, fits Wills well. She bears a strong resemblance to the skinny, squealing cartoon character, except that Wills doesn't need a muscle-bound sailor with a spinach obsession to protect her.

She peppers her sentences with the teenagerish "like," like, a lot, especially when she's discussing something that her sharp mind has trouble drawing a bead on. She talks slowly, carefully, in a low but confident tone. And she likes the phrase "It's hard 'cause . . ." She believes most things in life are hard, and she will say how come. Not that she can't handle it.

For her, tryouts are a formality. Berry knows she will need Wills's strength and resolve to help keep next year's young team focused. Even so, Berry plans to keep Olive Oyl in the back and to the side of Greenup's dance formations.

Wills joined the Greenup JV this past fall in the middle of the football season. After a couple of the varsity cheerleaders quit the squad—one because she was pregnant—and a couple of JV cheerleaders were bumped up to the varsity to fill their spots, Coach Peffer, who was Wills's algebra teacher, wanted to fill the holes left on the JV. He had worked with Wills when she cheered for McKell Middle, and he knew she could execute the tough tumbling moves required to cheer for Greenup, so he asked her to join up.

Wills mentioned Peffer's offer to her boyfriend, Jesse Stapleton, a football player for Greenup High. Jesse was very supportive. He didn't worry about the amount of time cheerleading might take away from his relationship with Wills. Rather, he told Wills how good cheerleading might be for her, what with the structure it offers, the camaraderie among the girls, and so forth.

Says Wills, "Jesse was like, 'Yeah. Go for it.'"

Wills wasn't so sure, however, because cheerleading is not her life. She likes the sport, particularly the high level that Greenup County dominates, but she's not willing to sacrifice her schoolwork for anything. During the four years she cheered in middle school, she had a good time. It kept her busy, productive, away from her father. But a lot has happened since middle school. Wills didn't try out for the Greenup JV during the spring of her eighth grade year because it didn't occur to her.

"So much stuff was going on with like, my dad and my mom and stuff," she says. "I just never even thought about it." Wills pauses, to think. She sits with her body angled to the right, her head twisted to the left. She's wearing an oversized forest-green "Greenup Cheerleading" tank top, which hangs loosely on her skinny frame. "Just like, my dad," she continues, "he drinks all the time and stuff, and well, he's been like that for as long as I can remember, and I guess I started getting older and wanting to do more, and he didn't want me to do stuff. He would, like, if I did something, he would hit me for something just, for something stupid."

Wills pauses again, looks away. She's an only child, used to solitude, to keeping herself to herself. She seems to be considering how much she's willing to tell.

"I would want to do stuff with my friends—little things, like talking on the phone. He was protective, really bad. I didn't really have very many boyfriends. I mean, I would talk to guys, but I would never go out or nothing. Me and Jesse had never really been out yet. But anyway, we fought all the time, my dad and me.

"My mom's not really capable of taking care of me, neither. So my grandmother had really took care of me most of the time. She lived with us. It was her house. She got it from my great-grandpa. It had been his house. We lived there for a while; then we moved away. But the other house we lived in, it flooded, so we had to move back.

"My grandma took care of me because my mom was like—My mom, she's thirty-seven, but she acts like she's probably about twelve, so she can't really take care of me. She's disabled, you know? She doesn't have the ability to be, like, an adult. She just kinda did some stuff with me, but she couldn't take care of me like my grandma. I think it's kinda my dad's fault, too, the way my mom was, because he was kind of overbearing, and he wouldn't let her do anything. She was born with it, but I think he kinda made it worse, kinda made her think that she couldn't do anything. Because he always told her, 'If anything ever happened to me, you wouldn't be able to do anything. You wouldn't have nothing.'"

Toward the end of Wills's eighth grade year, her relationship with her father, Danny, had begun to deteriorate. Wills's mother, Ruth, was powerless to stop it, and Wills's loving grandmother—Danny's mother—was too easily swayed by her son's arguments that the thirteen-year-old Wills deserved what was coming to her. Looking for a way out, Wills convinced her dad's brother, Bobby, to take her into his home and let her live with his family. That was "hard" because Uncle Bobby and his wife have three young children of their own.

"It also made it hard," adds Wills, "'cause my uncle Bobby, he was afraid it would cause conflicts between him and my dad, and he didn't want that, because, you know, he's his brother—his only brother, 'cause his other brother, Timmy, he was murdered. He and Timmy were friends. I guess they were drinking, and he just, I don't know. I was little so I don't remember. It happened in like, '82, and I was born in '81. I don't think I was a year old yet."

Coal Branch is the road Wills grew up on. It winds west from the Ohio River through the wooded hills in the north-central portion of Greenup County. Young tobacco leaves, green and leathery, sprout in rows along parts of it now. Thin trees cover everywhere else. The few houses are tucked back, at the end of dirt and gravel driveways, hidden by the trees.

When she was little, all Wills knew was Coal Branch Road. But when she moved in with her uncle Bobby in upper north Greenup, she saw other ways of being, and her resentment of her father and of the life he'd given her grew.

Asked what her father does for a living, Wills snorts. "Sitting on the couch, drinking beer, that's his job." Like when she cheers, her smile is forced, and it fades quickly. "He'll work sometimes. I mean, he's really smart. He could do just about anything he wanted to do. He can build houses. He went to college for I don't know how long, but he went to college. He didn't graduate high school. He only went to the eighth grade, but then he got his GED and went to college, a vocational college. He's worked so many different things. He used to drive a taxicab. He used to be a truck driver. And he can build houses. He just doesn't want to, because he thinks drinking is more important than everything else in the world."

Wills sees some good in her father. What makes her so mad is that he uses the good in bad ways.

"He knows how to manipulate people," she says. "He's done that for years with my grandma. 'Cause I know if it was up to my grandma, she would throw my dad out. I know she would, 'cause my grandma and me are closer than my dad and her. I guess it makes it hard on her because he's the only person my grandma has."

Wills admits that she provoked her dad back when it all hit the fan two years ago, but she's not the least bit apologetic.

"I guess it was like, he really didn't have any respect for me, so there was no reason for me to have respect for him. I guess I kind of added to the problem by, you know, when he would tell me to do something, I would be like, 'I don't want to.' He'd never done stuff for me, so I didn't see why there was any reason why I'd want to help him. Like my grandma, if she would ask me to do something, there would be no problem. I guess when you grow up, if somebody's not going to help you, there's no reason why you should help them. That's kinda how I see it."

A few weeks after Wills moved in with her uncle Bobby, during the summer after her eighth-grade year, her dad asked her to come back for a visit.

"I went home for three days, and he hit me and kicked me, and all kinds of stuff. So then, that's when I moved here." Wills motions to Pat Heineman, mother of Wills's good friend Angie Heineman. Mrs. Heineman has been leaning quietly against the side of the doorway to her living room, just listening. Now she speaks.

"In the beginning, I said she should stay with family," Mrs. Heineman says. "The first time Angie asked if she could come stay here, I said, 'You don't want to get in the middle of something.' I knew Rachel had an aunt, and I thought she should stay with family. That didn't work out for her, so

we discussed it, and we decided that it would be okay for her to stay with us. She's a good kid, and it's worked out fine. It was a big adjustment for Angie because she's an only daughter. And I'm sure it was a big adjustment for Rachel. But it's pretty well worked itself out. They love each other to death. But, you know, sometimes—they don't argue much—but at times, they just get tired of one other. In the beginning, they were like friends, they were really good friends. Now they're like sisters."

Mrs. Heineman gazes softly at Wills.

"We think the world of Rachel."

Wills nods at Mrs. Heineman, and adds, "She has legal custody of me."

The second day of tryouts is a lot like the first. The girls practice Hank Light's dance—"Can you feel the groove? Can-can-can-can you feel the groove?"—again and again. One part of it calls for the cheerleaders to jump up into the air, do the splits and touch the tips of their toes with their hands, and then, rather than landing on their feet, the girls must land on their rears. The dance picks up with the girls thrusting their hips up from the floor. For Rachel Brown, with her tender tailbone, every practice-landing on the gym floor, butt-first, hurts.

It doesn't feel good for the other girls either. But Rachel is really in pain. She doesn't want to seem like a crybaby, so she keeps going, although her grimaces grow.

While Berry watches the girls practice the dance, she tries to decide whom she's going to keep. Rachel Brown has almost got her standing down, and Berry knows that something in her head is all that's stopping her. The Greenup coaches haven't yet learned of the rift developing between Rachel and Kelena, and they figure that Rachel will probably get the standing mastered before the team's first competition on Labor Day weekend. Coach Peffer thinks she will. Berry hopes so too, but she isn't sure.

Then there's Miranda Elliott; she doesn't have much of a standing right now, and Berry thinks that she may not be enough of an athlete to pull it off ever. Miranda is the reigning Miss Greenup County Fair beauty queen. Berry thinks she may be "too much of a lady" and "not enough of a tomboy" to make it as a competitive cheerleader.

Berry turns away from the dancing cheerleaders and looks at Aimee Lewis, a freshman who cheered on the varsity last year, sitting out today's practice with a hurt knee, her crutches resting beside her. Last night at tumbling practice, Aimee was goofing around, trying to show how flexible she was. She pulled her right foot over her head and then, to be funny, pulled it behind her head—imitating a contortionist, or something. All of a sudden, her face scrunched up and she fell to the padded floor. She'd torn some cartilage in her knee.

No one knows yet whether Aimee's going to need surgery, or a long re-hab. If she has to take an extensive leave of absence from cheerleading, Berry will be left with yet another hole to fill.

Berry watches Aimee tickle the baby in her arms. The little boy belongs to the girl sitting next to Aimee, sixteen-year-old Amanda Dean, a Greenup High junior and former varsity cheerleader. Amanda had to quit the Greenup squad back in the fall when she got pregnant. Now, her baby boy is a couple months old, she's gotten herself in reasonable shape, and she wants to try out for next year's varsity. That's why she's here.

Despite her pressing need for qualified competitive cheerleaders, Berry won't let Amanda try out.

"She's got other things to be worrying about now, besides cheerlead-ing," the coach decrees. "I was a teenage mother, and I know."

Wills and a few other girls stop working on the dance and decide to practice their stunting.

Berry watches as three girls lift Wills into the air. "Straighten your leg!" the coach hollers. "And tighten your butt! Squeeze those cheeks!" Wills tries to balance on her right foot. She's wobbly. Clenching her teeth be-hind scowling lips and flaring nostrils, she manages to get control of her lanky body, enough to hold her left knee up to her chest and raise her fists over her head.

"There, that's it," says Berry. "Now. Smile!"

Wills isn't sure where she got it from. It may simply have come as a reac-tion to her unmotivated father. But from an early age, she has always wanted to be great at everything she does. Her pursuits began as diver-sions, ways of escaping from home, even when she couldn't leave. She read voraciously. Her favorite writers are Edgar Allan Poe and William Shake-speare, her favorite story "The Tell-Tale Heart."

In that old wooden house on Coal Branch Road where she grew up, her small, one-window room was her sanctuary. She had no siblings to play with, and no neighborhood friends, because out in the wooded hills there is no neighborhood. So she holed up in her room, and she read. In particular, she loved fantastic stories told in romantic styles, about things big and beautiful and far away. She also dove into the macabre—ghost stories, stories about death and dying, about murder. Wills began to write her own poetry when she was thirteen.

Wills also taught herself to tumble. When she was nine, she mastered a back handspring by flopping around on her parents' full-sized bed. She practiced tumbling runs on her front lawn. When she was thirteen, after throwing herself backward time and again into the grass and dirt, she learned to do a standing back tuck.

As Wills got older, cheerleading and reading and writing became more than avenues of escape; they became means to an end. If she worked hard enough at them, she could avoid her parents and their shabby life. Nowadays, when she talks about all the reading she's done, Wills calls it "studyin'."

"I worry that my grades will drop because of cheerleading because I won't have time to study like I always have. But really, I study more, because I think I'm not going to have time to do it. Schooling to me is really more important than cheerleading. But I just had to have something to keep me busy. I never wanted to stay home. I couldn't stand to be there. When I got older, I would come here"—the Heinemans' house is a mile and a half down Coal Branch from Wills's former home, then up a knobby hill along a nameless gravel road—"and I'd go to my other friends' houses. Or I'd stay in my room and read. I didn't study with my friends, though. When I study, I like to study by myself. I get more done."

Wills has always wanted to do big things, as a journalist, a poet, or maybe a doctor. She says it would also be great to win a national cheerleading championship. The problem is, she can't do that by herself.

Asked about Greenup High's cheerleading chances next year, Wills erases all passion from her face and speaks in a detached tone.

"It depends on if all the girls want to win, and they all give everything they have. That has a lot to do with it, 'cause a lot of the girls just don't want to. They like to party, and they just want to get the practicing over with. I know everybody wants to win nationals. I was with a couple of the girls the other night outside the Burger King, and they were talking. And there was some guy that was sitting up there and he was talking about cheerleading.

"He was saying we were crazy, and blah-blah-blah. He was saying, 'You girls are crazy. I was at a competition, and I was watching and some girl fell, and they just left her.'

"And I was like, 'We've kind of been taught to go on with the show.'

"And Amanda Kitchen was like, 'We're national champions.'

"And I was sitting there thinking, 'Well, last year's group was national champions, but we're not yet.' I was like, 'Maybe. If you-all want to work.'

"I mean I know they want to be, because they brag about it. Everybody's like, 'Yeah, we're national champions.' But that's last year's group. This year is a whole new ball game. I want to be able to say that when I know that *I* did it, not when the other group did it, you know?"

Listening to Wills, one can hear the echo of Shawnda Bates. There's the same blunt wisdom, the same absolute confidence. Like Shawnda, Wills has the makings of a strong team leader.

Asked about Miranda Elliott, the girl trying out without much of a standing back tuck, Wills says, "Oh, she makes me so mad. She won't even try. She hasn't even worked on [her standing] for tryouts. I mean, Rachel Brown, she's worked her butt off, and she's scared to do it. Candy doesn't really see. She yells at us and stuff when we won't throw things, but she don't understand it's something we have to get over ourselves. It's not something where somebody yelling at you trying to push you, it's gonna help. You have to do it yourself. For a lot of time, I was afraid to do bounders. Like Aubrey, she can't do full twists anymore. When we freak ourselves out like that, we kind of have to get over it ourselves, and nobody's going to be able to help us do that. It's a mental thing, a mental block, like when you write. You just blank out. It's the same thing. You can't concentrate on it. It's just like, 'I can't do it!'"

Somewhere inside, however, Wills believes she can do it. "Bounders" is the name for a tumbling run in which Wills has to sprint, dive into the air, push off the ground with her hands, flip over, and twist so that when she lands on her feet, she faces the opposite direction. Then it gets tricky. Immediately after landing, so as not to lose her momentum, Wills jumps and does a straight-legged back flip—a whip-back—lands on her feet, then does another back flip, this time with a tuck. For a while last year, Wills was "freaked out" by bounders. But she kept at it, and got it.

Wills is quiet now, looking out a window that provides a view down to Coal Branch from the Heinemans' hill, over a clump of trees and brush. Suddenly, she says: "Last year's squad was in the paper with the milk mustaches and everything. You know the ads in the paper, 'Milk. It does a body good.' Well, they had milk mustaches painted on all of them. If we do the same thing that last year's squad did, then we'll get to do that sort of thing, too."

And maybe her dad will notice. Maybe he'll give Wills some of the respect she requires of him if he is to get any respect from her.

Neither of Wills's parents saw her compete last year with the Greenup JV, nor has her father once seen his daughter cheer throughout Wills's five years as a cheerleader.

"My mom has," says Wills. "She came to a ball game once."

Wills isn't hopeful about having much family at her future performances, though. Ruth Wills moved away from her husband about a year ago, and since then, her daughter says, she's been much happier. Because of her mental defect, Wills's mom must live with someone who can take care of her. First, she moved in with a longtime friend of her family who had an apartment in Ashland. He took care of her, and she came to depend on him. So when he decided to move down to Florida, she went with him.

Ruth Wills left Greenup about a month before tryouts, despite Wills's pleas for her to stay. Wills says her mom's roommate and caretaker has talked about moving back to Kentucky within the next year, but her mom wants to stay in Florida. Apparently, she's got a new boyfriend down there who's offered to take care of her.

Wills has an affection for her mom, if not a dependence upon her. So she misses her. And the occasional long distance phone calls don't allow for much contact.

"I talk to my dad and my grandma," Wills says, awkwardly changing the subject. "I visit 'em. I think it hurt my grandma a little bit, me leaving, 'cause me and my grandma are really close. My grandma, she was like my mom to me, for all those years. I think it hurt her more than it hurt anybody when I left. She'll call me and I'll go down and visit her and stuff. But it's hard because my dad, he'll be down there, and when I go down there, they'll be drinking or something. And I don't go down very often. It kind of hurts my feelings, 'cause when I *do* go down there, they know I don't want them to drink, but they will anyways.

"Oh yeah, my grandma drinks too. She's not like him, but she drinks. And she knows that I don't like for her to drink. When I come down, she tries to hide it. You know, she'll be like, 'Oh, I haven't been drinkin',' you know. I grew up knowing how people act when they've been drinking. So I can spot something like that. I don't know if they just think I'm stupid"—Wills forces out a laugh, then straightens her lips—"or I don't know."

Many members of Wills's family are heavy drinkers, but Wills refuses to join them.

"I know I won't," she says. "I mean, I have friends that drink and stuff. I've had opportunities. I just don't. I know what it can do."

Only Linda Goble, says Wills, is as strict with herself when it comes to alcohol. Wills got to know Linda fairly well last year. As teammates on the Greenup JV, she and Linda talked a few times about their fathers, their families, "and stuff."

"We could relate to each other," says Wills, using the past tense the way kids do after a friend moves away, as if she's dead. "She didn't really like to talk about it, though. It doesn't bother me 'cause I think everyone pretty much knows the whole situation that went on with me. But Linda seemed like, I don't know, she wouldn't say much about her family. And I didn't want to press or anything. I think it's just about that that she was quiet. Because with her friends and stuff, she wasn't at all. She was real loud, and she was fun to be with. She was funny."

Before saying good-bye to Wills and leaving the Heineman household, I notice a picture of a little girl on an end table in the corner of the room beside the couch where I've been sitting. The girl in the picture has on a white dress tied at the waist with a pink ribbon, and she's kneeling in such a way that her feet and legs are hidden by the crinkly white folds of her dress, which spills daintily upon the floor, enhancing her doll-like look. The girl is smiling sweetly, and across her immature chest hangs a lavender sash that bears the words "Miss Ideal" printed in curly silver letters.

"Is that Angie?" I ask, figuring the girl in the picture can't be Wills.

"Yeah," says Wills. "She was five. They have those pageants every year over at the elementary school."

"It reminds me of Jon-Benét Ramsey," I say, citing a current tabloid sensation, the beautiful little child pageant star who was found brutally murdered—possibly by her wealthy parents—in the basement of her home. "Have you heard much about that?"

"Oh, that's all a bunch of nonsense," says Wills. "That happens to little girls all the time. Little girls get killed all the time. I just don't see why she should be any better than all the other girls that's happened to. People only care about her because her parents are rich, because of her status."

* * *

As the last practice before tryouts winds down, Berry gets ticked. The girls haven't been working as hard as they should. Maybe because it's not yet do-or-die time—that'll come the next day—or because there are so few of them and the cheerleaders think Berry will have to take them all. No matter, the girls' collective attitude has gotten Berry markedly ticked.

Berry tells the girls to sit down in the middle of the gym floor. Standing with her hands resting on her chubby hips, occasionally chopping the air and pointing for emphasis, Berry tries to frighten some intensity into her wanna-be varsity.

"I want you to be serious! I want you to learn this stuff well so when you do it for the judges tomorrow, they'll be impressed. If they say, 'Take ten,' I'll take ten of you. I'd like to have twenty, but it doesn't look like it's going to happen this year. Some of you have been lazy today—and yesterday—and I'm sick of it. You're breaking my heart. Challenge yourself. Get serious. Get serious about your appearance, your neatness. You don't need to go out and buy a seventy-five-dollar outfit for tomorrow, but you are going to dress the way we want you to dress. You are going to wear your hair the way we want you to. I've got to dress a certain way when I go to work. That's life. If you're going to be on this team, you're going to learn to conform to rules when you don't want to. But bottom line, tomorrow should be fun for you guys. Later on, it should be stressful and really hard. The Greenup County Varsity. That's what you're going to be. When you come in here tomorrow, I want you to remember what it was like when you were seven, eight, nine years old, and you looked up to the Greenup County Varsity. That's what you're going to be. Remember the tradition. I was skeptical with the small amount of girls that are here. But the ones that are here want to be here. And I hope you want to be the best. There's no way I want to be associated with anything but the best."

Chapter Seven

Survival

On Friday, the last and most important day of tryouts, the cheerleading hopefuls report to the gym after school wearing a great deal of makeup, and ribbons in their newly brushed, newly sprayed hair. All but three, Sarah Dickison, Amanda Kitchen, and Megan West, wear pressed short-sleeved collared shirts and nice tennis shorts with pockets. Sarah, Amanda, and Megan wear white jogging shorts with green-and-yellow "Greenup County National Cheerleading Champions" T-shirts.

"Girls," says Coach Peffer to the three differently dressed freshmen, "why'd you wear T-shirts?"

Sarah, Amanda, and Megan say nothing. They look at one another.

"You oughta be ashamed of yourselves," Peffer says.

There is a pregnant pause as Peffer watches the girls stare at one another some more.

"Well," he says, "nothing you can do about it now."

The graduating cheerleaders are here too. But because they'll only watch today and not participate, they wear their typical school clothes: tight blue jeans for most, and bright, colorful tops.

The seniors watch the younger girls turn tumbling runs, practice the dance, and run through the sideline chants each will perform individually in front of Berry's two judges.

A number of boys and a few girls are still hanging out in the gym on their way out of the school.

"The gym's gonna be closed, right?" Megan asks no one in particular. "Right? There aren't gonna be no kids in here, right?"

"I'm wearing the same shirt from tryouts last year, and I'm wearing the same shorts from tryouts two years ago," Kelena McClurg says to Coach Berry.

"That's great, hon," says Berry.

"Don't the boys have to leave?" Megan demands. "They're making me nervous."

Wills, quiet and focused, runs through the dance in her mind, doing the motions half-way as she stares straight ahead.

Jennifer Stuart asks how much time till tryouts officially begin.

Thirteen minutes, says Peffer.

Hearing that, Brooke Meenach blurts, "Oh. Oh. Oh my goodness."

A rectangular table sits on the right-hand sideline of the basketball court, with two chairs facing into the middle of the floor.

Rachel Brown stands off in a far corner of the gym with Hank Light. She practices her back tuck again and again and again, but always with Light spotting her.

In the right-hand bleachers up above the court, Rachel's mother and father sit quietly with ten other mothers, and many younger siblings. Shiritta Schaffer's mother has brought shiny chrome-colored balloons that say in assorted neon colors, "Good Luck!" "You're the Greatest!" "Make Us Proud!"

Two mysterious middle-aged women arrive and talk briefly with Berry and Peffer. The Greenup coaches give each of them pencils and a stack of ratings forms; then the judges sit down at the table facing the now quiet basketball court. Berry has recruited her sister, Sandy Rice, and her good friend Lisa Sloan, the cheerleading coach at Russell Middle School, to judge these tryouts, partly because they are knowledgeable cheerleading experts, mostly because the prospective cheerleaders don't know them from Eve.

Peffer figures that only fifteen girls will try out today. The two girls who transferred from Russell have been barred from the team, at least for now. The status of the girl from Boyd remains in limbo as well. There's no Linda Goble or Melissa Morris. Berry won't let Amanda Dean take time away from her baby. And Aimee Lewis is still recovering from her silly attempt at contortionism two nights ago.

Aimee sits on the courtside bleachers next to her crutches, her knee in a brace. Beside her sits Amanda Dean, watching the potential varsity cheerleaders loosen up and balancing her little boy on her knee.

Peffer writes the numbers "1" through "15" on torn-up slips of paper. Then he puts the numbered slips in a baseball cap and has each girl fish around in the hat, take a slip, and pin it onto her chest. The number each girl receives will be the position in which she will perform for the judges during each round of tryouts.

"All right. It's about time," Berry says.

Rachel stops practicing her back tuck with Light and takes a number. She gets "1." Wills gets "8."

The girls pin their numbers on their chests and assemble themselves on the court-side bleachers, across from the judges, across from their parents up above, across from Peffer and Berry, across from Aimee Lewis and Amanda Dean, across from the mellow, confident seniors sitting together on the gym floor.

And across from the girls' softball team. The softballers have an away game today, so they sit in a corner of the gym—wearing no makeup, un-flattering nylon uniforms, ratty ponytails shoved awkwardly under mesh caps—and wait for the team bus.

All is quiet. The two judges shuffle the scorecards. They pick up their pencils, looking solemn, serious. One says, barely audibly, "Number one, please."

Rachel Brown jumps up off the bench and screams, "YEAH! AL'RIGHT! GO! WHOOO! GO GREENUP! YEAH! WHOOOO! YEAH! WHOOO!"

Rachel settles herself in the middle of the court, about ten feet from the judges. She stands quietly at attention, her hands on her hips, a BIG smile wrapped around her face, and waits as the judges scribble on their score-cards, rating her for how well she "showed spirit." After Rachel has held that smile for about a minute, the judges look up and nod.

Rachel begins her sideline chant.

"ONE! TWO! THREE! FOUR! GREENUP! LET'S HEAR YOU YELL! GO BIG GREEN!"

All of the onlookers—except for the two judges and the twenty-odd softball players—yell, "GO BIG GREEN!"

Rachel repeats the chant. During the second "GO BIG GREEN!" she must do some sort of standing tumbling pass, one of her many chances to try the standing back tuck. She turns a back handspring followed by a back tuck instead—impressive, but not as difficult as a standing back.

Rachel bounds back to the other girls through applause and her own shrieks of "GO GREENUP! WHOOOO!"

One by one, the rest of the girls shatter the gym's silence by showing spirit and performing the sideline cheer.

Miranda Elliott falls forward on her back handspring, back tuck and opts to do it again. The second time, with lots of "Come on Miranda"s raining down on her from the bleachers, she doesn't put her hands down, but still stumbles.

Aubrey Warnock lands on her knees following her back handspring–back tuck, and chants "GO BIG GREenoh." Many can't help laughing, especially the girls on the softball team.

Berry tells Shawnda Bates to go tell the softball players to keep quiet.

As Megan stands at attention in the middle of the court, waiting for the judges to stop scribbling so she can perform her sideline, she mouths to everyone else, "I'm so nervous." Megan's cheer is shaky from start to finish. Her voice cracks, her tumbling wobbles. But it doesn't occur to her to try again. As Megan starts to walk out of the spotlight, one of the judges asks if Megan is sure she doesn't want another chance. Megan turns around, surprised, stares wide-eyed at the judges, nods, and mumbles, "Okay."

Wills does fine, although her handspring-back doesn't stay on a perfect line the way it should.

Next comes the dance round. In groups of three, the girls perform the dance that Hank Light taught them two days earlier to the beat of that throbbing *CANYOUFEELTHEGROOVE?* techno music. Rachel Brown wows the judges, smiling broadly, gyrating and hip-thrusting confidently. Wills, however, loses points for her choppy movements and tense smile.

After completing her dance for the judges, Rachel Brown works with Light on her standing back tuck over in the corner.

Meanwhile, the dance round ends and the running tumbling begins. Shiritta impresses Coach Berry by completing a pass that ends with a flip and a full 360-degree twist of her body. Wills nails her bounders and pumps her fist down toward the floor.

The stunting round comes next. Wills tries out her flying skills, and doesn't wobble as much as she had the day before. Berry whispers to Peffer, "Boy, she's *got* to learn to smile."

Whenever she isn't performing for the judges, Rachel Brown works on her back tuck in the corner of the gym with Light spotting.

Now for the final round of tryouts. The girls fan out in two rows facing the judges.

"Okay," says Berry. "Toe touches."

Rachel Brown jumps up, does the splits in the air, and reaches out her hands to touch her toes. The judges spend a few moments scribbling down their responses. Aubrey goes next. Then Miranda, Wills, and so forth, until all the girls have received toe-touch ratings.

"Back handspring," says Berry.

Beginning with Rachel, each girl turns a back handspring and the judges judge.

"Handspring back," says Berry.

One by one, the girls lunge backward, push off the hardwood, land on their feet, and turn a back flip with a tuck. Miranda stumbles a bit on hers.

"Standing back," says Berry.

The judges stare at Rachel Brown, who looks up at the gym's ceiling, sucks in her lower lip, and stiffens her arms beside her, fists aiming down.

"Come on Rachel!" her mother hollers. "Come ON Rachel," says Wills. For a few moments, the rest of the parents, seniors, and cheerleaders join in.

Then silence.

Rachel claps twice, still looking upward, and lurches back. But she puts her hands down, turning the trick into a back handspring, not a back tuck.

Feeling the horrible silence, Rachel mumbles that she would like to try it again. The judges nod.

Again Rachel stiffens her body. Again the small crowd is roused to cheer her on.

"Come on Rachel!"

"Pull! You can do it!"

"Throw it, just throw it!"

"You'll only know if you try!"

Rachel claps twice and jumps. She turns a back handspring.

The judges focus on the next girl, Aubrey, who hits her standing on her first try. Miranda comes next. As Wills has said, Miranda has hardly worked on her standing all week. Still, Miranda almost lands it now, stumbling slightly forward at the end.

"At least she threw it," Berry says to Peffer.

Coach Peffer sticks out his lower lip and nods. He's surprised and impressed. Miranda smiles giddily.

As the rest of the potential team members turn their standing backs, Rachel Brown's eyes become red and wet. At one point, she searches the bleachers for her parents.

"Toe touch, standing back," says Berry. "It's optional."

"Pass," says Rachel, her voice cracking.

The other girls each attempt the difficult combination of a toe touch immediately followed by a standing back tuck. Wills is one of the few who lands it, but she's anything but graceful. Only Rachel and Miranda pass.

While the judges bend over their scorecards to tabulate the final scores for each girl, Wills rubs Rachel's shoulders and whispers, "You're okay. You're okay."

Rachel watches the judges write down their ratings and comments. Eventually, Rachel gets up her nerve and walks out from under Wills's hands. She approaches the judges' table, and announces that she'd like to try her standing back again. The judges look back at Berry, who nods. The judges tell Rachel that'll be fine, and put down their pencils.

All eyes are back on Rachel.

"Just throw it, Rachel!" Peffer hollers. "Just throw it."

Rachel attempts the standing twice, and twice chickens out. She's about to go for it a third time when Berry interrupts.

"All right, okay," the coach says. "Fine. That's fine."

Rachel, sweaty, red-faced, breathing hard, her eyes bloodshot, frowns and walks to the opposite side of the gym. There, she sits down next to Wills, who does her best to console Rachel with her hands and her whispers. Rachel puts her head in her lap and covers her face with her arms to muffle what soon becomes steady sobbing.

While Peffer, Berry, and the two judges confer, Linda Morris walks into the gym with her daughter Melissa and Linda Goble in tow. They came by to say hi, and to wish next year's team good luck. Now, they sit down on the courtside bleachers behind the judges' table and wave to the girls on the other side of the court.

To Lisa Sloan, the judge from Russell Middle, Berry says covertly, "I'll take all of them, but I want you to call them out and tell them what they need to work on. They don't know you. They'll listen to you."

Berry, Peffer, and Sloan tell the girls to sit in the middle of the court. The cheerleaders are nervous, unsure of what's going to happen.

"Some of you need to lose some pounds," says Sloan, standing over them. "And some of you need to get your standing backs before you compete with the team. A couple of you had really bad motions on the cheers, and a couple didn't dance well. But you're all good cheerleaders, and I'm sure you'll make a great cheerleading team."

A bit of the tension lifts. Rachel Brown mops the tears off her face, as she looks down at the floor. She's too unhappy with herself to feel relieved.

"I'm taking you all," says Berry, "but Miranda and Rachel Brown must have their standing backs in time for Kings Island. It wouldn't be fair to the rest of the team to let you two compete without your standings. Climbing's going to be the hard part this year. But if you work all year, it won't be as stressful at the end. I personally think we can work with all of you. I think you're all good in your own areas."

Says Peffer, "You girls coming off the JV squad are really going to have to suck it up. That's the truth. Don't sit back. You've got to do more than just enough to get by. We all need to be strong in our appearance, in our dance, and in our attitude. Greenup County High School has won nationals more times than any other squad in high school or college. That's important. That's what I want it to be for you guys. I want it to be really important for you."

"So anyway," says Berry, "you are all varsity Greenup County High School cheerleaders. Congratulations."

Berry hugs Rachel Brown, then a few of the other young girls. Wills congratulates Rachel, hugging her and telling her that she's got the summer to learn the standing, she shouldn't worry.

After Berry walks away, the new Greenup team huddles up in the middle of the court, and the girls give each other pep talks. Berry plops down next to Mrs. Morris, whose two girls are off talking and laughing with the senior cheerleaders.

"I wish they hadn't gone," Berry says, following Linda and Melissa with her eyes.

"Well, there's nothing I can do," says Mrs. Morris.

"You can drive them every day," Berry says, shifting her gaze to Mrs. Morris and smiling. The two women laugh.

"You've given her the most stable home life that girl has ever had," says Berry. "And I've known Linda since the fifth grade."

"Oh, I know. She went home on weekends, and you could see the difference. If she spent more than one day there, there were problems."

"You'll get some recognition and love for it at some point."

"I know. I know."

The following day, Saturday, the Morrises went house hunting in Mason County. The two girls had fun looking at all the nice new houses and imagining their lives there. For the first time, they didn't resent the move.

When they returned to Greenup, there was a message for Linda on the Morrises' answering machine: Linda's mom wanted Linda to spend the night with her. So Linda called up her mom and asked in hushed tones when she should come by. Mrs. Morris, not wanting to get in the way, said nothing to Linda and dutifully drove her to her mother's house that night.

The next day, Sunday, when Linda returned to the Morrises, she told Mrs. Morris and Melissa that her mom didn't want her to leave Greenup County. Linda told the Morrises that her mom had cried, and said she'd miss Linda if she went so far away. Linda told the Morrises that her mom thought she might never see Linda ever again. Linda began to cry and told the Morrises that she didn't know what to do.

Later that day, after Melissa and Linda have left the house for a previously scheduled gymnastics lesson, Mrs. Morris sits at home, stunned, trying hard to understand how it can be that Linda won't be moving with her family to Mason County after all.

"It will be like Melissa losing a sister. It really will," says Mrs. Morris, looking out a window from her rocking chair. "They've got that close. In fact, it will be worse for Melissa. Because she clings to Linda, stays right by her side. That's her favorite spot. And now she's going to lose that. But she'll survive."

It won't really be worse for Melissa. Mrs. Morris knows that. As she says, Melissa will survive. What about Linda? Without the Morris family, will she survive? Mrs. Morris isn't sure. She looks down at her wall-to-wall carpeting, her end tables with their doilies, and her white wicker couch.

"Linda's birthday's coming up," Mrs. Morris says in a low, husky voice. "I was going to invite all her friends over and have a big party. I'm not going to be able to do those type things for her anymore."

Mrs. Morris doesn't believe that Linda's mother was thinking of her child's best interests when she put this pressure on Linda to stay in Greenup. Mrs. Morris thinks that Mrs. Goble worries most about her monthly welfare check. If Linda moves away with the Morrises, Mrs. Morris reasons, then Mrs. Goble might not receive as much money from the government as she does now. During last night's teary-eyed appeal, Linda told Mrs. Morris that her mom suggested that Linda go back and live with Shiritta Schaffer and her family. So Mrs. Goble is not trying to keep her daughter, says Mrs. Morris, just the money her daughter's proximity helps her receive.

"I can't make her do something that her family is going to be against," Mrs. Morris says in a helpless tone. "Her mother, when I first talked to her about it, was not agreeable to it. But then when I told her what-all I could provide her, she went along. Then Linda went over there last night—"

Mrs. Morris's voice trails off until, suddenly, her eyes flash angrily.

"I think she's afraid somebody will find out," she says loudly, heatedly, "report her to social services."

Then, as quickly as it came, the anger recedes. Mrs. Morris looks down.

"It's a bad situation," she says.

Within the week, Linda Goble moved back in with her mother and resumed her classes at Greenup High. Coach Berry gave her a spot on the cheerleading team, and Linda practiced as a member of the varsity squad for three weeks.

In late June, Mrs. Goble called Berry and told her enough was enough. Linda's mother could not allow her daughter to cheer anymore.

Kings Island

Chapter Eight

Equal Rights and All That Crap

"You have to push 'em," Candy Berry says. "Perfect example: There's a stray cat that made a home—a nest, so to speak. She was having kittens and I didn't know it, in my outbuilding back of my house, and the little window was open and she was crawling in and out of it and I noticed that. Then for about a week or two, we didn't see her. My husband went out to get the lawn mower or something, and he said, 'Candy, that cat is having kittens out there in that building.' And I said, 'Great.'

"So anyway, we watched it for a couple of weeks and left the door shut so no other animal could get in and bother 'em, 'cause she was protecting 'em. When they were about three or four weeks old, my husband went out and opened the door so they could get their legs about them and come on and see the daylight. And she—the mother cat—she brought them to the door and she would go down onto the grass from the building but the kittens wouldn't come down after her. And for two or three days, we noticed that happening. Mark left the door open and would put our dog up so it wouldn't bother them. Then, finally, on about the fourth day, one of the kittens took the leap and come out with her, but the other one wouldn't come down. We put a bowl of milk and everything but it wouldn't come.

"My whole thing, is even then, the mother cat had to nudge the one to go out and try it. So these kids have to be nudged sometimes. Some will take the leap and go, like Shawnda, I think Shawnda would no matter what, just for the challenge. She might not stay with it but she'd try.

Others, like Jess [Madden]—you know, she could be cheering at UK—
you have to nudge them a little bit. And they'll end up liking it just as
well. Now, the little kitten come out in the yard with her mother and that
other kitten."

It's a warm Sunday afternoon in early June and Coach Berry has driven
down Route 23 to a city park in Ashland to talk about her cheer-coaching
career. Susan Ray, Greenup's JV coach, has also come along. The two
women sit on a wooden picnic bench and lean their elbows on its tabletop.
They were a little late because of Greenup's Sunday-after-church traffic.

A fountain bubbles in the middle of the park. Oak trees arch over the
two women, providing shade from the noontime sun as the leaves rustle in
the mountain breeze. Pigeons and sparrows flutter around. Young families
walk the six-block circumference of the small park, pushing strollers, still
wearing their church clothes. Horseflies and bees buzz. Occasionally,
Berry interrupts her ruminations on the importance of cheerleading in her
girls' young lives to swat at a yellow jacket. As the conversation progresses,
small beads of sweat appear on her forehead, clinging to her makeup, and
she dabs at her brow with a handkerchief.

It's been more than a month since tryouts. With Berry's help, the two
girls from Russell High School and the girl from Boyd County High
School successfully appealed the Kentucky High School Athletic Association's ruling against their cheering for Greenup. Now they are full-fledged
members of the team.

One of the girls from Russell High, April Creech, who'll be a senior
next year, had to move thirty miles, into the town of Greenup, because she
wasn't able to prove that she was transferring for any "personal" reasons.
April had plenty of friends at Russell. But she takes her cheerleading very
seriously, and before she graduates from high school she wants a realistic
shot at a national championship. April will be the only senior on the
Greenup team next year without a white-and-pink national cheerleading
champion jacket in her closet. (Even the senior girl coming over from
Boyd won a national title as a member of the Boyd varsity in 1995.) So
April's younger brother, her mother, and the man her mother's living with
chose to uproot their lives to help April realize her dream.

Berry is happy to have the three new girls on her varsity, but she's especially happy to have April, who's a solid flyer. Now, Berry can use Wills—
who's gaining grace slowly but surely—Kelena McClurg, and April as her
flying corps, with Rachel Brown waiting in the wings.

Rachel Brown has already lost over ten pounds, and has only eight more to go till she'll be light enough to fly. But Rachel's as spooked as ever when it comes to the standing back tuck. The week after tryouts, Rachel threw the standing confidently for a few days, and landed it more often than not. Then, at the end of a long, tiring cheer practice, Rachel decided to test herself and try the standing even though she was physically exhausted. She jumped up, began rotating back, then inexplicably halted her spin in midair and planted her face on Greenup High's carpeted auditorium floor. Rachel got two shiny black eyes, her cheekbones swelled up so big that she could hardly see for three days, and she had rug burn on her face. In the three weeks since, Rachel hasn't attempted the standing without a spotter.

Rachel feels very much alone in her pursuit of the standing. Without a consistent standing back tuck, she's not really a varsity Greenup cheerleader. Berry has said so herself. And a number of the varsity girls still hold Rachel's rumored liaison with Kelena's boyfriend against her. At practice, the other girls can make Rachel feel unwanted.

Even if Rachel never gets her act together, says Berry, Greenup will have a team big enough to defend its all-girls large varsity title next February now that the three newcomers have been cleared to cheer.

Berry's excitement is tempered, however, by her concern for Linda Goble. Berry can't help worrying about that troubled little girl.

"I think it's a sad situation," Candy says. "I think the kid needs something positive in her life. It's sad, 'cause to me, she's going to be a lost kid. She did come back and work with us. After she found out she couldn't go with the Morrises, she talked to us, and we put her on the varsity squad. And she worked out for about three weeks with us. But she's back living at home and you know that lifestyle. There's no discipline and no restrictions. It's kind of a wild lifestyle. It's hard having a kid in cheerleading. You need to give her a lot of help, you know, just generally be an adult and a director for her. She doesn't have that."

Linda's difficulties remind Berry of a girl she coached back in the mid-1980s.

"The girl had a mother, and I don't know if her father was in the picture or not, but her mother had boyfriends and stuff. Her mother, 'course she got food stamps and all that stuff, but the mother would go to the store and buy groceries, then she would lock it up in her bedroom where her and her boyfriend could have it and the kids couldn't have it.

"You find that a lot in that caliber of family. The girl wasn't willing to give in to it. She was willing to fight it. And she did really good, and graduated from high school, and I know she took a few years of college. And she's married. She's got two kids. I don't know if she graduated college or not.

"Some folks here, well, I wouldn't necessarily say they're poorer, but they're more socially deprived, they're the farm people, the isolated people, the people that live up the hollers and all they see is their 'kinfolk,' as they say. Those are good people and they don't need anything else. I mean their life is good, you know. But we can let the kids see there are other options. It's like the old Walton's Mountain, I watched a replay of it the other day—I love that show—anyway, old John was talking about how John-Boy chose to go on and be a writer, but the other one, Billy-Bob-Joe-George or whatever, he chose to stay there and run the mill. So we give them the option.

"Cheerleading can put you in the right direction. I think working with discipline is the main thing. I think realizing you can accept a challenge, and at any time you can achieve that challenge, you know, hit it head-on. That's the one thing you gain from it, plus the discipline. Plus you learn to present yourself in the proper manner. You learn how to carry yourself because of the pride you develop. And you know, our program teaches appearance pointers, and a lot of things that a female needs in the world to be successful. We've taken kids to dinner who've never been to a dinner where there wasn't plastic silverware, or who've never been where there was a salad fork and a regular fork, a lot of the things that we take for granted. We'll take these kids places that they've never been, and they experience just normal things that they would never have experienced. So the social skills that they gain, for a lot of these kids is just unbelievable."

Berry feels that as a coach of high school girls, she should instruct them not only in cheer skills but in life skills as well.

"When I was little, my mom put my sister and I in ballet and tap and all that stuff," says Berry. "And I went to charm school—the girls die laughing, they say, 'What's charm school?'—well, when I was twelve and thirteen, we had to go. They taught us the proper way to sit, how a *lady* should sit in a chair, and you never chew gum in public, and you never apply your lipstick in public—things like that. So when I start this stuff with them, like we'll go out to dinner as a team—this has nothing to do with cheerleading but it all goes with this program—they'll get dressed up, and they'll come out and they'll have on a dress and bare legs, no hose. And I'm like, "'Scuse me! Anytime you wear undergarments, such as a slip or a petticoat, and you've got on a dress, you should have hose on! You finish your outfit out—unless you're wearing sandals or something.' It's really cute to see them then, by the time they're seniors, they never go to a dinner with me unless they've got their hose on, and their lipstick on, and their lip liner on, and"—Berry looks at me and motions across the picnic table—"things that you wouldn't understand, but it all goes to make them that special little person once they're out of high school. It makes the difference when they go for a job.

"There's this one little girl that I've especially took an interest in, Regina Woolridge," Berry says, thinking of a rising freshman on the new Greenup JV. "Her mother died when she was three. And she has lived with her father. You can tell she's never had the influence of a female on her. Like she never wears a ribbon in her hair or nothing. But she's such a loving kid, and the change in her the last two months is unbelievable. I mean she'll wear a little bit of blush and eye makeup when she comes to practice now and she's always got her hair in a ponytail. I mean, when she first tried out, she wore tops that would have fit me!"

Berry rears back and laughs.

"And big old blousy shorts. Now, she's wearing more tailored-fitting-type shorts and stuff, you know. I saw her yesterday and I was teasing her about something, and she said, 'Yeah, I'm fat.' And I said, 'You are NOT fat. You're not even chubby! You just choose to look that way, to hide your femininity.' And she said, 'Huh?' And I said, 'You just choose to hide what's there.' I said, 'You need to wear the smaller-fitting clothes.' And she said, 'Well, the clothes I wear is what my dad buys.'

"You know?"

Berry closes her eyes, smacks the picnic table, and laughs some more.

"But you watch. In another year, she's going to be a cute little girl. I don't know what she'll do in cheerleading, but she's going to end up being a *lady* at some point, instead of a tomboy that would have had to settle for something that she probably wouldn't have wanted. That's the whole key: not letting them settle for something they don't want. If they like themselves enough, if they're comfortable with themselves enough, then they don't have to settle. They can look for more. I think that's true."

Berry believes that cheerleading offers budding young women something that girls' basketball, track, soccer, softball can't offer: lessons in how to be a *lady,* how to be tough without imitating men.

"There's a lot of girls that don't want to be a jock, but they like the challenge of the athletics."

Enter competitive cheerleading. For many girls, it offers everything they want in a sport: rigorous exercise, physical challenges, high-stakes performance, all with a feminine softness. Other girls' sports can scrimp on the feminine part—especially, says Berry, if the coach is a man.

"I'm a firm believer that they ought to have female coaches, because there's a lot of things that females need to discuss with females, the same as I don't think there should be a lady head coach of a football team. Of course, I'm of the old school. That's the way my mother brought me up. There's certain things that ladies discuss with ladies, and gentlemen discuss with each other, and it shouldn't be brought out. I guess I'm an old Southern person. I never thought of it till I said it that way, but that's the way it sounds."

"You look at the girls' basketball team, for instance," Susan Ray pipes up. "For years they had two men as coaches. And they had no idea. The girls would wear white uniforms and black polka-dotted underwear. It would show through their uniforms at ball games."

"The girls' panties would show through," adds Berry, remembering, "and they'd never care."

"You know, the men would never think about that sort of thing," Ray says. "People in the stands would talk about how awful it was. Now, they've got an assistant coach who's a woman and she's done it right."

"Yeah," says Berry, "some of the girls will have bows in their hair now, or they'll wear the full-length underwear under their shorts so it won't show through, things like that that a woman would notice.

"So sometimes girls that play sports lose out. They're so geared on being like the boys, to be competitive with the boys, that they imitate the boys, instead of imitating another woman. Of course, Jackie Joyner-Kersee is a perfect example that that doesn't have to be, 'cause while she's very athletic, she's very feminine in her own way. I mean I'm not the little prim and proper, tiny petite lady either. But there are certain things that a girl needs to be taught."

Berry has no interest in holding women and girls back from anything they want to do. To her way of thinking, however, forcing girls to imitate the traditional traits of boys makes no sense. If girls want to be like boys, says Berry, that's fine. But it should also be fine for girls to act like old-fashioned girls without sacrificing their dreams, athletic or otherwise. Jackie Joyner-Kersee, as Berry points out, certainly hasn't sacrificed her dreams for her traditional femininity. She's won multiple Olympic gold medals in the heptathlon and the long jump, and was hailed by many during the eighties and early nineties as the best female athlete in the world. For Berry, women and girls should remain women and girls even as they invade traditionally male pursuits.

"In the eighties, a lady wasn't supposed to be feminine if she wanted to be a major contributing force in the workplace," Berry points out. "To be equal with those guys, she wore the three-piece suits, and double-breasted jackets and stuff to look like the guys so they wouldn't think she was different. That was when we were fighting for equal rights and all that crap, which I didn't agree with.

"It's the same in sports. Women's sports can have their own flavor and their own draw if they want to. They don't have to imitate the males. That's just like co-ed cheerleading and all-girl cheerleading. We can be as exciting as the co-eds. We don't have to imitate them. There's certain things we can do that they can't do. Like the strength in the tumbling, for one. Males are not as strong using handsprings in their running tumbling, solely because they're not built that way. They're not as flexible. And with the mounts, you'll notice there are no guys on top of those mounts doing heel-stretches. So there's a lot of versatility that a female can put into her routine that a male can't."

Despite the niche that cheerleading fills—as the only sport in which girls can be cute as well as tough, hard but still soft—cheerleaders regularly get drubbed by outsiders who call them silly, shallow, self-important, and ditzily unaware that they are perpetuating a sexist stereotype. Cheerleading is not politically correct.

When many people think of cheerleading, they immediately recall the 1992 media frenzy over the cheerleading mother from Channelview, Texas, who was charged with soliciting the murder of another cheerleading mother so that her daughter could make the local high school's squad. Every American media outlet—from *Life* magazine to *Donahue* to *Hard Copy* to the Cable News Network to *The Tonight Show with Johnny Carson*—followed the months-long story of the woman's arrest and subsequent trial. The media has portrayed cheerleading in pejorative terms ever since.

In January 1997, *The New York Times Magazine* ran four paragraphs under the heading "Get Peppy or Get Out" that took a selective look at American cheerleading.

"Once content with frothy squeals, today's cheerleaders can boast that their athletic, high difficulty displays cause more deaths and injuries than any high school or college women's sport"—a misleading statistic, considering more girls and women participate in cheerleading in high school and college than in any other sport. "Driven to interpersonal frenzies," *The Times* continues, "they can also get downright nasty."

The Times summarizes the state of cheerleading by relating three aberrant cheerleading anecdotes. One from Washington state, where two high school cheerleaders spiked the drink of a fellow cheerleader with ipecac syrup to keep her off the team because they didn't think she was good enough. One from Texas, where a girl confined to a wheelchair was declared ineligible to participate in cheerleading. And another from Virginia, where a cheerleading mother was convicted of misdemeanor assault for shoving, punching, and ripping the wig off of another cheerleading mother after an argument over a $5 fee for after-practice snacks. These examples, *The Times* contends, reflect cheerleading's "broader pathologies."

"We're the no-name sport," says Berry with gusto, her arms outstretched. "We're not a sport. We're not a performing art, like ballet. We're kind of the forgotten stepchildren. But we're not! We're like Cinderella! We're coming out!

"I thoroughly resent the way cheerleading is treated. We might have half of a percent of the kids that come through our program where it is not a strong positive influence on them. And I resent anybody that tries to tear down a program that can influence kids in such a positive manner, for no other reason than that they're jealous of it. Like when I was in high school, maybe it was the popular girls and the prettiest girls and the coolest girls. So everybody else was jealous of that one percent of kids. But it's not that way anymore. It's not the prettiest, the best liked, the best dressed. It's not that. It's kids that are strong in their skills and are willing to give up the time it takes to get even stronger. I mean, these kids give up a lot of time and learn a lot of discipline to be a part of this sport. And for them to be criticized and ridiculed—I can remember about four or five years ago, we went to a camp, a cheer camp, and we were at UK at the same time that there was a basketball camp and a soccer camp. They had females involved in all these camps, and we were constantly being made fun of."

Berry squeals, imitating her team's detractors. "'OOOh, TU-TU-TU-TU-TU, SIS-BOOM-BAH!' And all this stuff. And I looked at them, and I said, 'What is your problem?' This was females and males doing this. They were like, 'Ooooh, it's the cheerleaderrrrsss! Oh yeah! Cutie, cutie, cutie! Rah, rah, rah!' I resent that. I really do. Because if you give a cheerleader a challenge, be it to learn to make a basket from the three-point line, or to run the fifty-yard dash in a certain amount of time, they might not get right at the goal you give them, but they'll be darn near close. That's the type of kid that's in competitive cheerleading."

Berry isn't through.

"Band kids get made fun of, too. Why? Because they're perceived as—not unskilled—but the weaker people that you can make fun of, the funnier, the different. I was in the band, too. I know. Kids make fun of the band kids—'Oooh, they're weird. Oooh, they're strange.' But, you know, those kids have become part of that group to feel a part of a group. Maybe you've got an overweight girl who couldn't be a basketball player or a cheerleader because of her size and she chose not to do anything about it. Or you've got a little tiny boy who was too little to be in sports. You know, they need to belong in something.

"That's what I tell kids. My son was a football player. Now, he has a guy that's a best friend that helped with the flags and the band and sings and everything. Chris used to make so much fun of him. I used to say, 'Chris, he's not athletic enough to play sports. He wants to feel a part of something. Why are you making fun of him? Are you jealous of him? Are you threatened by him?'"

Berry takes on a deep, throaty voice to imitate her son. "'I'm not jealous of him. Why would I be jealous?'" She laughs. "You know, anybody that's different from us, we perceive that way, and we tend to make fun of. I don't know why, but I think that's the way everybody is. So I think it's that way with cheerleading, too. People who aren't involved with the sport and not interested in the sport make fun of it. My husband, to this day, when I've got ice skating on, he's like, 'Oh my God, you've got that ice-skating on *again*. That guy's got those tight pants on! Who cares?' You know, he don't like watching that. Anything like that, you'll find people who'll poke fun, be uninterested, and think it's totally unnecessary."

Until the 1960s and 1970s, rural Kentucky counties like Greenup had seven, eight, or nine high schools scattered throughout their sprawling hills. Before cars became affordable and most of the rolling Greenup roads got paved, it was difficult for schoolchildren to get around, so many schools were needed to serve the hillside population. Once travel became easier, the county school board consolidated Greenup's seven high schools into three to cut down on building and teacher costs.

The old-style Kentucky schools had rather small student populations, mostly about fifteen kids per grade; sometimes, only fifteen in the whole school. With such small numbers, the schools couldn't field many sports teams. They certainly couldn't muster a viable football team, which requires at least thirty boys, preferably many more. But they could put together basketball teams, which only need five boys, twelve at the most.

In the 1930s and 1940s, high school basketball became the most popular form of family entertainment in eastern Kentucky. Twice a week, folks could make their way to the local school's gym, or to a rival school's gym—still in the same county—and root for their boys. And when the University of Kentucky won three college basketball national championships, in 1948, 1949, and 1951, basketball became as important to Kentucky as bluegrass or the Derby.

Mason Branham, editor of the *Greenup News-Times*, puts it this way: "You've got people back here who haven't got much to be proud of, and here was something their boys done better than everybody else."

"And what goes with basketball?" he asks. "Well, cheerleading."

Nowadays, Americans tend to associate cheerleading with football more than with basketball—probably because of the popularity of the Dallas Cowboys' cheerleaders. As Branham points out, however, it's easier to lead cheers at a basketball game than at a football game. If cheerleaders ever influence the outcome of games, they do so at basketball games.

Candy Berry was born in 1950. By the time she entered Russell High School in the mid-1960s, basketball was the thing to do if you were a boy, and cheerleading was the thing to do if you were a girl.

"I had an older cousin that played basketball," Berry says, remembering her girlhood. "He was the coolest thing. He had a cherry-red convertible and he and all the cheerleaders and stuff would ride around. These three cousins of mine, they were all guys and they all played sports, and I always thought the girls that hung around them were the coolest things. They had the headbands and the pageboys and they were all cheerleaders and so I always thought they were the neatest. Of course, they paid attention to me because they wanted to date my cousins. But I guess that's where my interest in cheerleading grew."

Before her sophomore year, Berry tried out for the cheerleading team. First, she had to audition by herself in front of a panel of judges appointed by the school. They chose her to be one of five girls in her grade to try out in front of the entire student body. Berry's classmates then voted for their two favorite girls in each grade. One of their picks was Berry.

"I remember it was exciting," she says. "I always got into challenges and the thrill of doing stuff like that. So it was fun. One of my friends didn't make it and she was devastated."

After three years of low-impact cheerleading ("All we did were walkovers and splits. I don't think we did back handsprings. If we did, I don't think I did. I'd be able to tell. My head would be banged up."), Berry had to quit cheerleading her senior year when she got pregnant, then married. Still eighteen, she went to live with her husband, Mark Berry, who was a sophomore at Eastern Kentucky University, about three hours southwest of Greenup. There was only enough money to put one member of the young Berry family through college. So Candy took care of her baby and worked at a Bentley's pharmacy while her husband finished up school.

After Mark Berry graduated from EKU, he and Candy moved back to Greenup County, where he got a job at Ashland Oil and Candy got bored.

"At that time, I was too cool and too satisfied with where I was, you know, didn't think that I needed to have an education," Berry says. "Then the same lady that coached me in high school—she was still the cheerleading adviser at Russell—and she was like, 'Candy I need help with these girls. Everybody's going to competitions and stuff. Maybe you can come and help me.' I was like, 'Yeah, well, I don't care. I've got extra time.' There was no pay, of course. It was a free, gratis-type thing.

"Money's not that big a deal for me and my husband. We don't live a big fancy lifestyle. We have a nice, three-bedroom, ranch brick home. And you know, our son's gone to school and he's grown and stuff. But my husband and I made the decision years ago. I have a sister that's worked every day of her life and she's got anything and everything that she's wanted. That's the lifestyle she chose, and we chose a more laid-back-type lifestyle."

Berry became an assistant coach at Russell in 1973, when she was twenty-three years old. Competitive cheerleading had just gotten started. The National Cheerleading Association, headquartered in Dallas, began organizing cheer camps around the South in the late sixties, and started holding small competitions in the early seventies. Berry and the Russell High team went to an NCA camp during her first year as an assistant coach, in the summer of '73. The next year, however, a former college cheerleader named Jeff Webb, who had met Berry while working for NCA, started up his own cheerleading organization, the Universal Cheerleading Association.

"Jeff wanted cheerleading to take a different direction than what it was. He wanted it to be more athletic, and he thought it should be less of a performance-type thing. NCA didn't want to do that. You know, they started out in Texas. And that's all showboating. You've got those Texas Rangers, those little majorette things. That's their thing. Anyway, after Jeff and them made a break from NCA, they came to Russell and they did what they call a one-day clinic. When they came, they had their little onesie outfits, little cute onesie things—looked like something you might wear in P.E.—and they had 'NCA' on them. And they had these new, really neat patches that had 'UCA' on them, but they weren't on yet. It was their first clinic they were ever teaching. So I sat there and whip-stitched their patches on their uniforms for them. Jeff and I laugh about it now because he's took off and he's a *Fortune* 500 magazine person and I'm still"— Berry adopts a mock falsetto—"back home in Flatwoods.

"I was just kind of a path that they walked on to get to that major highway."

Until 1974, the rural northern end of the county had had three high schools: Wurtland High, in the town of Wurtland along the Ohio River; Greenup High, a half-hour north in Lloyd; and McKell High, up in South Shore across the river from Portsmouth. That year, the county tore down the old Greenup school, built a new, bigger school in its place, and turned Wurtland and McKell into middle schools. That was why students attending the new Greenup County High became Musketeers: they represented a union of three different schools, from three different parts of the county—all for one, and one for all.

In 1976, after two years as an assistant at Russell, Berry landed the head coach position at the new school. A native of Russell in southern Greenup, she arrived as a complete outsider, and she thinks that that helped her unify the cheerleading team—which, in turn, helped to unify the school.

"It was really hard for them all to pull together. But those kids were so ripe for knowledge and something to be proud of. And I came in as someone who wasn't from Wurtland, Greenup, or McKell. I was told you can't put too many McKell girls on the front row, and you need to put so many Wurtland girls—and I said, 'Now, wait a minute. These girls are all Greenup County kids. I don't know who's who. I don't know where they live. I don't want to know where they live. They're all going to find their niche the same as I'm finding mine.' So because I didn't care where they were from, that helped them, I think, to bond with each other better. Those kids just wanted to know things, wanted to experience new things. I guess they were like me. They liked the challenge of succeeding."

Back then, Berry didn't know much more about cheerleading than the girls she was coaching. She'd never had any gymnastic training, and she'd never cheered for a competitive cheer squad. Her boy, Chris, had grown old enough to attend elementary school, so Berry could go ahead and plunge into her work. She devoured everything there was to know about the sport. Berry went to clinics and watched the instructors teach new stunts. She bought videos that explained gymnastic technique.

"It was just hands-on learning," she says. "We'd watch those videos and go, 'Okay now, let's analyze that. Yeah, you oughta do it like this.' Then I'd try it out on the girls and think, 'Gosh, that's not exactly how that looked.' But you've got to remember now, see, I was in my early twenties then. I was willing to get down and get dirty, and do all that crazy stuff with them, and throw them over, and all that stuff. You just BS a lot, you make them think that you know this is the way this is supposed to be done. Convincing them that your way is the right way. So they'll go, 'Okay.'

"I loved the camps and the clinics. I would just walk around and watch everybody. I didn't care what my girls were doing, as long as they learned something. I was just fascinated by everybody's style. I was like this sponge that wanted to grasp all this other stuff and take it into our program. I think when you can't learn anything else, you're dead in the water. I just wish I had the time and the money and the energy to do it. [At the camps and the clinics,] I used to go outside and sit in the heat and never think about it. I'm at the point now that, eh, one or two hours outside is enough, and I'm ready to go back to the hotel and lay in the air-conditioning."

Looking back, Berry feels sorry for the girls on the Greenup High squads of the early seventies. They worked so hard, learned so much, and set the tone for the following decades of Greenup cheerleading greatness, but because national cheerleading championships didn't exist before 1980, they never got to compete for a national title.

Once a national competition came into being, Berry and her squad didn't wait long to establish themselves as the preeminent cheerleading team in the country. Greenup took second place in 1980, then won four championships in a row from '81 through '84. Berry and crew followed up with wins in '87, '92, and '94, before their most recent victory at the '97 competition. The Greenup JV won titles in '85—the first year a national JV competition was held—and again in '92 and '93.

At the '82 championships, Berry recalls, laughing, she realized just minutes before her team was about to perform that she'd made a mistake in dubbing the team's music. ("We did a *Saturday Night Fever* routine—'Ah, ah, ah, ah, staying alive'—you know.") As things turned out, two eight-counts, or about six seconds, were missing from the musical mix, and a woman working for UCA told Berry it was just too late to do anything about it. That meant the Greenup routine would have to be changed. The UCA official watched as Berry broke the news to the Greenup squad.

"Her mouth dropped open, like 'Holy crap, I can't believe she's telling these kids this,'" says Berry. "So we go out there and we do it and we ended up winning. And that UCA girl, she laughed. She said, 'Those little girls were like, "Oh yeah, no problem. You say it's no problem, then it's no problem. We'll do it that way.'" And she was right. That's the way they were. They were very gullible, but they were very intelligent, and they could just take things and run with them."

Berry learned early on the importance of maintaining her cool during important competitions. She has the rare ability to instill in her athletes the same relaxed yet focused sense of confidence and desire that she feels herself. After the national competition of 1984, however, a dam inside her burst and she cried and cried.

"That year, Bartlett went on and did really good, didn't have any major flaws," says Berry, speaking of the Tennessee high school that produced three national champion cheer squads in the eighties, but is now relegated to the all-girls' medium varsity division. "Bartlett had been our competitor back when there wasn't all these divisions, small, large, men, all that stuff. They had done a really good job, so I had gone to the girls and said, 'Okay, they nailed their routine, but your routine's better. Your routine's stronger. All you've got to do is go out there and hit it, and it'll win for you.'

"So they went out there, and in the opening running segment, two tumbling passes had mistakes in them. I won't say they fell, but they were not good. And they stumbled a little bit on putting a mount up. It went up, but it wasn't clean. They got almost to the end, where the second section of music starts, and the tape breaks. It's clearly UCA's fault, their equipment fails, the tape breaks. The girls all stop and kind of look at me.

"So I go over to Jeff Webb and he says Okay, you have two options. One, you can start right here—we can reload the tape and you can start right where you are and continue on. Or two, you can wipe out the whole routine and go again, but you have to go again *now*. Well, at that time, the routines were three minutes long. And we had gone through two minutes, thirty seconds of hard-hitting routine. But we had had what I considered three mistakes, minor that they were, but three mistakes. So I went out to the girls and I said, 'Well, this is the bottom line, your routine that you just did isn't good enough to win. But because the music screwed up, you get to do it again—if you want to. And you're going to, starting at the beginning, all over, right now, line up, and do it. And you better not make any mistakes.'

"And they did it. I mean they nailed everything. And we won. I felt so bad for Bartlett that I wouldn't go on to the floor and get the trophy and everything. Susan [Ray] and them were like, 'Candy!' I mean I was crying! I felt so sorry for them. The little Bartlett girls were just killed when we went out and did it the second time—it was so good. You could just see their faces were like, 'Oh, God!' So I felt so sorry for them. I said, 'Love their hearts, they worked so hard.' I mean we did screw up. We messed up. And by the grace of God, our music messed up too, so we got to go again and we won. That's the only year I guess I've ever been upset at a competition."

As Berry and her Greenup County cheerleaders continued to win championship after championship through the eighties and on into the nineties, the rest of the cheerleading world tried to learn as much as it could from them, much to Berry's surprise.

"Honest to God, we never really thought that we were *THE*— I mean, I do now. But I bet it took till '92 or '93 that I ever felt like people would say, 'Oh gosh, there's Greenup. Oh gosh, look, here comes Greenup County.' Till then, I never really thought about it but everybody else did. Those people from UCA would say, 'People call us in here all the time wanting to know what Greenup County is doing, they call wanting to know where you're going to camp.' And I was like, 'Oh yeah! Right! I know they're calling long distance wanting to know where Podunk High School is going to camp.'

"You know, you just don't realize that. Which is sort of where our high school kids are now. The kids today, they don't realize it, they don't realize what's involved. They don't perceive themselves as *THE*—in my opinion—*THE* premier all-girls' cheerleading program in the United States. Which is good, too, because if they realized that, they wouldn't be the normal type kids that they are."

The summer of 1996, someone from Los Alamitos High School, in suburban southern California, called up the UCA offices and asked when and where Greenup would be attending cheerleading camp. So UCA gave Berry a ring. Berry and the Musketeers would be attending a UCA camp at Morehead State University that summer, fifty miles southwest of Greenup County. The twenty girls on the Los Alamitos cheerleading squad, and their three cheer coaches, flew nearly 2,000 miles to Lexington, where they chartered a bus to drive the remaining hundred miles, just so they could rub elbows with the legendary Greenup County cheerleaders.

"When our girls met them," says Berry, "they were like, 'Why are they coming from California? What do they want to do this for?' And I'm like, 'Girls, if they're in cheerleading, this is the hot spot for cheerleading. Not just you-all, but there's other strong squads. There's Dunbar and Henry Clay and Boyd County right here at this camp.' And they're like, 'Well. Okay.' Then the girls meet these kids, and they're like, 'Did you know so-and-so had a movie filmed at her house? And so-and-so owns three Mercedes?' You know, they were all just fascinated by it. And they couldn't understand why anybody would be interested in coming to Kentucky."

Berry got a similar call from UCA two weeks before her interview with me. A cheer team from Merritt Island, Florida, had made plans to come to Kentucky and have their own brush with Greenup's greatness. But UCA assumed Greenup would attend the Morehead summer camp, as they had in 1996. Because of a scheduling conflict, however, the Greenup girls were actually planning to attend a camp in Lexington, three weeks later.

By the time that news was relayed to Merritt Island, the Florida team had already bought their airline tickets. UCA, not wanting to disappoint the Floridians, convinced Berry to bring the Greenup squad to Morehead to practice cheers and stunts with the Merritt Island girls two weekends from now.

"I was telling our girls about this the other day," says Berry, "and they're like, 'Why?'

"And I said, 'Why what?'

"'Well, why do they want to do this? They're coming from Florida? Here? For camp? They're spending all that money?'

"And I'm like, 'Yeah.'

"The kids just don't understand. They don't understand that other people see them that way."

What do other squads hope to gain by spending time with the Musketeers? Do they simply want to meet high school cheerleading's biggest celebrities?

"I think they all feed off of our—I don't want to say knowledge—but the attention that is paid to us, to the point that they aren't really jealous, but envious of that attention, and thinking that it's within their grasp if they just do this, this, and this. Then they work harder. I know that was the way with Dunbar [from Lexington, Kentucky], because Dunbar and some of the other Lexington schools, like Henry Clay, said, 'Well they're just a bunch of country hicks, farmer girls. If they can do it, I know we can do it.' Kind of negative, which really hurt when they did succeed. I mean I was glad when somebody from Kentucky succeeded, but not when they were nasty about it."

As always, there's a downside to success. Some want to tear you down. Others won't give you your due unless you surpass what you accomplished the last time.

Berry explains: "We've gone to competitions when we don't have all the standing tumbling that we often do. The comment on the judges' sheet will be, 'Standing tumbling not as strong as last year's.' Because one girl out of nineteen didn't land her standing. The majority of other squads don't even have half the girls do standing tumbling. We do everybody or everybody but one, and the judges pick up on the one, solely because they're used to us doing that.

"That's what I try to get across to my parents. Like if I've got a parent whose daughter doesn't do the standing tumbling, she'll say, 'Well, Bartlett doesn't all do the standing tumbling, Boyd County doesn't all do the standing tumbling, Dunbar doesn't all do the standing tumbling.' And I'm like, 'That's not Greenup County.'

"They expect us to do certain things. We have to do what's expected. If we do more than what's expected, we get extra points. If we do less, we get dogged. Whether or not it's still better than everybody else, it's not up to Greenup's par. And that's a shame.

"That's why I get mad at the newspapers. You know, they get tired of putting in that we're going to nationals or we've won nationals or we've won the state competition. Like, a picture! They don't want to put a picture in. Especially a posed picture. They're like, 'Everybody can put in a posed picture. Who wants that but a grandma?' And I say, 'A grandma!' People get tired of you winning, but they've got to understand that it's a different group under different circumstances every year."

Cheerleading, Berry believes, is "just as American as baseball and basketball," and it's not going away.

"You know, when you have the athletic sports, you've got the girls supporting them. That's the way it was when I was in high school. We were the support group, we were the supporters. Now, although it's not an official sport, it is a performing art of its own. It's gained its own notoriety. I've challenged the school for the last three years to let us take a survey of a couple ball games and just see what percentage comes in to watch the cheerleaders. 'Cause I tell them I know we have anywhere from twelve to fifteen percent to watch the cheerleaders.

"Cheerleading combines performance and athleticism and thrill all together. You've got the dance, which is performance. And you've got different types of dance—some is sultry, some is floor moves, and some is street dancing. There's a lot of girls who aren't good at running track, or haven't grown up with a basketball in their hands. And gymnastics is a popular sport on TV. So is ice skating. They both combine—to me—the same skills that you use in cheerleading. It's just something that the typical kid can get into.

"I don't see it getting much stronger, though. I see it leveling off. Basically because there's a lot of males in charge of athletic departments and school boards and stuff that are threatened by the growth of cheerleading. I think they don't like the challenge that it gives to their ball teams, and they're worried that equal funding will have to come about and so on. As long as we can be self-sufficient and don't have to challenge them and ask for their help, we're safe. If you challenge them much on it, then they're going to limit your program. Once we get a parent with wild hair that wants to challenge it, and we can't control it, then we've got a problem. Our program will go by the wayside."

But Berry doesn't foresee any parents with wild hair fussing in the near future.

"I don't think it'll be here with the Jetsons, in 2200 or something, but I think it's a tradition that's going to survive, because parents are always going to want their kids to achieve, and to achieve, they're going to have to learn and study. That means going to camps and having instructors. As long as that's there, those camps are going to reward people with jobs. It's a circle and it's going to keep going."

Specifically, Berry believes that all-girl cheerleading will survive despite the advent of coed cheerleading. She recognizes that coed squads now dominate the college cheerleading ranks, but she insists that all-girl cheerleading will continue to thrive, if only at the high school level.

"It's the same way I don't think the WNBA will ever overcome the NBA," she says, speaking of the newly formed Women's National Basketball Association. "I mean there's an interest right now in the WNBA. But I guarantee you if Michael Jordan was against them in the TV ratings, ninety-eight percent would watch Michael Jordan's team. And the WNBA wouldn't get anybody except a few females who would like to do what they're doing. That's because there's a lot of mothers that don't want their daughters to go in that area. And that's okay. To each their own."

Berry says that she once thought of coaching coed cheerleading "for about thirty seconds, that was it.

"I don't want to work with males," she says flatly. "Also, in our area, for males to be involved, they would be considered sissies or stranger-type kids and to me that would lessen our program. I and a lot of other people have worked really hard to have our program become elite, and I don't want anything to degrade it. I don't mean that badly to the one or two boys that would keep out. But I don't think it's fair to the next hundred girls coming up to deteriorate the program.

"It's just not the thing in this neck of the woods. It's the same how soccer is just now catching on in our area. You know, we're a little bit delayed. Last year was our first year to have a male soccer team at the high school. So, you know, we're maybe backwoods-y on some things. It will take another ten years for the interest to grow enough for our cheerleading program to be competitive with a coed squad—if ever.

"Basically, you've got a lot of single-minded male father figures who won't encourage their boys to do that because they see it as too feminine, so the numbers won't be there. And that's okay."

If Greenup County High School ever does create a coed cheer team, you can be sure the kids on it would take an awfully passionate approach.

That's just the Greenup County way. Whatever kids participate in outside of class, whether it's football, basketball, cheerleading, the marching band, the debate team, or the model U.N. delegation, they take it darned seriously.

"You find that in a small town, because money to participate in things like that is so hard to come by. So when children choose to participate, you want them to do the best they can. A lot of people in Greenup you would think are very poor. They're not. They work hard for their money, and therefore, they don't spend it frivolously. And when they do spend it, they expect to get something in return, 'cause that's the way their grandparents and parents have always taught them. So I think that's the reason you find people becoming so serious about sports and all that other stuff."

Berry doesn't want her girls viewing cheerleading as a matter of life and death, however. So she tries to take the blame for any mistakes away from the girls and put it on herself. At the national competition in 1995, when Shawnda Bates fell on her tumbling run, then dropped Jerri Floyd during a mount, Berry tried to make Shawnda and Jerri believe that it wasn't their fault, that they shouldn't beat themselves up for it. After all, Jess Madden had torn up her knee just two weeks before, causing Jerri to adjust quickly to the varsity, and Shawnda to adjust quickly to working with Jerri.

"I said to myself, 'They're not going to pull it off. I need to change the routine.' But I also said, 'If I change the routine and lessen it, we're not going to win.' So do I take that one chance out of ten that it's going to hit and give them that chance to win? Or do I lessen it and tell them from day one, 'The best you're going to do is fourth or fifth place.' I was like, 'Well, let's just go for it.' But I knew in my heart that it was going to fall. It was such an elite stunt, and Shawnda and Jerri were so nervous. So that was a coaching error. And I told them that. I should have changed the routine and been satisfied with fourth or fifth. Of course, they said, 'Oh, twenty-first is just about the same as fourth or fifth.' But it was horrible. Of all the years we'd ever gone, that was the most horrible. I don't ever want that to happen again. It's just like a plane crash. You might get back on the plane, but you sure as hell don't want it to go down again."

The following year, despite a rash of injuries to many of the girls at the beginning of the season, the Greenup team got back on the plane and flew it silky smooth, but still they lost, to Boyd County.

"We thought we had a really good routine. But I thought the two squads who beat us had equally good routines," Berry remembers. "Jerri Floyd sat on my lap after most of the squads had finished, and she said, 'What do you think?' And I said, 'I think you've gotten third place.' She just started crying.

"Then she looked up at me and she said, 'Did you not think we did good?'

"I said, 'Yeah, I think you did really good.' But, I said, 'These other squads'—one was from Tennessee, Houston High School—'they're unheard-of, they had a real strong ending, they're going to be up there. And Boyd County, they've been close every year, and they didn't screw up this year, and they're going to be up there. And you-all are going to be third.'

"Well, she was just devastated, and of course, it turned out that way, that we were third. You know, we're pretty honest with them.

"Anyway, after it was over, I asked them, 'Could you have done this routine any better? Were you not thrilled when you come off the floor?'

"'Yes.'

"'Why were you thrilled?'

"'Well, because we had all these injuries, and we done pretty good, we done a good job, better than we thought we would.'

"I said, 'That's the whole key, feeling good when you come off the floor about what you did. Yes, it makes it nicer when the judges agree with you. But those kids from the other teams have worked just as hard as you have.'

"So we went on and talked about it. And I said, 'The whole thing is to come here and have a good time and do the best you can.' And I said, 'You did the routine the best you could. We didn't give you a good enough routine. It's my fault. It's Hank's fault. It's Randy's fault. Because we did not give you-all a good routine. If you did the routine the best you could, why did you not win?'

"And they went, 'Because our routine wasn't good enough.'

"And I said, 'Right. So blame us. Don't blame yourselves.'

"And they're like, 'Okay.'"

Candy chuckles.

"So then we took off and went to the parks at Disney World and had a good time. It was hard when we come home though, and had to face the billboards from the Boyd County squad that won just miles from us.

"But it's supposed to be fun. When it's not fun anymore, you can't be successful. And it has to be fun for us, too. I'll know when it's time to quit when it's not fun anymore, when I'm too downtrodden about everything."

Berry has considered moving on a few times, either retiring from cheerleading altogether or taking a coaching job at a Division I university. But she always ends up back at Greenup County High School.

"It's easy. It's safe. It's fun. It's kind of like family. I've wanted to get out two or three times. But you kind of hate to because you know what it's meant to the other kids, and you think, 'If you could help one more kid, if you could help one more kid do something special with themselves.' You know, you just kind of hate to give it up. Also, during the week, it's something to keep me occupied.

"If I went anyplace else, it would be to the college level, and those kids already have experience. Most of those kids on college programs are elite kids one way or another, either because of what their parents financially can give them or what their skills have given them. So there's not a whole lot of new things that I can help them accomplish. That's the fun. Susan will tell you, I love going and working with her JV kids this year. They're good kids. They just don't have the knowledge yet. They're like, 'Oh man! I'm a Greenup County cheerleader! Teach me! Teach me! Teach me!' Don't get me wrong, they're still not elite cheerleaders on the junior varsity level, but I think they will be. Before, I thought, 'Love their hearts. Only their mothers will love them.'"

Berry has a way with teenage girls. She pushes them to work harder than they've ever worked in their lives, to be something that few people get to be—the best. The coach's one frustration comes from watching her girls lose their drive and ambition once they leave the Greenup program. Jess Madden and Jerri Floyd could be two of the best college cheerleaders in the country, but neither plans to cheer next year, nor are they doing much this summer. They were both recruited by UK but opted not to go, and they could have worked as camp instructors at UCA, but they turned that down as well.

"It's hard for them to break out," says Berry. "And I think that comes from the small-town attitude. Which there's nothing wrong with. Because that does protect you from a lot of things that you would experience otherwise. But it also keeps you from growing in other areas and that's not good. Of course, I've experienced that same thing. That's why my general attitude with speaking engagements is like it is." (Berry is always fending off offers to speak about cheerleading at events organized by UCA, the University of Kentucky, and others.) "As a young person, I was never privy to that kind of experience. I never got out in front of people."

So when Berry looks at Jerri and Jess, she sees her own insecurity, her own failings. Jess, she says, may be the best flyer Berry ever coached.

"She's extremely talented, so it's sad," says Berry. "Maybe she'll grow up a little bit and want to do something. She's not a very aggressive kid. She's very introverted, and you'd think with all the attention she'd gotten in cheerleading . . . But she's a team member. And that's the one thing about these kids. I get really mad at them when they go away to school, because I want them to be more outgoing as individuals. But we train them to be team members and tell them that not one person wins, the team wins. So they're so geared to being part of a team, it's hard for them to make a break. So maybe Jess will be able to grow up, I don't know.

"Shawnda and Kasey Dillow have both been teaching in Pennsylvania and here in Kentucky for UCA this summer. They went for a training session and have taught at three camps. They come home last night, and they told me how much fun they had and how great it is, and how they can't wait to get back on the road and go again. Whereas here's Jess and Jerri, still in the water so to speak, not growing and not doing anything. Shawnda and Kasey's had a lot of problems—like breakdowns on the highways, things they've had to grow from. And Shawnda's dad and I were talking, and he said, 'We sent away a little girl this summer, and a young lady come back.' Now, when she goes away to college, there's not going to be much thrown at her that she can't handle, and I really feel that because of cheerleading, she's gotten this opportunity.

"The ones that accept those challenges and go on and do something with their lives, in the long run, are going to be so much more well-rounded than those that have only seen that one side. That's what we want for them—to be more well-rounded. I want them to be able to do more and see more and get more out of life before they make those lifelong decisions like marriage and family and relationships and so on. I think the more they're exposed to, the better they'll be able to make those decisions."

Of all the things Berry wants to teach her cheerleaders, personal confidence is what she emphasizes most. Watching a cheerleading competition can be a lot like watching a car race: everybody's waiting for the wreck. Over the years, Greenup has set itself apart from all other high schools because time and time again its team has avoided the wreck. Berry has a knack for making her girls feel good going into their competition performances, so they don't even think about the possibility of a wreck, so they think good things and that's all.

Asked how she does it, how she knows just what to do and say so that her girls feel relaxed and confident before performances, Berry says, "I don't know. It's just somebody up above. I don't take the credit for that. There's got to be a higher being or something that enables me to calm down and think of those things. I don't know."

Berry leans back on the bench, holding the edge of the picnic table with her hands. While she thinks, a sparrow flutters behind her, the fountain bubbles, and somewhere a cricket chirps on and on.

"Feed off of your feelings when you've been competitive," she says finally. "You're already anxious. You're already agitated. Those things are going to get you the adrenaline and the strength that you need. But to get you beyond that, where you can't perform to the level that you've been trained to, is not good. I try to get them to focus on what's there, but not beyond what their skill level is. Maybe I could get them to be a little more hyper and a little more agitated, I don't know, that's just not me. I try not to do that with myself.

"I want them to be so confident and so proud of themselves that they have no question what they're doing when they go out there. I want it to be as if they're walking around this park here. It's just another thing that they are so comfortable with because they are the best. If you are the best at your skill, it will show and you will come out on top. The training and the practice times are supposed to make that happen. If you're nervous to the point that you feel challenged by someone else, then you're going to make mistakes. When your skill level and your practice schedule have made you the best, then those mistakes are not going to occur, just like with the fall we had in '95. We had to throw somebody in at the last minute. Our level was down. We knew it was. The girls were very unsure. I couldn't give them the confidence because I didn't have the confidence. And I think they fed off that, too.

"It's great to challenge them and see if they can do it. But they're kids. And they're going to be nervous and anxious. It's up to us, as the adults and the coaches, after we've given them the training, to decide what's right and what's not right.

"We really, really have the kids' best interests at heart. Because at our age, we've already done everything and achieved what we set out to. Now, we want them to see what it's like, to see what the feeling's like. The last time we won—not this year, but in '94—they did really good onstage and were thrilled to death. When they won officially—got the trophy and everything—they come off and was hugging me and some of the seniors looked at me and said, 'You know, when you told us the biggest thrill would be when we come off the floor knowing we done the best and felt like we were the best?'

"And I said, 'Yeah.'

"They said, 'Winning this trophy was nothing compared to what the feeling was when we come off the floor.'

"That's really what you want. You want them to be so proud of themselves and what they've achieved as a group, separate from winning the monetary-type thing or the trophy or something like that.

"You look at Katarina Witt. I watch her on the ice, and you know, her skill level's not high anymore, but she loves the performing and doing the best that she can do for her skill level. She's never disgruntled with anything. And then you see ones like Oksana Baiul, and those people that are doing it solely for the notoriety and not for the love of the sport. I guess I do it for the love of the sport and what it gives to the kids."

Chapter Nine

What's Good for the Boys Isn't Always Good for the Girls

From outside the University of Kentucky gymnasium, April Creech can hear Will Smith rapping the *Men in Black* theme through six-foot-tall speakers. She can hear 400 teenage cheerleaders shrieking, stomping, clapping on a hip-hopping stretch of bleachers. Curious, April peeks inside and sees the buff UCA counselors jumping and dancing on the gym floor, whipping the campers into a swelling cheer frenzy.

April's been to a UCA summer camp before, but never as a member of the Greenup County varsity. Now she's wearing a green-and-gold T-shirt with the letters "G.C." printed prominently across the chest, and when Coach Berry says it's okay, April swaggers into the UK gym, sur-rounded by her new teammates. Trying to take it all in—the rocking mu-sic, the raucous cheerleaders, the rambunctious counselors—April looks this way and that, her thin blond ponytail swinging back and forth across the nape of her neck. She feels the excitement bursting out of everyone around her; it mingles with an intense anticipation all her own. And she senses the pointing, the staring from the throng of girls on the bleachers once they recognize April and those with her as *the* Greenup County cheerleaders.

Almost everyone associated with Greenup County cheerleading has come here to Lexington for this first day of cheer camp: the nineteen var-sity girls, the twelve JV girls, Candy Berry, Tom Pack, Randy Peffer, Susan Ray. Only the team choreographer is missing. Hank Light is over 600 miles away, vacationing with his four best friends, getting a deep, dark tan on the sands of Myrtle Beach.

April Creech owes much of her involvement with elite competitive cheerleading to Light. Three years ago, he introduced her to the upper echelons of the sport. Since then, April has gotten closer and closer to the Greenup High program while Light has moved further and further from it. When they first met, April and Light were both leaping into something new—April had begun her freshman year at Greenup's cross-county rival, Russell High School, and Light had begun coaching an all-star cheerleading squad.

All-star cheerleading began in the late 1980s as an answer to school-sanctioned cheerleading. All-star cheerleaders don't cheer for a school. They are brought together by a coach, usually at a private gym, to compete against other all-star squads without ever cheering for basketball or football teams. All-star cheerleaders cheer only in competitions (UCA holds regional and national competitions in three all-star age groups: there's the youth all-stars, for girls under twelve; junior all-stars, ages twelve to fourteen; and senior all-stars, ages fifteen to seventeen). Their parents pay a lot of money for the use of the gym during practices, for equipment, for uniforms, and for the coach's time and expertise. A young person like Light can create a career—indeed, a lucrative career—as an all-star cheerleading coach.

Light first designed routines for the Greenup County JV and varsity during the 1990 season. By late 1993, he'd gained a great deal of experience as coach and choreographer, helping lead the Greenup varsity to a national championship in '92 and the JV to two national championships in '92 and '93. Then, when he watched the Greenup girls win their school's seventh national championship in early '94, again performing the moves he created for them, Light found the confidence he needed to head out on his own.

Light got the chance to work with Greenup cheerleading from Candy Berry, a longtime family friend, and for that he's grateful, but Light's always known that he would eventually move out from under Berry's critical eye. Throughout 1994, Light did some part-time work as a cheer and tumbling instructor at a gym in Ironton, Ohio. And when the autumn all-star season approached, he got permission from the gym's owner to hold tryouts for a new junior all-star team.

Fourteen-year-old April Creech made the squad. Devoted to cheerleading since she was five, April had continued her competitive cheerleading training by taking individual tumbling lessons from Light at the Ironton gym. As a freshman at Russell High, April couldn't cheer for her school because of an arbitrary school rule barring ninth-grade girls from the varsity squad. (Russell has no JV.) By cheering with Light's new junior all-stars, April could avoid taking a break from her sport.

Light, April, and the rest of that new team won UCA's 1995 junior all-stars national championship down in Orlando, but Light found that his fellow coaches at Greenup County were not as excited for him as he'd hoped. Light feels that Candy Berry and Randy Peffer and even Light's half-sister, Greenup JV coach Susan Ray, thought all-star coaching monopolized his time. Once Light took on the responsibility of April and the other junior all-stars, he stopped going to every Greenup High football and basketball game. And he stopped attending every varsity cheerleading practice and every JV cheerleading practice. Instead, he came only to practices at which he had to teach the girls a new dance, a new stunt, or a whole new routine.

Light continues to coach all-stars despite the grumbling of the other Greenup coaches. He has yet to win another national championship, but in early 1997 he moved to a gym in Hurricane, West Virginia, and tripled his chances, holding spring tryouts for three all-star teams—one youth, one junior, and one senior. Light doesn't worry that his heightened commitment to all-star cheerleading will further sour the Greenup coaches on him. Light says he stopped needing their approval four years ago, when he finally decided to tell them that he's gay.

By now, Light says that the Greenup coaches, the cheerleaders' parents, and the cheerleaders themselves have all learned to get past his homosexuality. Like the U.S. military, they seem to practice a "don't ask, don't tell" policy. The Greenup community may not approve, but they accept him— in part, Light believes, because of the confidence he has felt since coming out and coming into his own.

Still, Light plans to move away from the Greenup area next spring to a big city down south, which would make this season his last choreographing for Greenup High. Light wants to live in a larger city simply because it would offer more to do. And he prefers the Southeast because, for one thing, he likes warm weather, and for another, he wants to stay involved in high-end competitive cheerleading. Atlanta's the biggest city with both, so it's his first choice. Memphis, his second choice, isn't quite as big but, as the home base of UCA, it's arguably America's cheerleading capital.

Ultimately, says Light, he wants to move because Greenup County is no longer home for him. Both his parents have died and he isn't terribly close to his brothers and sisters anymore. He would have moved long ago if not for the success he's enjoyed coaching cheerleading at Greenup High. Now, at twenty-six, he feels it's time to make his own way, to find his own place.

April Creech loved cheering for Light's junior all-stars—the challenge of striving toward excellence, the thrill of competition, the pride of winning. It was great. Then came her sophomore year, when April first joined the varsity cheerleading team at Russell. Suddenly, she was miserable. She thought the coach was lousy, the other girls didn't take the sport seriously, and everyone at Russell—from the administrators to the wealthy student body—looked down their collective nose at cheerleaders.

In the middle of her sophomore year, April asked her mom if she could transfer to Greenup High, where, she thought, the students and teachers would respect her for who she was. But April was then only fifteen, too young to drive a car, and her mom, Deborah, didn't have time to chauffeur her an hour north to Greenup High every morning and home every afternoon.

After April turned sixteen and learned to drive, Deborah consented to the transfer. April left Russell in the middle of her junior year; for two months, she happily drove an hour to Greenup High each morning and an hour home to Russell each night. But the Kentucky state school board would not let her cheer for Greenup unless she actually moved into the Greenup High school district.

The board believed, Coach Berry says, that this ruling would dissuade April from leaving Russell. And they couldn't flat-out deny April's request for transfer because Berry could then complain that they were regulating cheerleading the same way they regulate official sports. (If they're going to regulate cheerleading as a sport, Berry insists, then they'll have to spend more money on it.)

In early June, a couple weeks after the state school board's decision, April's mother and her live-in boyfriend sold their place in Russell, bought a small brick house in the town of Greenup, then carted all of their family's belongings forty-five minutes north—all so April could cheer for Greenup County High School during her senior year.

Now, at this UCA camp, April's making her first public appearance as a Greenup High varsity cheerleader. From the bleachers in the UK gym, she looks out at the counselors pumping up the crowd. The Spice Girls have taken over for Will Smith, singing their hit song "Wanna Be."

"TELL ME WHAT YOU WANT WHAT YOU REALLY REALLY WANT!"

April's complexion can be sallow and her eyes tired, but now her whole face glows with excitement. She's found her way. She's found her place.

The Spice Girls fade out and a generic techno beat fades in. The college-age men and women who will run this four-day camp stand in a line facing the bleachers full of cheerleaders, and they chant, "Staff Beat Coming! Staff Beat Coming! Staff Beat Coming!" while clapping their hands over their heads and jumping and smiling. Most of the campers join in the staff's chant while clapping and jumping and smiling themselves. April and the Greenup girls are a bit more reserved. They seem nervous, uncomfortable.

"They're trying to be peppy," Susan Ray yells over the din of girlish squeals and pumping music. "But our girls have never been that peppy. It isn't that they don't want to be peppy. They just aren't." Greenup cheerleaders get peppy only when they need to—in competitions, before judges who will give them low marks if they don't. Here at camp, cheerleaders act peppy because they want to, not because they have to. Apparently, the Greenup girls don't really want to.

One by one, each camp counselor is introduced to the screaming crowd of campers. All of the counselors cheer for elite college programs, and at the sound of his or her name each takes part in an impressive partner stunt to demonstrate cheerleading expertise. All of the men lift a woman up into the air with one hand. All of the women display themselves precariously while perched atop the hands of a male partner. Except for the last camp counselor introduced:

"FROM THE UNIVERSITY OF LOUISVILLE, SHAAAAAWN-DAAAAA BATES!"

Shawnda sprints down the gym floor between the line of counselors and the bleachers, then does an elaborate series of round-offs, whip-backs, and tucks, ending with a full-twist flip.

That gets the Greenup girls peppy. Along with the rest of the crowd, the Musketeers yell long and loud for their former teammate.

As Berry has said, camp is supposed to be fun for the Greenup varsity, a time to learn some cheers, learn some stunts, bond as a team, and get some experience performing for judges.

Berry feels relaxed and confident about this year's team—for now, anyway. Rachel Brown finally conquered the standing back tuck a couple of weeks ago. She's consistently landing it now, and her confidence appears to be growing. As her confidence swells, so does her vivacious attitude. So much so that Berry recently demoted Rachel Wills from the first-string corps of Greenup flyers because the coach feels that Rachel Brown—if she can keep from being "Psycho Child"—will give the team a charismatic lift.

Some of the other Greenup cheerleaders roll their eyes at one another when Rachel mugs for an imaginary audience during cheer practice, but not Wills. Wills has never shown anything but respect for Rachel Brown. She admires her work ethic, her determination. And Wills isn't jealous of Rachel's good looks. It doesn't occur to her to be jealous.

Still, Wills hasn't taken the demotion lightly. Determined to take back her position as one of the top three Greenup flyers, she plans to go through camp error-free and show Berry how tough a flyer she can be. Of course, Berry's decision to go with Rachel Brown has more to do with grace than with toughness.

In April Creech, Berry's got both. April isn't a flashy flyer, like Kelena McClurg, but she's pretty and charming enough, and she never messes up. Even when her bases make a mistake, pushing her up unevenly or mistiming a lift, April manages to stay aloft. Rarely does she wobble. And you'd never know, says Berry, that April's only been on the squad for a month and a half, the other girls like her so much.

April's even-keeled. Confident, but not cocky. She's happy, but never gushes. Nice, but still genuine. In many ways, April embodies the sweetness-and-light cheerleader ideal that Rachel Brown aspires to.

April's never let that go-along-to-get-along veneer take precedence over what she wants, however. In keeping with Berry's mantra, April does not compromise.

The week before camp, April sat in the sparsely furnished den of her family's Greenup home, boxes strewn in the hallway, the walls bare, and described the way the folks at Russell High treated her. Cheerleading, she says, is not a second-class sport, even if some snobs choose to view it that way. And just because the kids at Russell come from wealthy families doesn't mean they're better than her or anyone else.

"Some of the dads are doctors. Some of 'em are lawyers," she says. "Some of the moms are nurses. One of my friends at Russell, her mom's an RN in surgery and her dad's a big executive at Ashland Oil. So she has money. Some people, they spend so much money on clothes and stuff. I mean, if you don't wear brand-name clothes and stuff at Russell, you're nothin'."

April says that at Russell Middle School, which feeds into Russell High, the cheerleaders receive fair support, but the middle school cheerleaders themselves "don't take it seriously. They're just on the team because there, it's like a name to be a cheerleader. You're, like, 'The Cheerleaders.' But that's only how it is in middle school. Once you get to high school, you get made fun of."

"How?"

"For just being a cheerleader. Like you can be settin' out there cheerin' and they'll be laughing at you in the stands."

As April continues, she occasionally lapses into the present tense. She's not yet over her Russell cheerleading experience.

"Our principal said if it was up to his opinion, he'd probably do away with cheerleading at Russell," she says. "'Cause we don't have anything. Greenup has a cheerleading room. We don't even have that. All of our stuff just gets thrown into like, this locker in the athletic room. It's baaad. . . .

"Russell's mainly rich people, so they don't care much for cheerleading. They support their football team mainly, and basketball, and if you play soccer and stuff, you get supported, too. But they look down on us, the cheerleaders. Basically, they don't see that there's any need for it. It's baaad."

During April's sophomore year, the team's faculty sponsor was fired; the new sponsor, according to April, was brought in because the Russell administrators figured she would do what they wanted her to do, not what was best for the squad.

"She doesn't know anything about cheerleading," says April. "I mean, she can't even put a routine together."

The Russell administration wanted the cheerleaders to provide encouragement for the boys' teams. They didn't want them to do their own thing. According to school rules, the cheerleading team can only compete twice a year—at Kings Island up in Cincinnati over Labor Day weekend, and at the Kentucky state competition over in Lexington in the spring, but never at the big UCA competitions like the Kentucky regionals or the nationals down in Florida. And if either of the two lesser competitions conflicts with a football game or a basketball game, the Russell cheerleaders have to stay home and cheer for the boys.

"At Russell, you weren't considered an athlete," April explains. "They considered you part of an activity, that's what they called it. At Greenup, they put you in with the athletes, you know? They make you feel like you're part of the athletic program. I guess they have more respect for their cheerleaders and I guess they have a lot of respect for Candy and Mr. Peffer, too.

"With the sponsor at Russell, whatever the principal and them said, she did. She didn't say, 'What about if we did this?' She'd just say, 'Okay, I'll do what you say.' They didn't have any respect for us. . . . They say they don't want you to be a competitive squad so much as cheerin' for the ball teams. At Greenup, they have a pep club that makes signs and kinda helps the teams. At Russell, they say it's up to the cheerleaders.

"At Russell, before every game, all that week, you'd be making signs and stuff for the teams, 'cause what you are, you're relied on to do that. It's part of your job, I guess. Instead of practicing, we would spend time painting signs. All of our cheerleading money, basically, went to paint, glitter, and stuff like that for signs. I mean, we got paper free from the newspaper, but they would call practices just to paint signs. And if you weren't there, you would get in trouble.

"For the football team, each cheerleader was assigned a certain player to make a sign for. Before every game, you'd have to make candy bags, too. You would take a paper bag, put their number on it, maybe put, 'Go Russell, Beat Something,' and you'd fill it. Each of us had to bring in two or three bags and you'd fill 'em with candy. That gets really expensive when there's like fifty football players, and you have to do it every game.

"They'd put the signs for the football players all along the fence on the home side, like up by the field house, all down that. They'd completely cover the fence. And the boys usually take them home after the games. During basketball season, they'd assign a player to each cheerleader again, and the signs are plastered behind the cheerleaders all on a wall back in the gym there. The guys usually come get 'em after the games, and if they don't come get 'em, they get thrown away and you've got to make a new one before the next game. Then you put 'em all back up again.

"I got sick of it. It's pretty tiring. I mean I guess that's good for the guys, but it's hard just painting signs all the time."

Years ago, the people who ran Russell cheerleading cared more about stunts and gymnastics than boosting boys' egos. When April was a little girl growing up in Flatwoods, another town in southern Greenup, the Russell cheerleaders received respect and admiration. They weren't the celebrities that the Greenup cheerleaders were and are, but no one made fun of them, and they went to the major competitions.

Not long after April's little brother was born, when April was five years old, her parents split up. April kept her mind off her newly divided family by cheering in a local JFL, a Junior Football League. In JFLs throughout the southern United States, boys ten and under play organized football while girls ten and under cheer for them on an organized squad. JFL cheerleading can often become comical because the girls involved don't give a rip about football. They pay little or no attention to the game, and cheer enthusiastically even as their football team—unbeknownst to the cheerleaders—gets trounced.

By the time April was ten years old, her mom was remarried, to a high-level executive at Ashland Oil. Ashland used to house its corporate offices in Boyd County, not far from Russell and Flatwoods, but in 1990, the company moved its headquarters to Lexington, taking April's new stepfather—and April—along for the ride.

April spent three years in Kentucky's capital city, where she continued her cheerleading and gymnastic training at a private gym called the Pep Club. But after April's sixth-grade year, her mom divorced the Ashland Oil executive. Without any family or friends in Lexington, Deborah decided to move herself and her two young children back to Greenup.

For a while, times were hard for Deborah, April, and April's younger brother. Steady income was tough to come by.

"My mom worked in Huntington [West Virginia]," says April. "She was a personal secretary for this older man. Because when we first moved back, she couldn't find work, and she was working at Wal-Mart for a while. And this man came in and asked her if she had any secretarial skills. He was looking for somebody. So she worked for him for three or four years after we came back. Then he got real old, and he couldn't keep up with the business, so she got laid off. And she was looking for a job again."

Before another job came along, Deborah moved in with a man named Rick Lambert, who works at the tri-state office ("serving Kentucky, Ohio, and West Virginia") of Gemini Corporation, a national fuel and gas company.

Although Deborah and Rick aren't even engaged, April calls him her stepdad. She gets along with him better than she did with her previous stepfather, whom she refers to as "the man my mom was married to at the time." April's biological father lives nearby in Ironton, but April hardly sees him.

"He's just never been around that much," April says. "I see his mom. I see my grandma all the time. But he works a lot and stuff, too, so he doesn't have much time. He works construction, I'm not sure what it's called."

April's mom has always been there. She was a high school cheerleader herself, at Ashland High School down in Boyd County, and she's done everything she can to support her daughter's cheerleading ambitions, including, of course, moving her family to the town of Greenup.

"My mom, she pushes me," April says. "She wants me to do my best. When I go to camp, I'm gonna get an application to try out for UCA staff. Already, she's really on me to fill it out and send it in. She's like, 'If you don't send it in, you're not gonna get to do it.'

"My mom says that she could see a complete change in me when I came to Greenup. I didn't have much self-esteem at Russell, because we got put down. So when I came here, it just built up my self-esteem."

April's found herself a steady boyfriend, Greg McKenzie, a nineteen-year-old senior at Greenup High, whom she's been dating since she first transferred last spring. Greg played varsity basketball at Greenup till he became ineligible after his fourth year of high school. He'll be entering his sixth year this coming fall and expects it to be his last.

Greg's family lives over on the other side of Route 23, on land tucked back in the mountainous woods. They raise cattle and grow fruits and vegetables to make money. Greg says he used to get in a lot of trouble by drinking, smoking marijuana, and as he puts it, "chasing girls." But for the past couple years, he's spent most of his time outside of school delivering pizzas for a Greenup restaurant called Giovanni's. With the money from that job, he's managed to buy a new maroon Chevy pickup with gold striping. Greg spends over $500 a month on car payments and insurance, but that's okay. He feels responsible for something.

Greg's never had a girlfriend like April. He spends almost every waking minute with her, and he can't stand to be without her. He's the only cheerleader boyfriend who attends the team's practices. And he recently got his truck custom painted with "Greg" in gold letters on the window behind the driver's seat, and "April" in gold letters behind the passenger's seat.

April has never known a guy to be so serious about her, so devoted to her, and she likes that. She and Greg are as intense about their relationship as they can be after only four months together.

April's brother, who's twelve now, rounds out April's support system. Not only did he take the family's recent move in stride, but he also hopes to follow in his big sister's footsteps. He wants to finish up his last two years at Russell Middle, then transfer to Greenup for high school.

"He plays football and basketball and baseball and everything," April says, "and at Russell, it's so much to do with politics, and who your parents are, how much they suck up to coaches, and that's how you get to play. It's all about who you are and who your parents are. I think Russell should probably be a private school because that's how they act.

"My brother, he has a major interest in football and baseball. He's not very good at basketball, but he tries. He respects cheerleaders 'cause he's seen me do it all his life. He thinks it's great. If every guy could be around cheerleaders, I guess they would, too." April laughs. "He's really supportive. He goes to all my competitions. And if he can't go, he gets upset about it."

Not everyone's like her brother, as April well knows.

"A lot of people don't see the importance of cheerleading. They're like"—April takes a disgusted tone—"'Cheerleaders.' You know? But if they would take a look, and see what cheerleaders really do, then they would understand. I would much rather set and watch cheerleading any day than basketball or anything like that."

The only cheerleaders most people see, says April, are the ones at pro ball games, who aren't the real thing.

"In the pros, it's not cheering. It's like dancing around. And they're just there in little outfits. That's completely different from college or high school. If the pros did cheerleading the same as us, I would love to cheer with them. But I would never do it right now, because they're just dancing.

They're just there, like the Dallas Cowboys cheerleaders, they're just there to be looked at. Like the Laker Girls and stuff like that, I mean, what's that?

"And that happens to us, too, and it bothers me. Sometimes, people just set up and say, 'Oh, look at the cheerleaders.' And they just *look* at us, as if that's all we're there for. But they don't pay attention to what we're doing. It takes the complete aspect of cheerleading away. You're there to be looked at and not to be cheerin'."

If only adults would take cheerleading as seriously as they take football and basketball, says April, then maybe boys would, too.

"This area's mainly dominated by guys. The people really support football and basketball. I mean, they're always in the newspaper and everything. If they could just come to a cheerleading competition and put it in the paper, like, 'Cheerleaders Win Kings Island' or something like that. That would make a difference. I think it would show that it's not so—" April hesitates, as if she'd rather not say the word: "Sexist." She takes a breath. "'Cause there *is* a sports section and we could be included.

"I think at Russell, even if they had won eight national championships, people would still care more about the football team. That's just how the people are. That's why I wanted to come to Greenup, because the cheerleaders, they get attention. When they win, they get the attention they deserve. But at Russell, we won state, we won the Kentucky state competition my sophomore year, and we didn't get anything. They were like, over the P.A."—April muffles her voice and mimics her old school's public address system—"'The cheerleaders won the Kentucky state competition.'

"And that was it."

April was the star of the Russell squad. She was the premier flyer and she counted a number of the girls on the cheerleading team among her best friends. But April decided she'd had enough of Russell cheerleading after the treatment she got when she hurt her back during her junior year.

"Last year for Kings Island, I was hurt. I had a back injury and couldn't compete," she explains. "And after that, I was nothin', you know? I had climbed before, I was the main climber for everything. Then after I got hurt, they were like, 'We don't need you anymore. You can just stand out front.' And I didn't climb hardly in anything. I tumbled out front mostly.

So I was like, 'That's fine. I'll show you.' So I went to Greenup, and now I'm climbing."

April isn't so sure whether the girls on the Russell team are her friends anymore.

"They *were*," she says. "Yeah, until I moved. They're jealous now. There was one girl, her cousin cheered at Greenup, and that's all she ever talked about, that she wanted to cheer at Greenup. But she can't, because at Russell, you don't have to be that great to cheer. And she's just cheerin' just to be cheerin' her senior year. She's really, I guess, jealous about it."

Meanwhile, in just a month and a half of summer practice with the Greenup squad, April's gotten everything she hoped for, and then some.

"It's really stressful at Greenup," she admits. "It puts a lot of pressure on you. And this is pressure that I've never had to deal with. And it's hard. They work really, really hard, and that's something I'm not used to, either. I'm used to if something falls, or if something's not working, the coaches saying, 'Oh, okay, we're not going to do that.' But here, you've got to do it. And if you don't, then you get in trouble, you know?

"At Russell, if you would try to throw a handspring-back, and it didn't hit, they would take you out of that part. Candy says, 'You have to hit it. It's not a choice.' If you don't want to, she's like, 'Yes, you do.' We have a lot of fun with her, and she can be hilarious. But when she wants to be serious, she is serious.

"Russell makes you think, 'Well, I don't have to try, because if I don't do it, it's not gonna matter, because I'll be taken out. If I don't wanna do it, then I'm not gonna do it.' But at Greenup, if you don't wanna do it, you're still gonna do it. Whether you like it or not.

"It's a really big step up."

April relishes the extra work, the added discipline, because she wants so badly to win a national championship. April knows the other girls on the Greenup squad want to win, too, but she thinks that she wants this year's national title just a little bit more. All the other seniors on the Greenup squad have been on a national championship team. Many of the sophomores and juniors have, as well. And the younger girls who haven't yet will be here next year, some the year after that, so they'll get other chances if this year doesn't work out. For April, this year is it.

"I want to win. I want it," she says loudly. "Not just, I mean I want to for the Greenup squad, but also to show the people at Russell that I can do it. 'Cause they always put me down, put everybody down."

When she went to Florida with Hank Light's junior all-star team and won that championship as a ninth-grader, April says, "I knew I wanted to go down and I wanted to win, because at Russell, people were like, 'Why're you on an all-star squad, you're not going to do anything.' And I really wanted to prove to everybody that we could. So I guess I wanted to win then too, but it's not as bad as now, because it's my senior year, and I'm just like . . ."

Her jaw clenched, her forehead wrinkling, April leans back in her chair and stares at one of the blank walls of her new home, as if she's projecting her hopes for the upcoming season onto the room's stark white expanse. She forgets to finish her sentence.

The third day of camp, the Greenup girls practice outside in the muggy Kentucky heat on a field near the UK gym. Candy Berry, Tom Pack, Randy Peffer, and Susan Ray all sit on lawn chairs, watching their girls take direction from the UCA staff amid the horde of cheer campers.

The Beastie Boys song "Brass Monkey" pumps into the humid air as Shawnda Bates and three other counselors teach the Greenup varsity some new mounts.

Berry looks smug as she watches Shawnda demonstrate the first stunt.

"All the bases are men," she observes, "except Shawnda."

A well-built young man wearing tight blue shorts and a tight white T-shirt walks by, between the Greenup coaches and the campers on the field.

"My, my, my," says Berry.

Susan Ray giggles. "Oh, Candy," she says. "For goodness' sakes, cut that out."

"What a nice view!" says Berry, looking after the man.

"Candy!" Ray whines.

"Don't tell me you aren't looking!"

A cluster of Greenup girls work on a dance routine with one of the female counselors. She explains how to do a move that involves rotating the hips, then pushing the pelvis back and forth.

"You don't want to be like super thrusting, like dirty," she says. "This is supposed to be PG rated."

BRASS MONKEY! THAT FUNKY MONKEY!

Berry watches sophomore Megan West practice the dance. "If Megan loses any more weight, I'm gonna sit her down," Berry says. "She's a bone."

"That looks like Linda Goble over there," says Tom Pack, pointing out a camper from another high school.

"Yeah," says Ray, "she's got the jawline."

"She sure does," Berry says with a sigh. "I wonder what that poor child is doing."

"Whatever it is," says Ray, "I'll bet it's scary."

From behind the row of Greenup coaches sitting and gabbing in their lawn chairs, Hank Light approaches. Then he stands, arms folded, and looks out at the wide grassy expanse full of cheerleaders.

Just in from Myrtle Beach, Light has an extremely dark tan all over his toned body. Highlighting his bronzed face, his hair gleams a brightly bleached white, and he wears a neat, equally platinum goatee, along with wraparound mirrored-lens sunglasses, and a small silver hoop in his left ear.

"Hello," Light says softly.

"Hey, Hank's here!" says Berry. The Greenup coaches greet Light and compliment him on his outrageous new look.

"My lan'," says Berry, squinting up at Light from her lawn chair. "You look like Dennis Rodman."

Chapter Ten

Different, but Similar

Hank Light will miss Greenup County if and when he leaves next spring. Well, no, he says, that's not true. He won't really miss Greenup County too much. He won't even miss the Greenup High cheer program.

He will miss the Greenup cheerleaders. The girls who compete for GCHS, he says, they're something special.

"I've never seen kids that dedicated to something," Light says. "You know, because these kids really aren't that talented as other places I've been. As hard as they work, it's just amazing to me. Of all the places I go and all the people I help, there's no kids I've ever run across like them, with their drive. Like I said, though, this younger bunch, they don't have the drive."

Sitting in the tidy, wood-paneled den of his duplex apartment in Ashland, Light explains why he lacks confidence in this year's Greenup varsity.

"Can the new girls get the drive?" I ask.

"I don't know." Light crosses his long legs and leans back, his right arm draped over the couch. "This will be an interesting year. You know, we went through this before. When I first started, it was the beginning of a dry spell. They had all this talent until '89. Then the talent kind of dwindled; '90 was like the bottom. Then we slowly built up."

When Light says that the new crop of Greenup cheerleaders lack "drive," he's not saying they don't work hard or don't want to win a national championship "really bad." Rather, he feels these new Greenup cheerleaders—including Rachel Brown, Rachel Wills, April Creech, Miranda Elliott, Amanda Kitchen, and others—aren't yet sure of their cheerleading abilities. They lack confidence, and they want something outside themselves—Greenup's cheerleading prestige, maybe, or the adulation of their parents and community—to give them the confidence they're missing. But confidence, Light insists, they've got to get that on their own.

The youngest of eight children from a wealthy family, Light grew up accustomed to pampering. When he was born, his father, a doctor, was already elderly, and his mother, a housewife, was middle-aged. Both had several children from previous marriages. Only Light's twin brother, Scott, has the same mother and father as he does. The rest of his brothers and sisters are half-siblings, some more than twenty years his senior. The half-sibling nearest Light's age, Greenup JV coach Susan Ray, is eleven years older.

"At one time, there were ten of us in the house," Light recalls. "And me and my brother, we were the babies. We were always in somebody's arms."

Somehow, Light became his own person. One of his older half-sisters, Lisa Ray, was a cheerleader at Russell High (Candy Berry, in fact, was one of her coaches), and Light loved going to the practices and watching, soaking up the intricacies of the stunts and the dances, the way all the brightly colored bodies danced together, flipped back and forth, hoisted each other up in the air. Still in his first years of elementary school, Light mimicked cheerleading moves that he saw his sister perform.

Then Light's father, who was over sixty years old when his twin boys were born, died of heart failure.

"Where I went to Russell, it was pretty wealthy people, like it is now, because it was pretty much the people that work at Belfont Hospital, the Ashland Oil people, and that. So these are people that get out. They travel and go places. You know, we always went on vacation. Every year. My parents went all over the world. They went to Hawaii and Mexico and Europe, and that whole school system at Russell was kind of like that. Then after he died, it was like a completely different lifestyle. It was like going from being rich, to not rich. And I was still in the same Russell school system. I was nine when he died, but it didn't really hit hard till a couple years later. He didn't leave that much, for some reason. I don't know all the details, but for some reason, it didn't happen. So here's my mom, a single mom, working with a nurse's salary supporting two kids."

Light quickly learned to do without the privilege of his early child-hood. His home in Russell, which had always been so full of people, emp-tied as his older siblings grew up and moved away. Meanwhile Light grew distrustful of those outside his family who offered help—the local Baptist congregation and the greater Russell and Greenup communities. A rural Holden Caulfield, the preteen Light thought most of the people around him were insincere phonies.

"I grew up in the church," Light says, leaning forward and flashing a wry half-smile. "To me, I learned at a very young age that all church around here was about who could wear the prettiest dress on Sunday. It was this big social event, basically. My dad was a doctor, so we were pretty social, and knowing what you know about these people, and seeing them at church every Sunday, it was like, 'This is a sham.' And it's still that way. It's just very social, and all about what the other people in the congrega-tion think about you. It doesn't have anything to do with what you should be there for. You're supposed to go, so you go. Now, I don't go like I should and I still don't even know, religiously, what my view is, even. But I think with everybody, it's what's here"—Light motions to his head—"what you think, and you don't go just to be there. You know, just because someone goes to church doesn't mean they're going to get their wings."

According to Light, Greenup County folks are terrified that their neighbors will form the wrong impression of them, terrified that some piece of prejudicial information will leak out to someone who will spread it through Greenup's ferocious rumor mill.

"It's like, people don't care what you do, as long as it's not wrong," says Light. "And as soon as you do something that they think is wrong, then everybody knows about it. Everybody knows everybody's business. It's crazy. I mean, it's hilarious to see how fast things get around to people."

And what's considered wrong?

"Anything that is different from what they're used to."

Light cites Greenup High basketball coach Randy Ward, who since getting fired in the spring has re-acquired his job.

"I'm sure you heard all this scuttle about Coach Ward when he took them to Hooters. But I mean, who cares? It's a restaurant. People here are like, 'Oh my God, he took 'em to Hooters! That's a titty bar!' But it's not, at all. I mean, *I'll* go to Hooters and eat. That got him run out on a rail practically. And Hooters is nothing. I mean it's not like he took 'em to a strip joint, but that's what it's coming across as. You know, it was on the news. I read it in the paper and I was like, 'Oh my God.' And that's pretty typical of around here. What they don't understand is automatically wrong. And most of the people that are all mad probably have no clue what Hooters even is."

Light isn't defending Hooters's objectification of women. He's defending the restaurant chain's overt sexuality. Unlike most Greenup residents, he doesn't think there's anything wrong with public displays of sexuality. Greenup residents, he says, don't care so much that Hooters waitresses have become objects to be leered at by men. Rather, Greenup residents dislike Hooters because they believe all manner of human sexuality ought to be kept locked away in an emotional closest.

Raised inside this sexually repressed culture, Light didn't know what to do when he began to feel homosexual impulses as a middle-schooler.

"I knew. You know? But I just thought I was the Antichrist." Light laughs. "I mean it wasn't that bad, really. I knew, but I kept it in. I never expressed any interest or anything. You hear about all these kids that have these experiences when they're like, ten. I wouldn't have known what to do if that had happened to me when I was ten."

"Did you have any crushes or anything?"

"No, never, not even. I mean I imagined a lot of things. But I never ever even *planned* on doing anything. I was like, 'Oh, it'll go away.' I never *really* thought that, but I guess it was there in the back of my mind. But it didn't go away. And finally, in college, I was like, 'I got to deal with this or I'm going to snap.'"

The other impulse Light had during high school that was purely his own drew him toward cheerleading. Light says he was "really popular" in high school, "everybody's buddy"; he "never missed a dance," although he didn't date, "girl-wise." But he was also short, fat, and prone to extreme shyness when around people he didn't know—all cheerleading liabilities, never mind that he was a boy.

So Light did the "right" thing. He played center for the Russell High football team.

"I was . . . ," says Light, then stops and gropes for the right word. "I was real heavy. I guess I was a late bloomer. Because I grew five inches after I graduated from high school. I mean, I always wanted to cheer, but instead I played football. Still, I always wanted to cheer and somehow I had a knack for it. Susan and Lisa were always involved with cheerleading, and I knew Candy all my life"—Berry had already won her first four national championships with the Greenup varsity by the time Hank entered high school in the fall of '84—"so I would be fifteen or sixteen and I would go to cheerleading practices with Susan and stuff, and I was intrigued by it. Then, somehow, I just started making up stuff. One day, they were like, 'Wow, that's a pretty good idea.' It just started from there. At Russell, I helped the cheerleaders while I was still a junior in high school. So I was playing football, then was over with the cheerleaders. It was interesting."

After graduating high school in 1988, Light entered the local community college in Ashland and began a physical transformation. As his body changed, so did his state of mind. Confusion gave way to confidence.

"My body completely changed," Light says. "I grew, and I lost all kinds of weight. It was like, while I was growing, my body used all that fat energy to grow. I think that's what it was saving up for. I completely became a different person, completely. It's pretty amazing. I mean, I wouldn't call and order food on the phone. And now I go anywhere in the country by myself. I mean I can go on vacation by myself and get along just fine. I was painfully shy, backward. In social situations, meeting people, uh-unh, no, it always had to be someone-else-making-the-first-move kind of thing. But now, I cannot *wait* till my tenth-year high school reunion next summer. I cannot *wait*. Because people won't know me. They really won't. Looks-wise and just my whole—I mean, I've always had a kinda happy-go-lucky personality, but I was always—like, in college, I never talked in class, I never got close to anybody. Then all of a sudden, the ugly duckling became a swan. You know? I really did. I was fat. I always thought I was ugly. Then I became this completely different person."

Light moved out of his mother's house at the beginning of his freshman year of college, got an apartment near school, and took a job doing administrative work so he could pay his own way. Emboldened by his new body, Light aggressively pursued cheerleading. He began taking tumbling lessons at a local gym, in preparation—he hoped—for cheering one day at the University of Kentucky. Also, Coach Berry took him onto the Greenup coaching staff and granted him full control over the choreography of Greenup's competition routines. But Light still didn't know what to do with his ever more insistent homosexual urges.

One night, he drove alone forty-five minutes down Country Music Highway, then east on I-64, crossed the Kentucky line into West Virginia, turned off at the second Huntington exit, and drove through the small Appalachian city to a bar he'd heard of. Out front, he parked. For two hours, Light sat in his car, thinking, wondering, wishing. Eventually, he went in and had a good time. He felt comfortable, unconstrained.

When he came back home to his Ashland apartment, to his Greenup friends and family, Light "like, flipped.

"I was like, 'This is just too much to handle,'" he says, his voice rising. "I didn't go back for a year. I guess it was the whole being-here thing, seeing people I went to high school with. You know, I was like, 'I can't handle this.'"

Upon completion of his two years at Ashland Community College, Light enrolled at UK along with his twin brother, Scott. They roomed together during their junior year, and Light had trouble finding time away from Scott to learn more about his budding homosexuality. "For forever," Hank says, "I didn't do anything unless it was with him."

Light did, however, go out for the UK cheerleading team. Or rather, he meant to. During the third day of clinics and practices leading up to the UK cheer tryouts, he tore the anterior cruciate ligament in his knee while landing a tumbling run on the UK gym floor.

In a detached tone, Light says, "I was gonna cheer for the JV squad and I blew my knee out. Completely. Stunning. During the clinics before the tryout. It was really weird because I don't know if I could have done it. Because I had been coaching for three years up till then. And it was real different being in the passenger's seat, so to speak. So I didn't even try to pursue it any further, because I had to have complete reconstruction on my knee. You know, that was right in the middle of the fall semester and I didn't have the surgery till after the school year was over in May, so it was seven months before I had the surgery. I did a lot more damage to my knee just by walking to class and that sort of thing. I've been coaching ever since."

Clearly, Light has enjoyed his coaching experience. But when he insists that it's all for the best that he's never actually cheered—in high school or in college—it's hard to believe him. Light has a way of downplaying the emotional intensity of some of his more difficult life experiences. When he talks in his matter-of-fact way about the death of his father, his arduous coming-out process, and the rupture of his knee on the eve of his first-ever cheerleading tryout, he keeps it all at a significant distance. And then he offers a positive spin. His father's death, Light says, helped him learn to take care of himself. Coming out in college rather than in high school, Light says, allowed him to live out his sexual adolescence as a mature twentysomething rather than as an insecure teen.

Asked if he ever attempted to cheer for UK after he blew out his knee, he says, "No. I never tried to do it again." He gazes down at the floor, then looks up. "Because I really don't think I would have liked it, to be honest. Plus, I don't think I would have been that good, and I don't like to be not that good."

The next year, Scott Light transferred out of UK and got his degree from Morehead State, leaving Hank alone and unfettered as a senior back in Lexington. In the fall of 1991, not long after he completed his six months of knee rehabilitation, Light went to a local bar—and once again parked his car outside, sat, and watched other gay men go in and out.

He grins. "Once I went in, you know, I was fine."

At UK, Light finally decided to let go of his shyness, to step forward and tell others who he really was. With the support of his college friends—some gay, some straight—Light decided to stop worrying about how Greenup folks would regard him once they knew, too. If his straight college friends could understand and keep loving him, maybe his family and friends back in Greenup could as well.

"One of my best friends in college was one of the first people I ever told and she"—Light pauses and smiles a full-of-himself smile—"wanted . . . to . . . go . . . out with me. I kind of ignored it for a while, then, finally, I told her. I think this is what made it so easy to tell other people, because she was like, she kind of just sat there for a minute. I was like, 'Ariana, what's wrong? Don't be mad at me.' And she was like, 'I'm not. I'm just glad you trusted me enough to tell me.' From that point on—I mean I didn't go on this big shouting spree down the street or anything—but it was easy. Telling my mom was the hardest thing I've ever had to do, but I think it turned out to be okay, too."

At the end of the fourth and final day of camp, every senior from every cheerleading squad tries out for what's called UCA All-Stars. Those chosen by the UCA camp staff earn the right to go to England and be a part of a UCA cheerleading float in a London parade—transportation and expenses *not* included.

The Greenup seniors probably won't go to England even if they qualify. The nineteen girls' parents have already shelled out $186 each for this four-day camp, not to mention the $50 outfit that got its only use at last night's dance competition. With long-sleeved black tops tied seductively over their chests, body glitter sparkling on their bare midriffs, tight black bell-bottoms, and black hairbands that let them dance with their hair flip-flopping all over the place, the Greenup girls easily won the dance competition, grinding out moves that Hank Light taught them.

Candy Berry takes stock of her varsity team. Will these girls be ready for the Kings Island competition a month from now? Miranda Elliott still can't do a standing back tuck without stumbling forward. She's even having trouble with her back handspring–back tuck, a move that any member of the Greenup varsity should perform easily. Aimee Lewis, still recovering from her injury during tryouts, has worn a knee brace all through camp and has sat out most of the more rigorous practices. On doctor's orders, Aimee is supposed to do knee-strengthening exercises for a half-hour once a day, but she has rarely kept to her regimen and is much farther away from stunting and tumbling than Berry would like. Still, the Greenup varsity won most of the camp competitions. (Although, without Dunbar, Henry Clay, or Boyd in attendance, they didn't face any serious competition.) If Miranda and Aimee don't come along as Berry hopes, the Greenup team should still have enough girls for Kings Island. Berry cares about those two, however, and she doesn't want to see them fall by the wayside.

Berry's greatest worry is that this year's seniors refuse to discipline the younger cheerleaders. Some of them, she's discovered, have even taken to talking behind their teammates' backs. Rachel Brown, it seems, has gotten the worst of it. Last year's seniors—Shawnda Bates in particular—never let the younger Greenup girls slack off at practice, and nipped any team feuds in the bud before they could hurt the squad's morale.

This year's seniors get annoyed when the younger girls goof off, but they don't confront them about it. Instead, they show their displeasure with their younger teammates in subtle, unproductive ways. With so many unproven girls on the varsity, the team needs a leader like Shawnda this year more than last, but—much to Berry's dismay—no one has stepped forward and taken charge.

As the UCA All-Star tryouts get set to begin, Hank Light walks into the UK gym with a young woman on each arm. Kristi Click and Sara Madden, former Greenup cheerleaders here to help coach the Greenup JV, have spent much of the past two days talking, laughing, and generally carrying on with Light.

Berry chuckles. "Here comes Hank," she says, "with his ladies of leisure."

Light feels that he and Berry are a lot alike. They're both "pretty domineering," he says. And at times, that can cause friction.

"You know, she'll say to me—this was hard for me to get used to, especially after I came into my own—she'll say, 'They're all yours today. Just go with it.' And she'll be having some big ol' conversation with somebody on the side, then she'll go, 'Stop. I don't like that. Change it.' Then she'll go right back to talking with 'em. And I'll be like—" Light drops his jaw in mock disbelief.

"As soon as she says that, the girls are like, 'Okay, let's do something else.' It's so frustrating for me because nowhere else I go do I have any restrictions. It's like, 'Do what you want. Make it up. We trust you, blah-blah-blah.' But with Greenup, Candy's like, 'No, ecchh.' You know? She'll just say, 'That's stupid.' We're all very honest and it gets hard at times."

However, Berry remains one of Light's favorite people, and he's extremely grateful for the opportunity she's given him to develop his coaching talent.

"Candy was always a good friend of the family, and she was my sister's cheerleading sponsor in high school. A lot of people would not have given me a chance. Having that chance, plus it being Greenup County, was this big springboard for me to leap onto. She's another one of these people who I don't think is content with the way her life turned out, so this is a way for her to help and do things for others. I think it's her way of reaching out. It's like her outlet. You know, she got pregnant in high school, so her life was pretty much set from that point on. Then she started coaching. She definitely has a unique characteristic because she became so successful, but I think it was just her way of living away from the life she had to live, because she had no choice, really. Back then, you know, the late sixties, you get pregnant, you get married, you raise the baby, obey your husband, blah, blah, blah. Then there was this cheerleading thing and she was going places. I think it's real similar to me, really. You know, different, but similar. Except I can get out. Because I don't have a husband or a kid."

Berry was one of the first Greenup people Light came out to. Soon after graduating from college, he took a few months off from coaching at the high school, to prepare himself. Then he phoned Berry and told her right then and there. She seemed to take it okay, and she urged Light to tell his sister Susan.

"It's weird," says Light, "because I'll open up to a lot of people except for the people closest to me. Actually, Susan and I would never have discussed it except I told Candy, and she kind of made it easier. Susan had the worst time with it. She was like, 'I don't want to talk about it. Just don't talk about it.' Finally, I was like, 'Look, you're going to deal with it and talk about it or you're not going to have a brother anymore.' Because I'm to the point with my life where I'm comfortable with it and those that aren't cannot be involved in my life. Finally, when I told my mom, I was like, 'Look, this is it.' You know, my mom died in '95. And thank God I told her before, because I would have been . . . It would have been awful."

With everyone else Light knows in Greenup—teachers and administrators at the high school, the cheerleaders' parents, the other coaches—he came out slowly but surely.

"I let people get to know me, and once they find that out, they don't care, it seems like. I've never run across anything that's too negative. I mean, a lot of times people take it in and act kind of different at first; then it's still me, so . . . You know? I always tell people, 'If you want to know, just ask, and I'll tell you.' You know, anybody. To me, it has a lot to do with me personally. And I don't care what they want me to say, I'll say what I want to say. But I guess if I found out it bothered someone, I wouldn't talk about it or expose them to it, yet I wouldn't get around it. You don't have to approve of it, but you have to deal with it as far as I'm concerned, because it's there. You can't just ignore it."

The cheerleaders have been the most easygoing.

"The kids, they're great about it. I don't go in depth with them or anything, but a lot of times, I like to talk with them because I don't want them to form the wrong kind of opinions. And I really think I've been a good example for them, so they'll maybe change their stereotypes."

Tom Pack, Greenup's young gymnastics instructor—who is heterosexual—moved in with Light a couple years ago and has proven himself very accepting as well.

"Tom's great," Light says. "Like my four friends were here this weekend, and he just goes about his thing and talks to them and so on. It's almost like he's amazed by it all, and takes it all in. I was more worried than he was about people talking when he moved in with me. I was like, 'I don't know if you should do this or not.' I don't care what people say about me. But it hasn't bothered him, either."

When Light thinks about how repressed Greenup can be, he finds the tolerance amazing. Even the mother who started the big scandal over Hooters and basketball coach Randy Ward adores Light.

"It's really weird," Light says, "because the parent that caused all that stink over Coach Ward, her daughter used to cheer, and she loves me. I just found it so strange that she would throw this big hissy over Hooters and she knows me. I mean, her daughter once didn't make varsity and it was this big thing at the school and I was the only one she liked. Because I helped her daughter before tryouts and stuff.

"I don't know why everyone handles it so well. I guess it's because I handle it well. Because I'm different, obviously. And some of the parents are as backward as anything, but they all seem okay with it. If they're not, they don't express it."

After Light came out, he pulled away slightly from the Greenup community and began to build his own life, apart from the closeted existence he'd known before. He stopped going to every Greenup ball game, every pep rally, every cheerleading function, every cheerleading fund-raiser. He was too busy dating for the first time, experiencing his first kiss, his first intimate relationship, his first breakup. Problems arose.

"Here I was, twenty-two," Light recalls, "never been on a date, never been out of town by myself, never traveled alone, and all of a sudden in this social thing, and I wanted to experience it for all it was worth. And that was right in the middle of the cheerleading, so I started doing all that and [the other Greenup coaches] were like, 'You weren't at the ball game Friday night.' And I was like, 'So?' I mean, you know? I said, 'Uh-unh. I cannot spend the rest of my life doing that.' So I just don't. It was to the point where I was comfortable with it, and if they weren't, then sayonara. The cheerleading wasn't that important for me to give up my other life for it. I wasn't about to. Because I'd just found the other life. I felt like, 'I've got a lot to do and I want to make sure I've got the time to do it in.' 'Cause I waited so long. It was almost like my mind and everything was sixteen, but I was twenty-two. It was wild. I mean I'd done nothing. I'd partied and all that kind of stuff in high school, but I hadn't done anything sexual."

Light believes that part of the animosity some of the other Greenup coaches felt toward him stemmed from their own dependence on the cheerleading team.

"I guess that's pretty typical of the area," he muses. "They've found this one thing, and it's their life. I mean they go to every ball game, function, I mean, they live it. And I just can't anymore. I used to, but I got to the point where I couldn't let it consume my life like that. I want the kids to be great. But everybody has their job and I do mine and then it's over. To be honest, I just don't want to end up like them."

For a while, Light dreaded going to Greenup High practices because of all the tension the other coaches thrust upon him. He stuck it out, however, and things eventually ironed themselves out.

"What bothered me more than anything was that a lot of people in my life seemed to like me better when I didn't like myself. Maybe it was because they were comfortable with me that way. Candy and Randy and Susan and them liked me better when I was miserable, but I don't think they knew I was miserable. That's the thing about it. That's where the resentment came in. But the more I got to understand myself, they got to understand me."

Light tries to explain what it's like to live in Greenup County.

"People here have so little self-esteem. They get in this slump when someone tells them something bad or they start having bad ideas about themselves, and then, where is there to go? I mean, there's nowhere to really go here. If you're somewhere where there's more to do, you put yourself in different situations and you see where you fit in. Here, you're in one situation and if you don't fit in, you don't fit in. But like in D.C., New York, Atlanta, even Memphis, anybody can find their niche. It's weird to me that I've found my niche here. Because I'm happy . . . here.

"I just want to experience something more."

Light gets frustrated by the Greenup girls' lack of perspective, their inability to see outside their limited world and imagine something better for themselves. Particularly frustrating for him is the situation with young Linda Goble.

"I'm a big believer in that you kinda create your own destiny," he says.

"I just don't see how people can stay in certain situations that they're in. And the whole backwardness of this area probably has a lot to do with why Linda Goble's staying here. Linda Morris has been more of a mother to her than her mother has ever been. To me, it's like, 'Don't even *think* about staying.' Her mom had her chance and she blew it. 'Course, that's kinda mean. I'm coldhearted about that sort of thing. People that I'm involved with—and it's weird, I guess, because I've never developed the sort of attachment that one day I'm going to, or whatever. But so far, it's been really easy for me to get rid of people. Because I've got too much to worry about without people trying to hurt me."

Light would like to imbue the Greenup cheerleaders—especially Linda Goble—with the same self-reliance.

"A lot of the girls have trouble seeing the big picture because of what they've been taught their whole lives. We try to help them with their boyfriend problems and stuff, and a lot of it's like, 'You don't need him. Go on!' And it's true. But these girls kill me. They stick with the guy that cheats on 'em, is mean to 'em. A lot of the time it might seem like a harmless high school thing, but look at their parents, they're doing the same thing. And the girls have seen that their whole life and they think that's the way it's supposed to be. And I think that's why they don't really see themselves for what they are, a lot of times."

Might there be other activities besides cheerleading that would be better for the girls? Better for their sense of themselves?

Light thinks a moment. "Yeah," he says, then pauses to ponder the question a bit more. "Well, actually, no, not around here. Because that will get you nowhere. Because you still have to live here. You do all this traveling and getting out in the world, but you still have to come home. And they're exposed to what they're exposed to at home. Southern women, I guess, came into their independence a little later, so cheerleading's this great thing because it's a way to be something and be a woman. In the North, they've been wearing suits and tennis shoes, you know?"

Regardless of the gender politics and regardless of whether he's living in Greenup or Atlanta, Light says nothing makes him happier than the sport of cheerleading. (For the record, he dismisses the notion that his interest in cheerleading has anything to do with his homosexuality. "People always say that if you're a guy cheerleader, you'd have to be gay," he says. "In fact, not even most of the guys, not even a *few*, are gay.") And he's hopeful that he can eventually make a good living by coaching all-star teams like the one with April Creech that he guided to the 1995 national championship.

Light could quit his part-time job as a financial aid counselor at Ashland Community College, buy a stake in a nearby gym, and devote himself to coaching cheerleading. But he doesn't want that sort of "anchor." He's intent on getting out.

"This will always be my home. I mean, I do feel that way about it a little. But I don't care if I leave. This will always be my home and it's nice to visit once in a while. But no, I am so thankful that I didn't turn out like my brother. He lives here, he's married, has a kid, but he could never leave here. And neither could his wife. They're both homey people. I was completely independent by the time I was eighteen. I guess it was because we had to be, because my mom moved back to work when I was nine so there we were, but somehow, my brother didn't get any of this. I don't know where I got it, but somewhere I did. Then finally, when I was eighteen, I was like, 'Okay, I was rich, then I was poor, and I like being rich a lot better, so I'm going to make sure I have what I want. And nobody's going to get it for me but me, so I'm going to go get it.'"

And how's he going to get it?

Through cheerleading, Light says, definitely.

"It's really odd. During the week, I have to be at work [at Ashland Community College] at eight in the morning, and I have to *make* myself get out of bed. I usually go to bed between eleven and twelve. But if I go out on a Friday night, get home at four in the morning, and have to get up at seven to go somewhere to teach cheerleading, I get up just like that. It's no problem. But I dread going to work at ACC so bad. I'm just not a desk-type pencil pusher. . . .

"A lot of it has to do with my own confidence. Because I didn't have very much. This cheerleading has given me confidence with myself, a lot—some people would say too much. You know, the most meaningful thing I've ever done is when my all-stars won the UCA thing three years ago. It was the first year I put them together. I put them together spur-of-the-moment, twenty kids from all different schools, not very talented, and I did it all myself. And you know, there are times when I think I need Greenup for me to be good. But then there are times when I'm like, 'I did this all by myself and nobody helped me and there was no Greenup on their uniform.'

"That win really gave me the confidence to go on. And it was interesting because it didn't sit very well with Candy and Randy and them. I don't know why. I guess they didn't think I could do anything by myself. A lot of them think they need the Greenup thing. Where I got into the problem with everybody is when I figured I didn't."

Chapter Eleven

Fight Greenup Fight

Autumn settles slowly over Greenup County. The air sweeping in from the Ohio River has gotten cooler, though still wet and sticky. The dark green blanket covering the hills is spotted with gold. People start spending more time outside, especially in the early evening, and they look forward to the football season with its cool Friday nights, full of cheering with friends and family in the high school stadium's stands.

The first gridiron game of the season, as always, features Greenup High versus Russell High on the Friday night before Labor Day. And during the week leading up to the Russell-Greenup grudge match—which will be played at Russell this year—the Greenup County Kiwanis Club holds a seven-day county fair, complete with carnival rides, corn dogs, country singers, a tobacco crop competition, a best-cow contest, and a beauty pageant. A sign hanging over Greenup's Main Street heralds this 1997 fair the county's "51st Annual."

On its second night, a muggy Tuesday evening, Candy Berry cancels cheerleading practice. With only four days till the Kings Island competition in Cincinnati, the Greenup varsity could use the work, but Berry doesn't want her girls to miss tonight's Miss Greenup County Fair pageant, especially since Miranda Elliott, the reigning Miss Greenup County Fair, will make an appearance.

Before school began, Miranda finally hit her standing back tuck. Now Berry can include her in the Kings Island routine without feeling that she's letting down the rest of the squad. Miranda's still shaky—she tends to stumble forward a bit on the landing—but Berry will keep her in the back left corner so the judges won't notice.

Rachel Brown, meanwhile, has regained her position as the team's Psycho Child. Since camp, she's had a number of little ailments, from a sore back to a sore ankle to periodic nausea. Berry doesn't trust her enough to use her as a principal flyer, so she's reinstated Rachel Wills, a.k.a. Olive Oyl, into the third flying position, alongside April Creech and Kelena McClurg.

Rachel feels bad about not getting to fly. She's having a hard enough time feeling like a member of the Greenup team, what with all the backbiting and gossip about her. Rachel was hopeful that as a flyer, she might win the girls' respect. Now she feels alone once again, and she's lost her confidence with the standing back tuck. At camp, Rachel appeared well on her way to hitting the stunt regularly. Now she hits it only once in a great while. Most of the time, she lands on her toes and lurches forward on the landing. Sometimes, she falls on her hands and knees.

Wills, meanwhile, is flying again, thanks to her boundless determination. Berry went with the super-skinny Wills because she's easy to lift, and despite her lack of show-stopping charisma, the girl has such resolve that Berry can count on her not to fall during competition.

Kelena McClurg has looked good as always, but April Creech is emerging as the strongest of Greenup's flyers. Of late, she's had the fewest mix-ups with her mounts. Maybe the upcoming Russell football game has given her extra incentive to perform well, to show her former school and her former town that she's better off without them. Or maybe she wants to show the Russell football players and cheerleaders who vandalized her new Greenup home that they don't intimidate her.

The weekend before this pageant—notably, the last weekend before the Russell-Greenup game—a handful of Russell students left a not-so-subtle message on April's car and on the front yard, porch, and walkway of her new house.

"It said 'RHS Was Here,'" said April, sitting with her boyfriend, Greg, in the Greenup High gym. "It was in shaving cream or silly string or something. There was a tank top that said 'Russell Cheerleader' on it on my front porch. By the mailbox there was a sweatshirt with pom-poms. On the hood of my car, there was a sweatshirt that had a big 'R' on it. Then there was a visor on my mirror, like a sun visor on the side mirror that said 'Russell Cheerleader.' Then on my car's antenna, it had a hat that said 'RHS Cheerleading' with two bows clamped to it. And there was a maroon-and-gold streamer wrapped all around my car." April smiles. "It was baaad."

Greg's not smiling. "They'll get theirs," he says, his close-cut, rusty red hair bristling. "You bet. They'll get theirs."

Greg and April are engaged now. Back in July, Greg drove over to Lexington to pick up April from the cheerleading summer camp and take her home to Greenup. During the drive, he mentioned to her that some day, maybe after high school graduation, he'd like to marry her. April didn't take it too seriously at the time, but she indicated that she could imagine such a thing. Two days later, Greg bought her a half-carat diamond ring. So now he's got more monthly payments to make on top of those for his truck.

Back in July, Coach Berry thought she had a fairly tough team. But a team's flaws become magnified the week before a competition, and Berry now feels that she's going into Kings Island with the least-prepared squad she's ever had.

During the first week in August, Hank Light hurt his right elbow lifting one of his all-stars. He didn't think much about the elbow at first; it was just sore. He choreographed most of the three-and-a-half-minute Greenup routine for Kings Island during the week after the injury, and taught the girls everything except the dance. Then he noticed that his entire bicep had moved down underneath his arm—"like Bugs Bunny when he's a boxer and makes a muscle."

He went to a doctor, who told him he'd snapped the tendon that connected his biceps muscle to the bone in his arm. The doctor ordered immediate reconstructive surgery.

During the following week, Light was good for nothing. His arm was black and blue and horribly sore from the surgery, so he couldn't choreograph the Kings Island dance.

With two weeks before the competition, Coach Berry needed a dance, and soon. She hired an all-star coach from Ohio to come to Greenup High and teach the cheerleaders a dance. But at the last minute, the woman canceled. Berry had to hire a second cheer instructor, and this one wasn't able to teach the dance till Friday, one week and two days before the scheduled competition.

"Normally, we're doing the routine full-out two weeks before," says Berry. "But this time, it's the week before and we're still making changes."

Aimee Lewis has presented a further frustration. Aimee still hasn't recovered from her knee injury. For a time, she appeared to be okay. She stopped wearing her knee brace shortly after camp, and her doctor cleared her to flip and tumble. So Berry told Light to include Aimee in the Kings Island routine. Then, the week after Light gave the Greenup cheerleaders their marching orders, Aimee's knee popped out of its socket, crumpling Aimee and the squad's routine. In great pain, Aimee popped it back in. But then it popped out again. Berry had no choice. She had to take Aimee out of the Kings Island routine and jury-rig the choreography to make it work with one less cheerleader.

Berry knows that her girls must accomplish a great deal during the final two practices on Wednesday and Thursday if they are to win their sixth straight Kings Island Cheerleading Championship. But this Tuesday night at the Greenup County Fair is a time to relax, a time to eat funnel cakes and take a ride on the Ferris wheel, a time to watch the beauty pageant.

Berry came to the Greenup County Fairgrounds early this evening to make sure she got a good seat. She's chosen a spot in the middle of the bleachers outside a fenced-in showring. On the showring's dirt floor stands a T-shaped plywood runway covered with green felt. At the back, partially attached to the runway, there's a stage with a green plastic awning. Parked behind the stage is an old—but still shiny—chrome trailer, the dressing room for the pageant contestants.

Berry's husband and son stayed home tonight, but the entire Greenup cheerleading team is here, as is the coaching staff—except Hank Light. With the smell of tobacco, cows, pumpkins, and fried dough hanging in the air, the sounds of flirtatious adolescents giggling and squealing, the pageant will go on for more than two hours. The twenty-odd contestants—ranging in age from fourteen to twenty-one—will strut their stuff in swimsuits, then evening gowns. There is no talent competition.

While the judges tally up their scores, varsity Greenup cheerleader Miranda Elliott—in her final appearance as Miss Greenup County Fair—will deliver her speech about what an honor it's been to represent her county over the past year, take a turn around the showring on the back of a white Ford Mustang convertible, and finally, walk down the runway, displaying her body with exquisite control.

Berry will lead a standing ovation.

As darkness sets in over the fairgrounds and the local Kiwanis Club

president introduces the first pageant contestant, Berry smiles content-
edly. Nights like these, everything seems right in the Greenup world.

Little seems right the following afternoon.

Berry and assistant coach Randy Peffer arrive late to practice because
they have to pick up the three new signs that the Greenup girls will use at
Kings Island. (They read, "Fight Greenup Fight.") Berry has left the
squad's seniors to take charge and get the practice going.

Senior Jennifer Morgan—known as Shmorg—stands and watches her
younger teammates gossip about boys and their new classes and last
night's pageant. They're not stretching, they're not loosening up, they're
not practicing their tumbling.

"It's time to go," Jennifer says to herself.

"Well, tell 'em to get going," says JV coach Susan Ray. Berry didn't
leave Ray in charge: she wants the seniors to learn some leadership.

Shmorg, unaware that anyone could hear her mumblings, turns around
and looks at Coach Ray, then looks back at her teammates.

"Yeah." She sighs. "They'll get mad at me if I do. But Candy and
Randy'll get mad at me if I don't."

"Well?"

"And they're my friends."

"You want to win, don't you? You've got to push 'em if you want to win.
You remember how Shawnda was, don't you?"

"Yeah."

"They might get mad at you now, but they won't when y'all win."

Shmorg walks over to the rest of the team. In as friendly a way as she
can, she tells the girls they should start stretching, then practice their tumbling. The Greenup cheerleaders continue talking and giggling, but they
also get a move on.

Of all the returning seniors on the Greenup varsity, Shmorg has made
the greatest effort to become a team leader, but she doesn't quite have
what it takes. She's tried to reach out to Rachel Brown, to make Rachel
feel supported, but the rest of the girls haven't followed her lead. The team
is still splintered over boyfriend issues—a couple of girls besides Rachel
have recently been accused of flirting with boyfriends not their own—and
the squad needs a strong leader to mend the rifts.

Wills might have what it takes. She's certainly willing to push when her teammates goof off, and she has led a subdued campaign to let the jealousies go.

Wills has also reached out to the three cheerleaders who transferred to Greenup High from Russell and Boyd, particularly April Creech, with whom Wills has become fast friends. But Wills is a junior, and this is only her first year on the varsity. Despite her strength of character and spirit, Wills needs more varsity experience, and she needs to improve her shaky flying, before she can lead this team.

After stretching out, the cheerleaders form two lines; in pairs, they turn cartwheels across the floor. Then they turn front handsprings from one side of the gym to the next. Then a series of back handsprings, and then running tumbling runs with a combination of front handsprings and back handsprings and back tucks. Finally, the girls turn standing tumbling runs, in which they jump backward into a series of flips.

Berry and Peffer return with the "Fight Greenup Fight" signs.

Shortly thereafter, Amanda Kitchen complains of a headache, and asks Berry for some Tylenol.

"Here, I've got some Excedrin," says Berry. "It's better for a headache." She looks closely at Amanda's tall, skinny frame. "Did you eat anything today?"

"Yeah."

"Well, Kelena had a headache a couple days ago because all she'd eaten was a Reese's cup and something else stupid. If you don't want to eat much, eat a banana or yogurt or something."

"I ate today. I ate plenty," Amanda says.

"Okay," says Berry. "I'm only asking."

Once the girls have loosened up, Berry has them practice the last bit of the routine. In time to a throbbing dance beat, both Kelena and April get thrown up into the air by six girls each while Wills poses in between, standing on the hands of three other girls. The first set of bases catches Kelena; the other set catches April. Each set of bases then pushes their flyer's body up over their six heads until she's lying face up on top of their hands. They spin the two girls' horizontal bodies around in a complete circle, like pizza makers spinning crust dough. After that, the bases push Kelena and April into standing positions. The routine ends with Kelena and April aloft, fists up and out.

I ask Berry how Hank Light makes up such unusual cheerleading maneuvers.

"Hank makes up nothing," Berry snaps. "He just copies a lot."

Berry tells Aimee Lewis to cut off the music. Since deciding that Aimee cannot cheer in the Kings Island competition, Berry has had her come to practice and operate the team's boom box.

Now, Berry wants the girls to practice the dance, then go right into the two basket tosses, the pizza spin thing, and the final pose.

The girls get ready. Aimee cues up the music.

"All right, girls," says Berry. "Exaggerate!"

In a pyramid formation, the squad runs through the dance. One moment in the choreography calls for each girl to assume a pose reminiscent of the "voguing" popularized by Madonna in the late eighties. Rachel Brown, placed front and center for the dance, strikes a strong yet coy stance. With her feet planted wide apart, her knees bent, and her arms up and flexing, she turns her head to the right, flips her light brown ponytail, and smiles sideways. Wills looks down at the floor during her pose, and her gangly body looks like a puppet's, held up at the joints with string.

Later in the dance, the girls turn sideways and squat down, then kick out toward the imaginary audience à la the Spice Girls, the British pop act that advocates "girl power." Trying to exaggerate, they all grimace while kicking, and some grunt.

"Come on!" Berry yells. She's taken off her pumps and is standing barefoot with her hands on her hips less than a yard in front of the dancing girls. "When you squat, your butt better almost touch the ground!"

After the cheerleaders finish with the two basket tosses and the rest of it, Berry offers her humble opinion.

"POOO-PY!" she pronounces. "Girls, you've got to sell it. You're not selling it. Come on. I want big cheesecake smiles."

Berry has them do it again. And again. And again. For over an hour, the team runs through the dance and the ending. A few times, Kelena's bases fail to get her upright after the pizza spin, which annoys Berry.

"We've got two days, girls," she says. "You better figure it out. Now!"

As she watches the dance and that final stunt over and over, Berry picks nit after nit. Shmorg needs to widen her stance when she strikes her pose. Wills needs to keep her head up and "smile, darn it." Berry decides that Wills, as third flyer, should be doing more. So she adds a new lift to the routine. Wills must now climb atop her two bases on one foot and hold her other foot bent at her side, like a flamingo, then pop down and back up for the final pose with April and Kelena.

At five o'clock, Berry tells the girls to take a break and "eat a banana or something."

"Does it look better?" Rachel Brown asks.

"It looks good," says Berry as she slumps down onto a courtside bleacher. "It couldn't win nationals. But it might win Kings Island."

The varsity girls wander in and out of the gym during their five-minute break. At the same time, the JV girls report for practice, among them Linda Goble. Susan Ray recently convinced Linda's mother to let her cheer—part time, at least—with the JV. Linda wouldn't agree to it unless her good friend Jessica Garthee joined up with her. Like Linda, Jessica was on last year's JV team and tumbles and stunts well enough to cheer for the varsity. But she had chronic back problems at the end of last year's push toward the JV nationals and decided not to try out for the varsity in the spring.

The JV doesn't practice every day, so it's a limited time commitment. Still, Linda often ends up spending the night with Jessica after JV practice so that she doesn't have to worry about convincing her older sister or her mother to come pick her up.

The Greenup coaches managed to scrape together enough money to pay Linda's way to Kings Island. The JV team won't compete this year—they're not ready just yet. But Ray wants her girls to make the trip and cheer on the varsity, to help them gain solidarity and see what a competition is like. Linda, of course, is a far better cheerleader than most of her JV teammates, but she's happy to be back on a team.

Tonight, when she walks past the varsity girls—some of whom greet her with warm smiles—Linda has trouble looking at their faces, and she can barely mumble her hellos. With the exception of her good friend Shiritta Schaffer, whose family now also gives her a place to sleep on occasion, the varsity cheerleaders intimidate Linda. They all seem so strong and confident, and they know that Linda had to leave the varsity because of her family problems. The varsity girls make Linda feel ashamed somehow.

Gymnastics guru Tom Pack has arrived, and Wills asks him to help her with the troublesome "bounders" tumbling run. At the far end of the basketball court, under the red, white, and blue of the American flag, Wills runs and flips while Pack makes sure she doesn't fall on the hardwood.

The rest of the squad sits down on the floor in front of Berry and munches chips and sodas from the school vending machines outside the gym. Brooke Meenach takes off her right shoe and complains to Berry about her ingrown big toenail. Back in January, shortly before last year's nationals, Brooke's doctor told her to stop cheering till the toe got better. But with nationals coming up, Brooke couldn't consider such a thing. "I won't go to *that* doctor now." She laughs.

Brooke keeps picking at the toenail. "I already had one ingrown toenail on the big toe in my *left* foot."

The constant hard landings after flips and tumbling runs induce this painful problem. Picking at the sore toe, Brooke suddenly cries out and stands up.

"Go on and walk it off and cry a little bit," Berry tells her.

Brooke turns her back and limps a couple of steps on her one bare foot. Then she halts and cries quietly. Wills, finished practicing her bounders now, walks over and stands beside her, rubbing her back and talking in soothing tones.

"Why do you pick at it?" Berry asks. "Why do you do what makes it hurt?" She raises and lowers her arm: "'It hurts when I do this. It hurts when I do this. It hurts when I do this.' Then don't do that!"

Sniffling, Brooke hobbles back to her shoe and sock, mumbling to herself, "My toe hurts when I'm standing. My toe hurts when I'm sitting here. My toe hurts when I'm just . . . being."

As Susan Ray herds Linda Goble, Jessica Garthee and the rest of the JV team over to the school's cafetorium for their practice, Coach Berry rounds up the varsity girls and has them practice their dance again. For another hour, until six o'clock, the Greenup girls run through the routine, grunting, grinning, and voguing till they can do it without a thought.

At six o'clock, Berry tells them to switch gears and spend the last hour of practice working on sideline cheers for the coming Russell football game. By Friday night, the Greenup cheerleaders must know the words and motions to over fifty short chants, as well as five elaborate cheers complete with stunts and gymnastics.

Berry decides to begin with the five cheers. First, she turns to Aimee Lewis and asks her if she feels sturdy enough to cheer at the Russell game. Aimee looks down at her hands.

"If you say you're cheering, you got to be there," says Berry, "whether you're in agony or what else."

Aimee nods and says she'll cheer at the game.

"Okay." Berry turns away from Aimee and stalks off, muttering, "I'm tired of changing it and changing it and changing it. By George, if you say you're going to be there . . ." Berry whirls around. "All right, girls. Line up for 'Two Bits.'"

While chanting the classic, "Two Bits! Four Bits! Six Bits! A Dollar! All for Greenup County! Stand up and holler!" half of the Greenup girls perform three mounts, with Wills, April, and Kelena doing the flying, while the rest turn a standing handspring to a back tuck.

Afterward, Berry moves in and starts fiddling with the cheer to make it as good as it can be. She has the cheerleaders doing flips in front break off into two groups and do two small stunts of their own. The only problem is that there's an uneven number to divide. Berry designates Rachel Brown the odd girl out.

Rachel seems disappointed at first, till Berry tells her that she gets to stand front and center with a big forest-green megaphone and shout at the crowd through her killer smile.

Nervous and excited about her new assignment, Rachel talks to herself. "This is so cool," she says. "How do I hold it?" No one responds. Rachel feels a chilliness from the other cheerleaders.

"Like this, I guess. Or like this? And when I'm not using it do I put it down like this? Oh, it's heavy!"

"Rachel!" Berry hollers, turning momentarily from her work on Wills's bases.

Rachel smiles self-consciously. "Sorry!" She giggles. "I'll be quiet."

The Greenup team practices the "Two Bits" cheer again and again. Berry changes things slightly each time, making the routine that much flashier, that much more exciting.

It's clear that the girls don't care about this ball-game cheer as much as the competition routine. The intensity has left their eyes. And as the night grows older, the girls talk when they're supposed to be working, a transgression Berry cannot abide.

"Candace. Megan. Shut up!" Berry yells suddenly. "I will not be disrespected. You guys will run up and down all four sides of bleachers after practice as punishment."

Rachel, with only her big green funnel to play with, seems particularly bored. Once, between run-throughs of "Two Bits," her teammate Sarah Dickison grabs at Rachel's new toy and accidentally jams its metal mouthpiece into Rachel's jaw. Rachel drops the megaphone and grabs her sore mouth. Sarah apologizes profusely, but Rachel walks away, not wanting to draw negative attention to herself.

"I'm okay," she says, shooing Sarah away. With tears in her eyes, Rachel glances furtively about to see if Coach Berry and the other girls are watching. But they're all focused on other things, and they missed Sarah and Rachel's horseplay. "I'm okay," Rachel says again.

Eventually, Berry decides she's had enough of "Two Bits." Frustrated, she grumbles to Coach Peffer that she'd wanted to work on all five ballgame cheers tonight, but now it's ten of seven and the team's mastered only one cheer.

For the remainder of practice, Berry has the girls practice sideline chants.

> *Green! [Clap-clap.]*
> *Green and Gold! [Clap-clap.]*
> *Green and Gold, Beat Those Devils!*
> *Go Green and Gold! [Clap-clap.]*

After one such chant, Rachel pulls her foot up from the ground and winces, having felt a sharp pain through the ankle she sprained a year ago. Rachel closes her eyes then opens them wide in an effort to hold back the tears.

"What's wrong?" says Berry.

"Nothing." Rachel looks down, holding her sore foot off the ground.

"Come on, what's wrong?"

"Nothing."

"Then why're you crying?"

"My ankle just hurts, that's all. I'm okay."

"I just broke my leg," says Jessica Newell sarcastically, "but I'm okay." The rest of the team laughs.

"Okay, girls," Berry says. "Enough. Go home."

Surprised, Rachel looks at Berry. Then she looks down and shakes her head. She doesn't want practice ended on her account.

"Candace. Megan," says Berry. "Don't forget to run those bleachers."

That Wednesday night, Candy Berry got a call at her Flatwoods home from Pat Heineman, Wills's foster mother. Wills had done something wrong and needed to be punished for it. Mrs. Heineman said she'd almost kept Wills from going to Kings Island, but after much thought had decided that Wills would just miss cheering at the Russell football game on Friday night. And Mrs. Heineman thought Berry should know.

Berry thanked her for calling, said good-bye, and hung up. Great. Now, she had to change that dang "Two Bits" cheer all over again. Fantastic.

At cheerleading practice the next day, a Thursday, Wills explains:

The previous Tuesday—the day Berry gave the cheerleaders the afternoon off so they could go to the Miss Greenup County Fair pageant—Wills had planned to get a ride home from school with Angie Heineman, her good friend and foster sister. But Angie wanted to drive another friend home from school and hang out at that friend's house before heading home herself. So Angie told Mrs. Heineman that she had to make up a test that afternoon, that Wills would wait for her, and that was why the two girls would come home late.

"It was Angie's lie," Wills says to Berry. "I just got caught in the middle of it."

On Wednesday night after practice, Mrs. Heineman questioned Angie and Wills. The two girls stuck to their story, but Mrs. Heineman had talked to Angie's teacher and knew Angie hadn't taken a makeup test that afternoon. She busted the girls for fibbing.

"At first she was going to keep me from Kings Island," says Wills, a slight smile hovering on her lips, her eyes wide. "Can you imagine?"

"No, honey. I can't," Berry answers.

"I would've cried and cried and cried."

Berry laughs. "You wouldn't have been the only one crying!"

"I mean, I would have thrown a fit," says Wills loudly. She stares hard at her coach. Wills is serious. "I would have moved out."

Susan Ray watches Wills walk down from the small stage of the Greenup High auditorium, away from the coaches and down to the carpeted floor below, cleared for now of chairs. There, Wills joins the rest of the varsity girls stretching in preparation for practice. This afternoon, the boys' basketball team has the gym till seven o'clock, so the cheerleaders must settle for this tiny auditorium if they want to practice before then.

"I've never seen Wills get really mad or upset over anything," says Ray.

It's six o'clock. Berry scheduled the practice late because the squad needs the gym to work on their competition routine. The auditorium is only good for sideline-chant work. The girls will review the numerous

ball-game cheers till seven; then they'll relieve the boys of the gym and
work on their Kings Island routine till nine, maybe later.

This will be Greenup's last real rehearsal before the competition on
Sunday. They can't practice Friday because they've got the Russell game
after school. They can't practice Saturday because that's their day to drive
up to Cincinnati, check into their hotel, and have some fun at the amusement park. And Sunday they've got the preliminary round in the early afternoon and finals in the evening.

While the girls stretch, Berry distributes copies of a handwritten
memo that details what they should wear for each of their various team
functions over the next three days. For tomorrow's school-wide pep rally,
they should wear their yellow "GC" T-shirts with their black "swimmies"
(tight lightweight shorts), and white ribbons in their hair. To the ball
game tomorrow night, they will wear their gold "GCHS" vest with
matching skirt, gold bodysuit, gold tights, gold bows—not ribbons—in
their hair, which should be "*major* curled," and they should bring their
new gold-and-white poms. For the bus ride over to Kings Island Saturday
morning ("leave school at 8:30 A.M."), the girls are to wear their black
tank tops with white swimmies and a white sports bra, and their hair
should be "pretty"—which means it should *not* be in a ponytail, but worn
down and well styled. Finally, for the competition on Sunday, the girls
will wear their "new gold" vests, green swimmies, white bodysuits, gold
tights, white ribbons in their hair, and "good" white socks. Before their
performance, they will take off the green swimmies and change into their
"new gold" skirts.

"Any questions?" Berry asks.

"Yeah, I've got a question," Brooke Meenach says. But Berry, who's already climbed the three steps back up to her seat on the stage, doesn't hear
her. Brooke asks her question anyway, quietly and to herself: "Why can't
you let us out at eight?" She presses her face against her legs, stretching
her thighs. "I've got three tests tomorrow. Geography, English, and U.S.
history."

Berry pulls a packet of chants out of her shoulder bag and tells the girls
to line up in sideline formation.

"Wills," Berry says. "You can practice with us. Just go over in the back
there." Wills nods and takes her place in the back left corner of the three-
row formation. The other girls watch her curiously.

"Wills gets to do the pep rally tomorrow, but not the ball game," Berry tells the team. "She's been a bad girl." The other girls are real curious now. Those near Wills break ranks to ask her what happened.

"Oh, Angie lied and I got caught in the middle," Wills says, unembarrassed.

"She almost didn't get to go to Kings Island," Berry continues, trying to get a smile out of Wills. "Yeah. She's been a bad girl."

Wills can't help it now. She smiles a broad, natural smile.

"Woo woo!" Brooke hollers.

"Go, Olive!" says Rachel Brown.

Wills is laughing now. She's not self-conscious in the least. She likes playing the tough girl.

"All right, girls," Berry says. "Straighten up. Who's going to start us off? It's the first quarter and we're on defense."

There's a three-second pause. The Greenup cheerleaders stand in their three rows, feet shoulder width apart, fists on hips.

Shmorg steps forward and yells, "Tighten! Tighten! Tighten up! That line!"

The rest of the girls pick up the chant, and the whole team yells, "Tighten! Tighten! Tighten up! That line!"

"Okay," says Berry, looking at her five pages full of cheers. "One for the offense."

Another couple moments of silent standing.

Shmorg steps forward again.

"T-O-U! C-H-D! Oh! Double-U! En! Touchdown! Let's win!"

Again, the other cheerleaders follow suit.

"Another one for the offense," says Berry. "Someone other than Shmorg."

Long silence. Berry can't take it. She slaps the rolled-up packet against her knee and points it at the team.

"Have you-all been memorizing these like I told you to?"

No answer.

"When I give you something to learn on your own, that means I don't have time to fool with it in practice."

Berry pauses. The cheerleaders stand silent as ghosts, unwilling to make the noise necessary to breathe. Even Susan Ray and Randy Peffer, who've been joking with each other about Peffer's smelly feet, perk up and pay attention.

"You-all are big girls!" Berry continues. "You should have learned this by now. That's part of time management."

For the next hour, Berry pushes the Greenup girls to take the sideline chants seriously and to make their motions crisp. The squad works hard, running through over fifty chants before the clock nailed to the auditorium's brick wall strikes seven. But the girls have something else on their minds—the Kings Island competition. Despite Berry's ranting and raving, they know that few people outside of a handful of cheerleader moms and two or three little girls will watch them on Friday night over at the Russell High School field.

Toward the end of the hour, Berry takes some time to reconfigure the "Two Bits" cheer to accommodate Wills's absence.

"We need a flyer," Berry says. "Who wants to be the flyer?"

No one says anything for a moment. Then Rachel Brown, smiling meekly, raises her hand.

"All right, Rachel, come on, let's see if you can do it." Berry seems tired. In an effort to pep up both herself and the team, she yells, "Do y'all think she can do it?"

The rest of the girls halfheartedly answer.

"Yeah."

"Okay," says Berry, "show her how."

Rachel's feeling very self-conscious, and she babbles excitedly as the team practices this boring cheer with her flying in the middle of the formation. The other girls don't care nearly as much as she does, and when she makes a couple of small mistakes despite her do-gooder zeal, some of the others smirk knowingly at one another.

At five minutes to seven, Berry tells her cheerleaders to take a break, then head over to the gym and practice their tumbling in preparation for the final competition rehearsal. The cheerleaders drink soda and water and chomp on chips in the auditorium for a few minutes, then cross the school's main hallway to the gym.

The boys' basketball practice has officially ended. "Officially," in fact, it never began. According to Kentucky state rules, high school basketball teams cannot officially practice till late November, and it's barely September now. Many schools, like Greenup, get around that rule by holding "unofficial" practices, organized and run by the players without any help or urging—in theory, anyway—from the coaches.

Despite the time, the boys are still running up and down the hardwood, playing a full-court game of b-ball. The more daring cheerleaders, including Brooke Meenach, and seniors Libby Barber and Jennifer Stuart—

called "Stu"—tell the boys that it's past seven o'clock and they need to clear out. It's the cheerleaders' turn to use the gym.

The boys don't respond. They just keep playing their game.

"Y'all need to go," says Stu. She claps her hands condescendingly and walks onto the court. "Come on. Time to break it up."

The biggest of the boys—nicknamed Sumo because of his heft—turns toward the cheerleaders as he's running down the court. He motions toward them and says, "Why don't you just cheer on the sidelines?"

"NO!" Brooke bellows.

Libby sprints onto the court and turns a series of flips and twists right into the middle of the boys' game. Sarah Dickison waits until the boys have brought the ball near her, then runs in, flipping over and over, again ruining the basketball flow.

The red-haired, broad-shouldered Stu—one of the bigger, taller cheerleaders at about five feet, eight inches—watches Sumo run down the court. As he nears her, Stu acts as though she's going to run and tumble into him. Sumo pulls up, closes his eyes, and throws his hands over his face, flinching miserably. Stu and a few other cheerleaders laugh at him.

Soon, with more and more cheerleaders flipping through the game, the boys give up. They gather their sweatshirts and their ball and walk off the court. Sumo, who's hot and bothered from the game, struts over to Stu and gives her a big, sweaty hug, much to her disgust.

"I still love you," he says mockingly as he rubs his body against hers. He lets her go and smiles at her. Stu snorts, trying to look unimpressed.

The rest of the cheerleaders follow Stu's lead and actively forget that the boys ever got in their way. All business, they go through their warm-up routine of cartwheels followed by walk-overs, then round-offs, then running tumbling, then standing tumbling. The boys, who now find themselves completely ignored, leave the gym.

Berry orders the girls to practice their partner stunts for Kings Island. The group at stage left hoists Wills, the group at stage right pops April Creech into position, and the group in between hoists Kelena McClurg. For the competition, each flyer must balance her right foot on her bases' hands and hold her left leg bent in the air—again, like a flamingo—with her fists up and out. This pose is called a liberty. After holding the liberty for a few beats, the flyer will then let her left leg hang straight down, her arms by her sides, and balance herself as her bases carefully rotate her in a full circle. This move isn't as difficult as some of those done by last year's team at the '97 nationals—that heel stretch Aubrey barely held, for example—but it's the hardest move this year's team has learned thus far.

Wills, Kelena, and April pop up into the liberty position. Berry watches from a nearby bleacher with her arms crossed over her chest. The flyers then relax their poses and brace for the slow rotation. Suddenly, Kelena's hips jut left; then she teeters back to the right and crashes. One of her bases, Candace Adkins—a junior who, like April Creech, transferred from Russell to cheer for Greenup—stands between Kelena and the gym floor. Kelena slams into Candace, who in turn slams into the floor with Kelena's weight bearing down on top of her. Candace can't use her hands to break her fall because she's going backward, but she does manage to turn sideways, so that her left forearm and the left side of her body hit the floor first. Then her head rocks the hard court with a *thwack*.

The other girls stand silently, looking at Kelena and Candace sprawled on the floor. Kelena sits up, tears in her eyes. She's crying from fright, mostly: Candace took the brunt of the fall.

Candace rolls over, whimpering quietly. Her right hand rubs her sore left arm; she feels her head for the swelling lump, then rubs her left arm again.

Stunned, the other cheerleaders don't know whether to approach their fallen teammates and console them, run for help, or what.

"You're okay," Berry says calmly as she lifts herself off her bleacher seat and walks slowly through the cheerleaders to the site of the accident. "I saw it. You're okay." Berry's talking to Candace, but in effect she's talking to all of the girls.

Berry helps Candace up off the floor and feels for the lump on her head. "Look," she says, smiling, gently running her fingers through Candace's hair, "it's already swole up." Berry tries to make eye contact with Candace, whose face is still squinched and wet with tears. She hugs Candace and says, "You did good." The girl begins to sob into Berry's chest. "It's okay," Berry says quietly. "Cry. It's okay."

Eventually, Berry lets Candace go and walks back to her seat. Candace is indeed okay, although her left arm's going to be sore. The other cheerleaders are comforting her and Kelena now, patting them on their shoulders and backs, talking with them in low tones.

"They would've made fun of her at Russell for stuff like that," says Berry. "I'm glad she can cry in front of us." Now it's time to get back on the horse.

Berry sits up and claps her hands. "All right, girls. Come on. Let's do it again."

The Greenup squad tries the three partner stunts with their three liberties and the three rotations. This time, Wills is wobbly, but she doesn't fall. Kelena, still spooked, watches the floor anxiously during the rotation.

"That's good," says Berry, after the flyers float down to the ground on the arms of their bases. "Does it feel good?"

Kelena nods. So does Candace, rubbing her arm.

"Okay. Let's see the whole thing. From the beginning."

The time limit at the Kings Island competition is three minutes, thirty seconds—one minute, fifteen seconds longer than at nationals. So it's rather exhausting. After a female voice yells through the boom box, "NASTY!" the music pounds away, and the girls all turn standing back tucks. Miranda hits hers, but Rachel Brown takes a big step forward when she lands. A few girls turn tumbling runs across the floor; Libby Barber finishes the gymnastic portion of the routine with an impressive standing tumbling run back toward the rest of the girls dancing behind her. After this short dance comes a series of quick group mounts with basket tosses thrown in, all in time to the grinding music.

Now the partner stunts. Aimee Lewis shuts off the music, and the girls chant, "Fight Greenup Fight!" as Wills, Kelena, and April pop up into the air and balance on their teammates' hands. Each girl strikes the liberty pose, but Wills teeters immediately—then, as she begins the slow rotation, loses her balance and falls into her bases' arms.

Berry emits a sharp sigh.

Next, the girls stand in three rows until the music comes back on; then they all turn back handsprings straight into a back tuck. Rachel lands hers rather well this time, but Miranda stumbles forward a bit.

The cheerleaders assemble in dance formation. They flash their big "cheesecake" smiles when they bump and grind, and they snarl sexily when they karate kick at the audience.

After the dance come the basket tosses, then the pizza spins and the final pose. But Kelena can't get upright, so she ends the routine still lying back in her bases' arms.

Berry holds her head in her hands for a moment, then looks up. "I've never had a group that the night before was falling on stuff," she whispers to Peffer.

Shmorg can't hear Berry. But, this being her third year on the varsity, she knows how strange all the falling is. As the rest of the team collapses to the floor, breathing hard, pulling at their sticky T-shirts to fan their faces, Shmorg paces back and forth and kicks at the floor.

"What's wrong?" Susan Ray asks her.

"I'm just . . ." Shmorg pauses. "Frustrated."

"HA!" says Berry. "YOU'RE frustrated." She looks at her watch. It's eight-forty-five, fifteen minutes before she's supposed to let the girls go home.

"All right, come on," she says. "Let's get this."

Berry has Wills and her three bases work on their partner stunt again and again. Wills pops up, she rotates, she spins down. She pops up, she rotates, she spins down. Most of the time, she stays up the whole way through—wobbling—but most of the time isn't good enough for Berry.

Stu sits down on a bleacher beside Brooke; together, the two girls watch Wills struggle to get the mount right. "Candy's going to get real frustrated," says Stu. "Then Candy's going to change the routine the day before. And we're going to forget how it goes. I just think we should do the whole thing again. We'll get it."

Wills's problem is that she's having trouble keeping her body stiff and straight. If she relaxes for a moment, her bases will have a hard time keeping her upright. As Berry likes to say, holding up a loosey-goosey flyer is like holding a big balloon full of water over your head. In the end, you're going to get wet.

After working with Wills till past nine o'clock, Berry decides that she's done as much for Wills and her bases as she can.

"All right," she says. "We're going to do it one more time. Hopefully, that'll be enough."

Shmorg calls the Greenup cheerleaders into a huddle in the middle of the gym floor. Once all the girls have formed a circle with their arms wrapped around one another, Shmorg tries to talk tough.

"There's no one to blame, y'all," she says. "We're all in this together. So don't be defensive. Just do your part and help the rest do their part. Okay? 'Team,' on three. One, two, three . . ."

"TEAM!"

The girls line up and wait for the music to begin.

"NASTY!" the tape player squeals.

At the end of her intricate tumbling pass, Shiritta turns a flip with a full twist, then stumbles and falls forward. Wills makes it shakily through her partner stunt without falling. But then, at the very end, Kelena once again fails to get upright and hit that final pose after her pizza spin.

"AAAAH!" Berry yells.

"I think we're just tired," one of Kelena's bases, Sarah Dickison, mutters between gasps for air.

"You're TIRED?" screams Berry. "That don't make no sense! April's side is tired too!"

Berry slumps down on the bleacher and arches her head back with her arms crossed over her face. Then she looks wide-eyed at Peffer. The usually expressionless Peffer silently acknowledges Berry's anger with a raise of his eyebrows and a slight shake of his head.

"April's group," says Berry quietly, still lounging on the bleacher. "Do it again. Kelena's group, find your counterpart and watch what they're doing. Whatever they're doing, that's what you *should* be doing."

April, Kelena, and their twelve bases pick themselves up off the floor and try to forget how tired they are. Kelena's bases spend a few minutes figuring out which of April's bases is each one's counterpart. Then with Kelena's group closely studying every move, April's group throws April up into the air, catches her, lifts her up over their heads, spins her horizontal body all the way around, then pushes her up till she's standing on their hands.

"Do you see what they did that you need to do?" Berry asks.

Kelena and her bases aren't sure. They want to see it one more time. So again, April is thrown into the air, pushed up and around, then straightened out.

"Got it?" asks Berry.

Kelena and her bases nod quietly, avoiding eye contact with the coach.

"Okay, now you do it," Berry says.

Kelena's six bases throw Kelena up into the air, they catch her, push her up over their heads, then, with remarkable grace, they spin her around and slide her into a standing position.

"That's wonderful," says Berry, rising. "That's not just good. That's wonderful. Look. You're just nervous because you're missing your leaders from last year. They were good, but you girls are just as good as they were. You need to forget about last year. You girls are pretty and talented and tough. Forget about last year. You girls, this year, can do it."

The Greenup cheerleaders line up for one last run-through. As Aimee Lewis rewinds the tape, Wills hollers, "We've got to quit on a good one, guys!"

"Yeah! Come on, guys!" yells Brooke.

As the music starts up, Rachel waits that one beat and then, with the rest of the Greenup team, jumps up, flips over backward with her body in a tight ball, and lands straight and sharp on her feet. During the opening tumbling runs, she beams. It's not often she hits a back tuck like that.

The girls roll through the group stunts. Then, during her partner stunt, Wills teeters—but refuses to fall.

After the chant portion, the girls again wait for the music to start, and Brooke yells, "Think positive, guys!"

Rachel still feels great about her back tuck. So she sells the dance and sells it hard, smiling and posing and thrusting like a champ.

At the end of the routine, Kelena's crew makes the pizza-spin ending look easy.

Berry, leaning back on her bleacher, rolls her eyes and smiles with her mouth hanging wide open. These girls can perform flawlessly when they want to.

"All right," she says. "Sit down. That was much better."

Chapter Twelve

Faith on Three

Hot. Humid. Sweltering. Gross. The whole world has become one big steam cooker. Autumn—which began to creep over northern Kentucky and southern Ohio before the Greenup County Fair—has fled. And summer, that muggy Ohio River Valley summer, has chosen today, Sunday, the last day of the Kings Island cheerleading competition, to make its final blistering appearance of the year.

The Greenup cheerleaders won't perform in the preliminary round until after three in the afternoon. But the girls and their families had to check out of their hotel at eleven A.M. to avoid paying for a second night. Before leaving the hotel and making their way here to Paramount's Kings Island amusement park northeast of Cincinnati, the girls dolled themselves up for the competition—in keeping with Coach Berry's memo—by curling their hair, putting on their makeup, and donning their pressed uniforms—save, of course, for the skirts.

Now, all dressed up with nothing to do, the Greenup cheerleaders sit in the heat and wait. In the back of the sprawling Timberwolf Amphitheater, the girls have found the only bit of shade created by some small amusement park trees. There they try to relax on the amphitheater's flat, backless benches. There's not one cloud in the blindingly bright blue sky, and soon the cheerleaders find themselves hunched over on the uncomfortable wooden bleachers, holding their faces in their hands to keep the sun from their eyes, wishing they could compete already and stop thinking about how hot they are.

The ride closest to the amphitheater, Amazon Falls, drenches all its passengers in cool, refreshing—albeit rancid—amusement park water. Throughout their nearly four-hour wait, the Greenup cheerleaders must grit their teeth and listen again and again to the delighted squeals of freshly dunked park patrons enjoying the Amazon Falls.

The ongoing cheer competition—now featuring the small varsity teams—provides the only diversion. But even when you have a keen interest in competitive cheerleading, watching mediocre squads, each with fewer than ten girls, perform one after another can get old.

Why couldn't today's weather be like the weather two days before? On Friday, for the Greenup-Russell football game, the air was cool, the sky was clear. It was a beautiful autumn day.

During the Greenup High pep rally that morning, the whole school was charged for the coming season opener. Fall is one of the happiest times of the year in Greenup County. It's not too cold, not too warm. There's the Greenup County Fair in September. There's the Old Fashioned Days festival in October. There's the economic boon that comes from the harvest of tobacco and other crops. There's football season.

The pep rally began with the high school drama club performing a skit that featured three big boys wearing white T-shirts, red skirts, and red yarn wigs, so that each looked like a burly incarnation of Raggedy Ann. In front of the entire twelve-hundred-kid student body, packed into one side of the gym's bleachers, those boys in Raggedy Ann drag hopped up and down and bumped chests with one another in a parody of Russell High cheerleaders. A girl playing the part of a TV news reporter approached them with a microphone:

"We're here live with the Russell High School cheerleaders on the day of the big game against Greenup County. Are our sources correct? Have you really lost your two best cheerleaders to Greenup County?"

One of the husky cheerleaders answered:

"Oh, we don't need Candace or April. They can go win a national championship with Greenup. We've got McDonald's! You know, Big Macs, french fries, McNuggets. That's all we need! Yeah!"

The students in attendance laughed and clapped and hooted. And the boys playing the Russell cheerleaders whooped, jumped up and down, and bumped chests. Then one of them grabbed the microphone from the reporter and hollered:

"And we don't know HOW that happened to April's house!"

"I'm sure you don't," the reporter replied, retrieving her microphone.

Again the student crowd broke up laughing.

Later, the drama club staged a mock football game. Three big boys wearing shoulder pads and football jerseys stood in for the Greenup team and three skinny girls in Russell High T-shirts stood in for the Russell team. On the first play, the three girls on the "Russell team" had the ball and tried to score at the other end of the basketball court, but were swarmed by the three boys on the "Greenup team," much to the delight of the Greenup High students. On the second play, "Greenup" had the ball and, while one of the boys carried two female members of the "Russell team" down the court, scored emphatically.

Susi Daniels, an English teacher, a one-time assistant cheer coach and currently the school's pep club sponsor, then introduced each and every one of the fifty football players, with the student body shrieking its approval after each name read. Toward the end of those introductions, the Greenup cheerleaders huddled at the side of the basketball court and said the Lord's Prayer together. Daniels then told the assembled students:

"Here at Greenup County, we have another tradition. The Greenup County cheerleaders are competing this weekend at Kings Island. We need to get them psyched up, too."

As the cheerleaders took the gym floor to run through their competition routine, the football players all applauded. But some other boys seated down on the front bleacher wailed like sirens. And they didn't stop when the routine began. As Megan West held up her "Fight Greenup Fight" sign, one boy stopped his irritating siren scream to tell her that her sign was upside down when it wasn't. Megan kept her cool and ignored him. Toward the end of the routine, Greg McKenzie, who was sitting near the disruptive boys, came over and shut them up, clamping his hands over their mouths and telling them in sharp whispers to keep it to themselves.

Meanwhile, the cheerleaders hit everything. Rachel Wills's partner stunt had a slight wobble, and Kelena McClurg's pizza spin worked beautifully.

Afterward, the football team led a standing ovation for the cheerleaders, who bounded off the floor confident and happy.

The game that night went off pleasantly enough, but Greenup didn't win. Russell High traditionally has one of the best football teams in the state. Greenup does not. And the game was held on Russell's home turf, which didn't make things any easier for the football Musketeers. The Greenup boys did better than expected, however, tying the game at 21 with under five minutes to play before Russell pulled out the win with a late touchdown.

It was weird for April, cheering against Russell on its own field. She had trouble getting into a rhythm at first and cheered tentatively, watching the other Greenup girls for cues, not really belting out the chants. By the end of the game, however, she was cheering full-out, without a hint of self-consciousness. Afterward, the Greenup cheerleaders lined up and shook hands with the Russell cheerleaders in the middle of the field, just like the two football teams. April hugged one Russell cheerleader lightly, then waved and smiled at some other students on the Russell side of the field before rejoining her new teammates and new classmates on the Greenup side.

Randy Peffer stopped Greg in the stands before he left the game that evening: "I don't want you fightin' tonight."

"Why'd I want to fight?"

"'Cause of April's house."

"How'd you hear about that?"

"I know everything. So you just stay on our side and they'll stay on their side."

"Okay, okay," Greg muttered, smiling and shaking his head as though shocked by the implication. "Nothing's gonna happen."

Nothing did.

And now, Greg's here at Kings Island—along with eight other cheerleader boyfriends—to applaud April during her first competition with Greenup High.

The assembled boyfriends could be enjoying the park's various rides today. They don't have made-up faces, or nicely styled hair, or uniforms to keep clean. Still, many of them sit on the not-so-shady bleachers, patiently waiting out the day with their girlfriends.

Not Greg, however. He's never been to Kings Island, and he wants to try every ride.

The same goes for Linda Goble and the rest of the Greenup JV. They, too, have come to Kings Island to support the varsity girls, but they don't see why they can't enjoy the park's amusements at the same time. Occasionally, Linda visits with Shiritta here at the amphitheater, but she and Jessica Garthee spend most of their time on the park's many rides. Linda's favorite, it seems, is the Amazon Falls. Whenever she returns to the amphitheater, she's sopping from head to toe, her rusty red hair matted down her back.

There's a strange tension in Linda today. She's happy to be here having fun at Kings Island, surrounded by her JV friends. But there are times when she looks at the varsity girls with an expression of jealousy and regret. She enjoys the freedom of wearing an old T-shirt and shorts and running around wet and unkempt, but a part of her would rather be stuck on an amphitheater bench with the varsity, her face covered with makeup, her hair dry and held back in a ponytail, her body tucked into a clean, tight uniform.

Greg, fresh from another roller-coaster ride, comes bounding up to April. He's been exploring the area around the amphitheater with another cheerleader boyfriend, whose bare chest was once covered by a "Greenup County" T-shirt.

"Some girl obsessed with Greenup County came up to Matt and asked how she could buy a Greenup shirt," Greg tells April and any other cheerleaders who'll listen. "She said she'd pay twenty dollars. So Matt said, 'You can have this one,' and he took off the shirt he was wearing and sold it to her! For twenty bucks!"

"What's he gonna wear now?" April asks, squinting through the glare of the sun, trying to sound amused.

"Oh, he's got another shirt in his car. But he says he might sell that one, too!"

April and the rest of Greg's audience laugh.

Greg sees Coach Peffer walk by, so he jumps up and tells his story again. Peffer listens with a calm smile and acts surprised on cue.

"Hey, have you seen my new tattoo?" Greg asks. He pulls back the sleeve of his shirt to reveal a small red-and-black design on his right shoulder.

"That's not real, is it?" Peffer says, genuinely surprised this time.

"Sure it is."

"It's not permanent, though, right?"

"Yeah. I already had one."

Greg reveals another tattoo on his left shoulder.

"Don't get any more tattoos," Peffer says sternly.

Greg shows him the new one again. "But the design. Don't you like the design?"

"It's fine. Just don't get any more tattoos."

In the preliminary round, Greenup looked strong throughout the routine except for Wills's super-shaky partner stunt. Olive Oyl weebled and wobbled but she wouldn't fall down. Coach Berry and the rest of the Greenup squad hope she can pull off the high-wire act one more time in the finals.

It's three-thirty now, and the sun hasn't let up. After their preliminary performance, the Greenup girls all walk over to a juice stand near the amphitheater and, with their parents' money, each buys a five-dollar bottle of fresh-squeezed lemonade. As they huddle around the juice stand, sweating and breathing hard, a short, dark-skinned woman with curly brown hair, who appears to be in her mid-fifties, approaches the team.

This woman and her husband drove for over ten hours—nearly 500 miles—from Bryan, Ohio, up in the northern part of the state, just so they could see the Greenup County cheerleaders up close and in person.

"We never miss you guys on TV," the woman tells the girls, "and I just had to see you in person."

The Greenup cheerleaders don't know what to say.

"You were wonderful," the woman continues. "I'm so thrilled to tell you so."

There's a pause as the Greenup girls stare at her, blank-faced, then the cheerleaders look at one another and try to figure out how to respond. They all smile warmly at their fan, thank her effusively, and take turns hugging her.

As they return to the amphitheater, the cheerleaders wave good-bye to the woman and smile at her some more.

"That was so *nice*," says Rachel Brown.

"It was a little weird," says Rachel Wills.

Greenup's toughest competition here at Kings Island—and possibly throughout the season—will come from Paul Lawrence Dunbar High School of Lexington. The Dunbar cheerleaders won the national championship back in 1995, the year Shawnda Bates fell badly, and they posed a significant challenge to Greenup in 1997 until one of the Dunbar girls fell in the finals. Dunbar has lost only a couple of cheerleaders from last year's strong team, so this year they've got experience and confidence to go with their usual cheerleading skill.

Normally, Boyd County High School would also pose a significant threat, but the Boyd program has nose-dived into mediocrity, not even making the trip to Kings Island this year.

As long as Wills stays up on her partner stunt, no one, not even Dunbar, should keep Greenup from winning this competition again this year. From what the Greenup coaches saw of Dunbar's routine during the preliminary round, there's a lot of talent on the squad, but it looked rough, unpolished. Greenup practiced all summer, while Dunbar took the summer off and hasn't spent much time preparing their routine for today. Once the Dunbar cheerleaders get a chance to practice consistently and hone their skills, they may prove a force to be reckoned with.

Hank Light, his injured right arm in a sling, is here at the back of the amphitheater, talking with the Greenup cheerleaders about their preliminary performance, giving them pointers on their stunting and dancing. Light hasn't worked with the Greenup girls much this weekend because he was busy preparing his three all-star squads for the Kings Island all-star competition, which ended late last night. His senior all-stars took third and his junior and youth all-stars both finished second. Not bad, considering Light's torn tendon. Now, he can finally focus his attention on the Greenup varsity and help them prepare for the coming finals.

An announcement comes over the amphitheater's public address system:

"Now, please welcome a team that has won six national college cheerleading championships, and in nearly twenty years has never placed worse than third—the University of Louisville varsity cheerleading team!" The Greenup cheerleaders, parents, and coaches all yell and clap as U of L— with the help of freshman Shawnda Bates flipping back and forth across the stage—puts on a spectacular exhibition.

Afterward, Shawnda visits with the Greenup cheerleaders. The girls gather around and tell Shawnda how beautiful she looks and how good she was up there with the Louisville team. Shawnda smiles and hugs them. Then other Louisville cheerleaders walk by and call to her. Just like that, Shawnda leaves the Greenup girls, with a wave and a "Good luck!"

* * *

Greenup will be the very last team to compete in the finals.

Before leaving the amphitheater to warm up, the Greenup varsity watches Dunbar perform. The Dunbar squad appears tough at first, hitting a number of tricky tumbling passes, but the Dunbar girls can't hide their lack of preparation. During a group mount, the right side collapses; a flyer falls on a partner stunt.

Dunbar's problems are only a slight consolation to the Greenup cheerleaders and their coaches. A similar fate may await them.

Berry turns away from the Dunbar performance, wipes the sweat from her forehead, and sighs. "I can't wait for this day to be over."

Outside the amphitheater, the girls practice their tumbling across the park's concrete walkway. Linda Goble and Jessica Garthee have just doused themselves in the Amazon Falls. Wet and sloppy, they sit on a nearby wooden fence and watch the varsity warm up.

Rachel Brown attempts a standing back tuck and stumbles forward. She stomps her foot against the pavement and grunts angrily. "My standings suck!" she bellows.

Rachel landed her standing at the beginning of the preliminary performance, but she stumbled a touch. She's sick, sick, sick, of worrying about this one maneuver.

Shmorg tries to comfort her. "It's okay," she says. "You'll get it." She awkwardly hugs Rachel, who frowns and pulls away.

Berry has the girls get together so they can run through the dance. Aimee Lewis, all dressed up in her perfect cheerleader attire, can now perform her only real duty here at Kings Island—turning the music on and off. Despite her injury, Aimee came here for the competition at Berry's behest. If she's a member of the team, Berry believes, she should be at every competition dressed just as they are.

As the girls dance, Berry stands behind them, hands on hips, watching carefully. Satisfied, she has the team practice the partner stunts. Wills, April, and Kelena rise up into the air on the hands of their teammates. They all hit their liberty poses, but before the rotation begins, Wills falls into her bases' hands.

"All right," says Berry. "Try it again."

Again Wills, April, and Kelena rise up into the air. This time, Wills and April stay up, but Kelena falls.

Berry rolls her eyes, as though she's too exhausted—from the sun, from the hours of waiting, from the endless practicing—to care.

Over the public address system, a voice announces:

"Greenup County High School. Greenup County High School. Please report to the warm-up area."

"Okay," says Berry. "It's time."

The Greenup squad walks through the bleachers down through a doorway that leads to a gravelly road hidden from the amphitheater audience by a ten-foot wooden fence. Across a portion of the road lies a narrow mat.

Wills doesn't seem worried about her partner stunt. Right now, she's loosely talking with Jessica Newell and laughing about something. But her bases—Emma Hood and Shiritta Schaffer—are a wreck. They confer anxiously over how best to hold Wills's foot steady during the partner stunt. They raise their hands over their heads as though they're holding the foot, and whisper about where their arms and hands should be and when.

Berry hasn't come back here with the team. Instead, she's sitting with the parents and boyfriends in the bleachers, leaving Peffer and Light to take care of the girls. The two men say nothing to the cheerleaders. They simply watch them warm up and occasionally spot tumbling runs.

Rachel Brown practices her standing back on the old mat lying on the asphalt. This time, she falls forward on her hands. She stomps away, tears welling up in her eyes.

"Rachel," says Shmorg, "that mat's hard to tumble on."

Rachel ignores her.

"I'm serious," says Shmorg.

Brooke Meenach is stressed about the dance. Berry has put Brooke at front and center of the Greenup dance formation, so she's the most visible member of the squad and the only one who can't see anyone else while dancing. With a terrified look on her face, Brooke runs through the dance again and again, thrusting and voguing while counting to eight over and over.

Shawnda Bates shows up.

(Berry has asked her to go backstage and give her old teammates a pep talk, because, as Berry put it, "They won't listen to me. Maybe they'll listen to you.")

"Come here, guys," Shawnda says. "I want to talk to you." With a gesture of her long arms, she gathers the Greenup girls together in a huddle.

"You can do this," she says. "You know you can. I know you can. You're Greenup County cheerleaders."

Led by Shawnda, the cheerleaders chant the Lord's Prayer in unison.

"Faith, on three," says Shawnda. "One, two, three . . ."

"FAITH!"

"I'll be pulling for you," Shawnda says. She hugs a few of the girls and returns to the bleachers.

As the Greenup squad starts up the stairway to the stage, Aimee Lewis hugs every one of her teammates.

Then Peffer, Light, and Aimee walk around to the other side of the stage, where they will watch the team perform from the wings. Berry is in the front section of the bleachers with Linda Goble, Shawnda Bates, and all the cheerleaders' parents and boyfriends.

Before their team is introduced, the Greenup faithful cheer loudly:

"WE! ARE! GREENUP!" Clap-clap-clap-clap, clap-clap.

"WE! ARE! GREENUP!" Clap-clap-clap-clap, clap-clap.

The Greenup girls run out onto the stage, yelling and whooping and smiling. They take their positions. The first trick of the routine will be the team standing back tuck.

From behind the curtain just offstage, Peffer says, "Pull, Rachel. Come on."

The music begins.

"NASTY!"

Rachel Brown stiffens her arms and lunges backward, but she doesn't fully tuck herself into a ball, which throws off her body's rotation, and when she puts her feet down, she's leaning too far forward. She falls onto her hands and knees.

"Come on, Rachel!" Peffer yells. "Come on. Keep it going."

"Keep it UP!" Light screams.

Shiritta stumbles a touch on her full-twist flip, but mostly the tumbling goes well. The group mount hits, as always. Then come the partner stunts.

"Oh, Jesus," says Light. "Here we go."

Wills faces Emma and Shiritta. With her back to the audience, she steps onto their hands with her right foot. As her bases pop her up into the air, Wills spins around so she faces the crowd. She hits the liberty position, her fists up and out, her left knee bent. Her hips wiggle to the right, her fists wiggle to the left, but she gets herself back under control as the slow rotation begins. Emma and Shiritta strain to keep themselves underneath her.

"Oh, God," Peffer says. He bends over behind the stereo equipment backstage and doesn't see what happens next.

Wills's right knee bends and shakes, her hips rock erratically back and forth, to the left, to the right, to the left again. Like Olympic weight lifters, Emma and Shiritta clench their trembling arms and hold on desperately to Wills's foot above their heads. Slowly, slowly, Wills's body turns all the way around.

The stunt ends and Wills pops down lightly to the ground.

Light raises his eyebrows, opens his mouth wide, and sighs.

The rest of the routine goes smoothly. April continues her faultless flying, while Kelena and her bases manage to hit the pizza-spin move at the end.

"I watched most of it that time," Peffer says to Light, smiling.

"Yeah?" Light teases. "Well, good for you."

Berry rushes to greet her girls as they come down off the stage. She goes after Wills first: "Rachel Wills? Did you hear me yell? I said, 'Don't you dare fall!'"

Wills laughs, and Berry hugs her.

"I was thinking, 'Oh my God! Stay up, Rachel! Stay up!'" Kelena says, smiling.

Says Wills, a big, toothy grin spread across her face, "*I* was thinking, 'I'm falling. I'm going to fall.' Then I thought, 'I can't fall. I can't fall.' I wasn't coming down unless they dropped me. There was no way I was coming down."

Emma is worried that Wills was so shaky that the judges will deduct a lot of points.

"You did fine," Berry tells her. "You did just fine. You kept her up there. Look, you're a kid. You did the best you can. If you were a pro, you'd get yelled at. But you're not a pro."

Emma lets some of her tension go, breathing deeply. Then she smiles and shakes her head. "That was the hardest thing I've ever done."

Rachel Brown, meanwhile, is off crying by herself. She doesn't care about Wills staying up on her partner stunt; she doesn't care that the team probably performed well enough to win the competition. She missed her standing back.

Rachel's father comes backstage and tries to console her, but she won't listen to him.

Linda Goble runs over and gives Shiritta a big hug. Shawnda has come

back here, too, and she congratulates Shmorg, Kelena, and the other senior cheerleaders.

None of the boyfriends have come back to hug and kiss and congratulate their girlfriends. They all wait for the cheerleaders to come to them.
Only then will the boys praise the girls.

April enters the amphitheater, smiling, looking forward to a hug from
Greg. But she can't find him. He's not with the other boys. He doesn't
seem to be here in the amphitheater at all. April's smile fades and her
brow furrows as her eyes dart about in search of her boyfriend.

The Greenup squad won the Kings Island competition for the fourth year
in a row. Dunbar, despite all those falls, finished third.

Greg missed the team's big performance. Shortly before the finals began, he planned to ride the Beast, a big wooden roller coaster at the far
end of the park. The line was longer than he'd expected, but he still decided to go for it. Afterwards he ran back across the park to the amphitheater, but the finals were already over.

April glared at Greg and asked him where he'd been. Then she turned
her back on him.

April avoided Greg the rest of the evening until the awards ceremony,
when the Greenup girls ran up onstage and accepted the enormous trophy, jumping up and down and screaming in victory. After that, she was
too happy with herself to stay angry with her boyfriend.

At nine P.M., the girls walk back to their families' and boyfriends' cars to
begin the three-hour drive home to Greenup. As Rachel Brown wends
her way through the now dark amusement park, she's quiet and sullen.
Her parents, walking beside her, can feel their daughter's frustration.

"Well, you guys did it," her dad says eventually. "It was tough, but you
did it."

Rachel keeps her eyes on the ground and says nothing.

"Come on, honey," her mom says. "You won."

Rachel looks up and her mother can see the tears glistening in Rachel's
eyes.

"I was the only one who didn't hit it, Mom. The only one."

Regionals

Chapter Thirteen

Queen Candidate

After the win at Kings Island, the Greenup cheerleaders relax. Too much, perhaps. They've just won first place in a tough cheerleading competition despite their status as Berry's "least prepared squad ever." Clearly, the girls feel, they aren't Berry's least talented squad ever.

The coach has conceded as much. But she's also tried to convince her girls that talent will take them only so far. Hard, regular work, she preaches, is necessary to win a national championship.

The Greenup girls have difficulty recognizing that. Their upcoming competitions—UCA's Kentucky state regionals in late November, and nationals in February—lie off in the indefinite future. Many of the varsity cheerleaders feel that hard work can wait. Some have come down with chronic ailments—bad backs, sore ankles, shin splints—which allow them to sit out the daily practices, the sideline cheering at Friday night football games, and the tumbling workouts at Tammy Jo's on Wednesday evenings.

Aimee Lewis, whose knee got plenty strong by late September, has missed almost a month of school, complaining of a pain in her abdomen that doctors can't explain.

Emma Hood also missed a month of school—and cheerleading—with a bad case of bronchitis.

With homecoming fast approaching, the Greenup cheerleaders have become further distracted by boys—as if boys hadn't posed a big enough distraction already. All that drama over who's "snaked" whose boyfriend refuses to die down.

This sort of fighting over boys is typical teenage-girl stuff, to be sure, but Coach Berry can't stand it. She says she's never had a team so torn up over such things, and she's sick of her girls' blaming one another for their boyfriends' infidelity. If a girl has an encounter with another girl's boyfriend, the wayward girl is reviled, and the boy gets off scot-free. To Berry, that makes no sense, and she's told the cheerleaders so. The pride of winning a cheerleading national championship and the subsequent bonds forged with victorious teammates will outlast any high school romance, she says. "And I know. I've been around."

Still, the cheerleaders won't take her word for it. No matter how much she pushes, Berry's girls—her kittens—refuse to leap out of the protective darkness they're used to.

The competition for the coveted titles of homecoming queen and her attendants has gone on for about a month now. Any senior girl can be elected homecoming queen at Greenup High. And the senior girl who finishes second to the queen in the school-wide vote becomes the senior attendant. Underclass girls vie for freshman, sophomore, and junior attendant positions.

Back in September, each of the fifty Greenup High homerooms nominated its own homecoming queen or attendant candidate. The students then voted for their four favorite homeroom nominees, cutting the field from fifty to sixteen. The top four vote-getters of each grade became the 1997 senior, junior, sophomore, and freshman candidates. Ultimately, the entire student body casts secret ballots, selecting the four girls they like best.

Only pep club sponsor Susi Daniels knows the results of the final vote, and she's not saying until the big announcement at halftime of the homecoming game against the West Jessamine High School Colts, on Friday, October 24.

Among the sixteen celebrated candidates, three are varsity cheerleaders. Sarah Dickison is in the running for sophomore attendant. Kelena McClurg is a candidate for homecoming queen, and, after only four months as a student at Greenup High, so is April Creech. April's renown as a cheerleader who transferred from Russell High, combined with her soft-spoken confidence and general niceness, have already gained her a measure of popularity. She has few friends apart from the other cheerlead-

ers and Greg, but, like any American high school student, April doesn't need friends to be popular.

This Thursday night, a day before the big game, Greenup High will stage a modest homecoming parade. April will ride down Main Street sitting on the back of a luxury convertible, from the county fairgrounds to the county courthouse, and all the onlookers will see that she is "Senior Candidate April Creech."

April would be more excited about her queen candidacy if she and Greg could work out their relationship. Only three months old, the couple's engagement seems doomed.

Greg has had his eye on a fourteen-year-old freshman at the high school. So heading into the weekend before homecoming, he told April he wanted to take a break from her, then went on a date with the younger girl. (April's scornful teammates call her the Twin because she happens to be one of a pair of twins.) As of Thursday, the day before the homecoming game, two days before the homecoming dance, Greg is planning to take the Twin to the dance—not April, the supposed love of his life, whose diamond ring he's still paying for.

April, meanwhile, has no date; she feels she must wait out Greg's "girl chasin'." She believes he'll come back to her eventually. Like the other Greenup girls who consistently forgive their philandering boyfriends, April's afraid to express her anger and bitterness to Greg for fear she'll lose him. So she keeps it all bottled up inside.

Thursday afternoon, the varsity girls gather in the auditorium and make colorful construction-paper chains, which will serve as decorations for the dance Saturday night. The Greenup cheerleading program will receive all the proceeds from the dance, so they must work to make the room pretty.

As part of their broader homecoming duties to pep up the football team and, by extension, the entire Greenup community, some of the girls prepare a candy bag for each football-playing boy, and others carry pieces of the "Greenup County Cheerleading" float to a pickup truck in the school's parking lot.

Greg walks into the auditorium, where he encounters a few girls sprawled about, writing cute messages—"GO G.C.," "BEAT THE COLTS" "GOOD LUCK BOYS"—on little white bags, then stuffing the bags full of candy. He's wearing brown overalls because today is "Farmer Day," when Greenup High students show their school spirit by dressing like farmers.

Randy Peffer asks Greg if he'll help out with the cheerleaders' many homecoming responsibilities.

"I don't want to decorate," Greg says, looking down disdainfully at the girls with their felt markers, candy bags, and colored construction paper. "But I'll lift and bring stuff out."

Peffer directs Greg to a large oblong piece of plywood painted to look like a football. Greg heaves it up over his shoulder and walks out of the auditorium toward the school parking lot. As he goes, April looks up from her candy bag and watches him with that tired look of hers. Once Greg disappears through the auditorium door, she shakes her head and looks back down at her work.

There are fifty-five football players, Peffer calculates, so each of the cheerleaders should decorate at least three bags.

"It's the Colts, Libby, not the Cougars," Peffer says, smiling.

"I was thinking of last week."

"That was the Jaguars."

A few other girls laugh.

"Yeah," Libby says, smiling. "So?"

"Colts plus Jaguars, so you got Cougars?"

Libby returns to her bags, wearing a wider smile. "Yep," she says.

"Give me someone to make a bag for," Brooke Meenach says to anyone who's listening. "I like it better when they're personalized."

"How about Chris?" says Peffer.

"I want to make one for Chris," Rachel Brown interjects.

Brooke grins. "I had him first."

"Don't fight, girls," says Amanda Kitchen acidly.

"But who should I make mine for?" Rachel asks, whining a little bit.

"Sam," says Peffer.

Rachel considers. "What's his number?"

"Sixty-two."

Rachel sighs. "Okay."

Rachel has tried to stay focused on her cheerleading amid the social pressure building toward homecoming weekend. Her date will be her cousin, obviously not a romantic prospect.

Unlike many of her teammates, Rachel came away from Kings Island humbled, not cocky. The memory of her missed standing back tuck dogs her still. Determined not to mess up again, she has retreated emotionally from the rest of the team, and has practiced her standing relentlessly—at cheer practice, at her private tumbling lessons with Tom Pack, at the team tumbling workouts at Tammy Jo's. Rachel's hard work—her determination to master her cheer skills all by herself—has allowed her to stop worrying so much about what her teammates think of her. And when Rachel stops worrying, the Greenup coaches believe, she can do anything. Indeed, during these last couple weeks of October, Rachel has hit her standing—when she's tight, when she's loose, when she's fresh, when she's worn out, when she's on a mat, when she's on the gym floor, whenever. The problem is that she's had to cut herself off from many of the other cheerleaders to do so.

Aubrey Warnock hands Peffer one of her bags.

"What do you think of this one?" she asks him.

Peffer reads aloud, "'Win, so we can all have a happy Thanksgiving.'"

The girls laugh, except for Rachel Brown, who's focused on the bag she's making for Sam.

April Creech doesn't laugh, either, because Greg has re-entered the auditorium.

"So," says Peffer, "do all of you have a date for homecoming?"

The girls don't answer.

Looking down at her candy bag with its array of alternating yellow circles and blue stars, April says loudly, "I don't."

Peffer turns to Greg. "You're going with the twins?"

"One of them," April states, her eyes still focused on the bag.

"Yeah, one of them," Greg mumbles.

Candy Berry walks in.

"Me and Kelena and Holly all have the same outfit," says Rachel Brown, trying to join the homecoming conversation but oblivious to the tension between Greg and April.

Berry sits down on a big, cushiony chair on the auditorium stage as Greg walks quietly out.

"Me and Krista have the same outfit, too," says Megan West.

"Well then," says Berry, breathing hard from her walk from the school parking lot, down the school's hallway, and across the auditorium stage, "they must be nice outfits if you all chose them. So you'll all look cute."

"I guess I'll just take off my jacket," Megan says.

"Oh! Someone pushed Ms. Jackson's buttons today," says Rachel, again trying to engage her teammates. "Oh, man! She was hot!"

"I hate it when someone pushes my buttons," Brooke Meenach says, grinning. "That's almost as bad as when someone frosts my cookies."

The cheerleaders laugh. Rachel smiles uncomfortably.

"Olive Oyl?" says Peffer—he's busy taking stock of the girls' parade uniforms. "Where are your poms?"

"They're at my house."

"Well, before the parade, you're going to have to get them."

Rachel Wills looks at Coach Peffer and furrows her brow. To get her poms before the parade, she'll have to ask Angie Heineman to bring them, and soon. But Angie probably just got home from school, and she's not going to want to turn around and come back. She has to pick up Wills late tonight after the parade ends at eight P.M., and Angie's already not wild about that.

Wills has had a tough couple of weeks. While practicing a mount here in the auditorium in early October, she fell and split her chin wide open. She says she's never been in so much pain. Her head ached for weeks afterward, and she had to get five stitches. She still has three butterfly bandages under a big bandage on her chin, and she thinks she'll be left with a prominent scar. To make matters worse, she got braces recently. The bandages, the probable scar on her chin, plus the metal studs on her teeth make her feel less than glamorous—all with homecoming right around the corner.

As she says, "It's been hard."

Looking serious, Wills walks out of the auditorium and heads over to the school's office to call Angie.

While Wills is gone, Greg returns, wearing a black hooded coat and a creepy mask reminiscent of the hauntingly disturbed face in Edvard Munch's painting *The Scream*. It's the same mask worn by the killer in the hit horror flick *Scream*.

April sighs, throws down her marker, and lies back on the carpeted floor.

"Oh, he's so stupid," she whispers.

Greg walks over near April and stands above her.

With haste, April sits, then stands. "Greg," she says, jabbing her finger at him, "you get away from me with that mask!"

"Is April afraid of the mask?" Peffer asks with a smirk.

When Greg doesn't back off, April runs away to the other side of the auditorium.

"She sure is," says Greg. He takes the mask off, revealing a broad, mischievous grin.

From across the room, April tries to look at Greg with an angry, sullen expression. Against her will, she smiles. Slightly.

That night, April comes to the county fairgrounds in her grandmother's red Mercedes convertible. Eight flashy convertibles are needed to carry the sixteen homecoming queen and attendant candidates along the parade route, so April's grandma Creech—the mother of April's AWOL birth father—volunteered herself and her Mercedes. Mrs. Creech has tacked handwritten signs on either side of the car:

> SENIOR CANDIDATES
> APRIL CREECH
> HEATHER BENTLEY

The other Greenup cheerleaders have already arrived and are still busy putting the finishing touches on their float, which consists of a flatbed trailer with a hardwood deck blanketed by a plastic green rug, much like the fake grass used at goofy-golf courses. On top, the girls have mounted the big flat wooden football that Greg helped carry and, on either side of the football, two big flat wooden megaphones with "G.C." painted on them. The girls have also printed "MUSKETEERS" on both sides of the float with zillions of yellow plastic strips forming the letters against a backdrop of zillions of green plastic strips. On the back of the float stands an arc with two large wooden letters positioned within it, a "G," then a "C," all covered with thin plastic strips of green and gold and black.

A half-hour before the parade is scheduled to start, the Greenup cheerleaders staple the last of the colored plastic strips onto their float.

Greg's here. He and a couple of his friends each have a *Scream* mask and they're having a grand time scaring the Greenup cheerleaders. The members of the Greenup pep club are also here. They're dressed in overalls and will ride in a trailer pulled behind a tractor. There's the "Lady Musketeers" soccer team assembled near a white pickup with handmade signs tacked all over it saying, "Greenup Ladies' Soccer" and "Go Ladies' Soccer!" There's the fifty-some Greenup football players—all squished into two long flatbed trailers which will be pulled by pickup trucks, and there's the Wurtland Elementary School cheerleaders, standing in uniform in the bed of another pickup truck, yelling in their high-pitched young voices:

"WE'VE GOT SPIRIT! YES WE DO!

"WE'VE GOT SPIRIT! HOW 'BOUT YOU!"

The Greenup cheerleaders holler back:

"WE'VE GOT SPIRIT! YES WE DO!

"WE'VE GOT SPIRIT! MORE THAN YOU!"

The sun has begun to set, and as the sky darkens, the air gets cooler, crisper. April has dressed up in a stylish cold-weather outfit; she wears navy blue slacks with a dark green turtleneck, a peach blazer, and matching peach gloves. She's blow-dried her blond hair and applied hairspray to give it a full, fluffy look that it doesn't usually have. She also wears a heavy dusting of blush, which makes her normally pale cheeks glow.

As April stands beside the Mercedes with her grandmother and waits for the parade to start, Greg keeps his distance. April's grandma doesn't much like Greg, and Greg knows it. So he flirts with the other Greenup cheerleaders.

Wearing his mask, he walks stealthily beside the cheerleaders' float where it sits on the side of Main Street, outside the fairgrounds. Rachel Brown, busy stapling plastic strips with Aubrey Warnock—one of the few cheerleaders she can confidently call a friend—doesn't see Greg coming. Suddenly, he jumps up in front of her, making her scream. Aubrey, mocking Rachel, screams as well. Rachel smiles at Aubrey and says, "Let's get 'im."

The two girls jump down off the float and chase Greg while screaming at him as loudly and shrilly as they can.

The football players follow Greg's lead. From their cramped seats in the flatbed trailers, they hurl candy at the cheerleaders—the same candy that the girls gave them in those painstakingly decorated candy bags. Tootsie Rolls, miniature Three Musketeers, and little bags of Skittles whistle through the air and hit the girls harmlessly. In return, the girls pick up as much of the fallen candy as they can find—underneath their float, on top of the float, out in the street—and throw it back at the boys, all the while shrieking and giggling. Rachel Wills mostly keeps out of all the candy throwing and screaming, and concentrates on the last bit of float preparation.

The sun has almost completely set now, and soon the show will get on the road.

Randy Peffer and Susi Daniels arrange the parade participants in order of increasing importance.

At the head goes the ladies' soccer team, then the four freshmen homecoming attendant candidates—two girls sitting atop each of two convertibles—then the pep club's "Farmer Country" float pulled by that tractor, then the sophomore attendant candidates riding on their convertibles, the Wurtland Elementary School cheerleaders, the junior attendant candidates, the varsity Greenup cheerleaders standing on—or running and flipping beside—their float, then April and the rest of the queen candidates, and last, the football team.

By the time the parade begins, the sky has darkened completely. It's a cloudy night, so there's no moon out and only a handful of stars. The few street lamps here on Main don't cast much light on the parade.

Out of obligation or from a sense of community, the Greenup residents who live along Main Street step outside their houses, walk to the end of their front yards, and watch the parade pass by in the dark. April sits atop her grandma's Mercedes and waves to everyone she sees—probably no more than thirty people—most of whom force smiles themselves, and wave as the parade goes by.

One old couple stands out in front of their little wooden house with blank expressions on their faces, their hands in their jeans pockets to protect them from the nipping cold. Neither the old man nor the old woman wave or smile or anything. They stand there, hands in pockets, and watch.

In celebration of Halloween's imminent arrival, the Greenup cheerleaders throw candy at the old couple. Most of it lands on the street with a clickety-clack. Some of it whizzes by and lands in the couple's small, neat yard. They look at each other, then at the candy on the street. Then they look back at the cheerleaders whooping and hollering ten feet away.

Some of the cheerleaders walk behind the float, turning cartwheels, smiling, waving, flipping. The cheerleaders don't care that their audience isn't terribly excited about the parade. The girls came here to perform, to show spirit, to inspire, and they're going to give it everything they've got.

April and the other senior candidates pass by the old couple now. The man and woman watch solemnly as April waves and smiles at them and still they don't respond. After the football players roll by quietly—an anticlimax, after the raucous cheerleaders—the elderly man and woman, their duty done, walk slowly back into their house.

The most excited parade watchers are the children. They scramble about on their hands and knees—to the dismay of their parents—trying to gather up as much of the candy thrown by the cheerleaders as they can find on the dark street.

Suddenly, Greg and his two friends, all wearing their *Scream* masks, jump out from behind a roadside hedge and rush at the cheerleaders, who shriek, then giggle. April, perched atop her convertible, watches this scene unfold in front of her. She purses her lips for a moment, then turns her attention to the other senior candidate riding with her and makes small talk.

As the procession reaches the county courthouse, everyone gets down from their pickup trucks, their trailers, the one float, and their convertibles. Susi Daniels hosts a small pep rally around the flagpole in front of the dark, cold courthouse steps.

Tomorrow's homecoming game will be a big one for the Greenup footballers. If they win, they'll clinch Greenup's second division championship in a row.

"We're proud of you!" says Daniels.

The small gathering of parade participants and some of their parents whoop feebly.

"You've accomplished a lot!" Daniels continues.

The supporters whoop again.

"And you're going to win tomorrow night!"

"Yeah! All right! WHOOOOO!"

"And you're going to win districts!"

"WHOOO! Yeah!"

"And you're going to go on and on AND ON!"

"Yeah, Yeah, YEAH! WHOOOOO!"

April leaves with her grandmother before the pep rally ends. She doesn't care much about the football team, and she's cold from riding through the dark for an hour on that convertible. But mostly, she's tired of watching Greg's antics.

The rest of the cheerleaders stick it out because it's their duty to do so. Right now, they're lining the courthouse steps, backlit by the fluorescent bulbs glowing from the courthouse hallway inside. As a few football players make short speeches about tomorrow night's football game, the girls clap and cheer and jump up and down—to keep warm as much as to show their spirit.

"We're going to win tomorrow night," the football captain bellows. He pauses. "We're going to win tomorrow night," he says again. "Yeah!"

The cheerleaders hoot and holler approvingly.

"We thank you for all your support," the football coach says. "We're all real proud of the guys this year, so come out tomorrow night and be a part of history."

At the end of the pep rally, most of the cheerleaders pile into their parents' cars and drive off. Rachel Brown, smiling, happy, bounds up to her parents, hugs her dad, then gets in the family van and heads home. Rachel Wills, waiting on Angie Heineman to pick her up, notices her boyfriend, senior footballer Jesse Stapleton, leaving the courthouse with a few of his buddies. Not wanting to be left waiting for Angie all by herself, Wills calls out to him.

"Hey, Jesse!"

He has his back turned and is talking with friends as he walks away.

"Hey, Jesse!" Wills calls again, and skips up behind him.

Jesse and his three friends turn around.

"Where're you going?" Wills asks.

Jesse's buddies look at him, then at Wills, then turn and slowly amble off. Glancing sideways, Jesse notices them go.

"Home, I guess," he says.

Jesse cares for Wills, but right now, he doesn't know what she wants from him. And he doesn't know what to do with his buddies looking on and all.

"All right," says Wills cheerfully. "Well, see you tomorrow." She gives Jesse a big hug.

Jesse hugs her back awkwardly, his left arm around her, his right hand still in his jeans pocket.

After Jesse heads off to catch his friends, Wills paces back and forth in front of the courthouse. Most everyone has left.

"Where are you, Angie?" Wills mutters to herself, looking around. "Where's my ride?"

Randy Peffer asks Wills if she's okay.

"Yeah, Angie's supposed to get me. I'm all right."

Peffer waves good-bye, and leaves Wills alone in front of the courthouse, waiting in the cold for her ride home.

* * *

The following morning, Greg tries to make up with April. He tells her that he's missed her. That he doesn't want to go to the homecoming dance with the fourteen-year-old "Twin." That he hopes he can still go with April. That April's still his fianceé. And that he still plans to marry her. If she'll have him.

April takes Greg back, and the reunited couple appears very chummy at the school's midday pep rally. During the show put on by the pep club in the Greenup County gym, Greg lies on his side next to April near the edge of the basketball court, his head and shoulders propped up on his left elbow. April sits, legs crossed in front of her, wearing her pep rally uniform, her pom-poms in her lap. She and Greg laugh and whisper to each other while the pep club performs.

A pep-club boy wearing enormous eyeglasses does a dead-on imitation of Harry Caray, the longtime play-by-play announcer of the St. Louis Cardinals and Chicago Cubs. The boy sits on a couch in the middle of the gym and—in Caray's distinctive style—he announces that it's time for the *Harry Caray Show.* His guest? Greenup High football coach Gary McPeek.

The gray Greenup sky has poured down rain all morning, and the local weather report calls for the rain to continue on into the night. So the boy playing Caray makes a bunch of jokes about football in the rain, in the mud, and so forth, and Coach McPeek laughs along good-naturedly.

The boy asks McPeek whether he plans to take the team out to celebrate if they win the game and their second district title in a row.

"I don't know," says McPeek. "We'll probably go our separate ways, you know, each celebrate safely on our own."

A kid yells from the bleachers, "Take 'em to Hooters, Coach!"

April and Greg look at each other, and they giggle with the rest of the student body. Coach McPeek widens his eyes and tries not to look uncomfortable.

"Well," says the young Harry Caray, "Hooters does have great wings."

Again, everyone laughs.

Later, April pulls herself away from Greg and performs with the cheerleaders in the middle of the gym floor.

"HEY FOOTBALL TEAM!" the varsity girls holler. "HOW DO YOU FEEL?"

The football team, standing beside the cheerleaders in five rows of ten players each, hollers back, "WE FEEL GOOD, OH WE FEEL SO

GOOD, HOOOAH!" And as they grunt, the footballers all put their hands on the back of their heads and thrust their pelvises forward.

The cheerleaders then chant "We! Are! Greenup!" and the student crowd joins in. Greg and another boy down on the gym floor run toward each other, jump into the air, and bump chests. Then they both stumble backward and fall to the floor on their backs. Greg lands right in front of April, Brooke Meenach, and Megan West. Brooke and Megan can't help but laugh. April just smiles, rolls her eyes, and shakes her head adoringly, all the while waving her pom-poms at the crowd.

The rain keeps pouring down throughout the day. By the time April and the rest of the Greenup cheerleaders arrive at the Greenup High field around seven-thirty P.M., the Greenup High parking lot is one big puddle. The normally grassy area around the football field stands is one big *mud* puddle. And the rain doesn't stop. Sometimes it drizzles lightly out of the cold night sky; sometimes it zips down hard.

April's mom and the man she lives with, Rick Lambert, brought April here tonight. Together, the three of them try to stay dry and warm by huddling under the narrow awning over the small concession stand behind the bleachers.

"Careful, honey," April's mother warns, "your makeup'll streak, and your hair—"

"I'm fine, Mom," April snaps. "I'll be fine."

Greg arrives carrying an umbrella, and April turns to her mother.

"I'm going to go find a seat," she says.

April takes Greg's arm, ducks under his umbrella, and walks off with him down the muddy corridor between the bleachers, toward the football field.

April and Greg have made plans to watch the game with Kelena—the other cheerleader who's in the running for homecoming queen—and Kelena's controversial boyfriend. The two couples find seats in the front row.

The rest of the Greenup cheerleaders run out onto the track between the bleachers and the field, while the small audience applauds. The cheerleaders wear stiff, bright yellow rain pants and raincoats, with their hoods pulled tightly over their heads. In keeping with Greenup homecoming tradition, the JV will cheer with the varsity tonight. Coach Berry planned to have JV member Linda Goble do some flying, but because of the rain and the girls' cumbersome gear, she has told her squad not to do any mounts or stunts. No tumbling, either. The girls will simply perform chants, chants, chants, and more chants.

For now, the cheerleaders stand, hands on hips, and wait for the football team's big entrance. Brooke Meenach breaks ranks to tighten the tie string of her hood. "I was so looking forward to this game," she says, "and now I just wanna go home."

Eventually, the football team enters. The parents and students who braved the weather cheer as enthusiastically as they can. Then the game gets under way.

From the opening kickoff, the Greenup team appears to have West Jessamine well under control. It's a sloppy game, with no passing, lots of fumbles, and slipping and sliding all over the field. The Greenup team always manages to get the better of things.

Still, it's hard for the cheerleaders or the Greenup fans to get too excited when the weather's this horrible. April, for one, looks very unhappy. She huddles between Kelena and Greg under Greg's umbrella, and frequently looks up at the scoreboard to see how much time's left before the half.

Linda Goble, Rachel Brown, Rachel Wills, and the rest of the cheerleaders keep cheering and cheering. Whenever the rain slacks off a bit, they loosen the tie strings of their hoods, and pull the suffocating yellow plastic off their heads, revealing their frizzy hair and streaking makeup. But when the rain picks up, they must tie their hoods back over their heads before they get drenched.

Halftime finally arrives, so April takes Greg's umbrella and goes off to find Rick Lambert. Greg was going to be April's escort for the homecoming queen presentation ceremony, but since their breakup Mr. Lambert agreed to escort her. Despite April's recent reconciliation with Greg, she thought it best for Mr. Lambert to accompany her tonight. Many of the homecoming candidates will be escorted by their fathers. Mr. Lambert's at least something like a male relative, although technically, he's not even her stepfather.

April and Mr. Lambert walk arm in arm, Mr. Lambert carrying the umbrella, around the fence from the bleachers to the track. There, April stands and waits at the back of the line of homecoming candidates and their escorts. She's all decked out in her slacks, blazer, and high heels, her makeup still in good shape, her hair beginning to sag. The rain slaps down onto the umbrella above her and onto the concrete track all around her.

Soon, Susi Daniels welcomes everyone to the 1997 Greenup High homecoming game and thanks the crowd for coming out to support their football team. She then turns to the homecoming candidates. One by one, she introduces the girls vying for freshman, sophomore, and junior attendant, and finally the four girls hoping to become tonight's homecoming queen.

When April hears her name, she and Mr. Lambert walk down the track to an arch made of gold-painted metal tubes interwoven with green plastic vines and white, red, and yellow plastic roses. Daniels tells the crowd of April's interests—"she enjoys cheering for the Greenup County High School cheerleaders, and hopes to cheer for the University of Kentucky someday"—and April and Mr. Lambert turn, face the audience, then walk through the arch. The umbrella doesn't fit under the arch, however, so Mr. Lambert takes the umbrella and scoots around, leaving April to walk through unprotected. As Mr. Lambert joins her on the other side, April brushes the falling water out of her face. Together, they stand and smile through the rain as April's mother and a woman from the *Greenup News-Times* take their picture.

They then step to the side and wait as Daniels introduces the last of the candidates. April fiddles with her homecoming candidate corsage, a yellow carnation held to her blazer by a thumb-sized football pin.

Daniels reveals the winner of the school-wide vote for freshman attendant. The crowd of anxious friends and parents emits a squeal. Then Daniels reads the name of the new sophomore attendant. Again the crowd erupts. The new junior attendant. The fans yell.

Daniels waits a moment for the audience to fall silent. The two football teams have returned from their locker rooms. Behind the left-hand end zone, they stand silently, their helmets protecting them from the rain, and watch the girls waiting with their escorts.

"The 1997 senior attendant—" Daniels begins, "and remember, this is the girl who's runner-up for homecoming queen—is . . . Kelena Mc-Clurg!"

The crowd cheers. April smiles, relieved—she's still in the running for queen. Then, as she feels the pressure of the coming announcement, her face clouds over. But she quickly forces a big, toothy smile, while wiggling her knee back and forth nervously. Daniels reads the name, and it's not "April Creech."

April stops wiggling her knee and keeps pushing out that smile. After a moment, she looks over at the winning girl receiving her crown, and applauds.

Rick Lambert says nothing to April. April says nothing to him. She doesn't even look at him as he walks her back around the chain-link fence to the muddy bleacher area.

There, Greg meets her.

"I wanna go," April tells him, removing herself from the crook of Mr. Lambert's arm.

Greg says okay, and the young couple walks back through the bleachers toward Greg's pickup. April's mom catches her before she leaves.

"Where're you going, honey?" she asks her daughter.

"I don't know, Mom. Greg's, I guess."

"Okay. Well, don't be out too late."

"I won't, Mom."

Like the rest of the cheerleading team, April must return to the high school at nine tomorrow morning to help decorate the auditorium for tomorrow night's homecoming dance.

After saying good-bye to her mom, April looks down at the muddy path leading out toward the parking lot. Greg offers his arm, but she ignores him, stepping carefully into the mud one heel at a time. On her second step, she slips and nearly falls. Instinctively, she catches Greg's arm and rights herself. Not taking any more chances, she walks the rest of the way steadied by her boyfriend.

Chapter Fourteen

Candy Says, Candy Says

"Susan made it sound like we were going to be coaches, so we sort of got suckered back into it," says Linda Goble, describing how the Greenup JV coach convinced her and Jessica Garthee to rejoin the junior varsity back in September.

Jessica Garthee, sitting beside Linda, laughs at the word "suckered."

Linda smiles. The two girls are sitting on brown plastic chairs in an otherwise empty dance studio at Tammy Jo's gym, where the hardwood floors are waxed and mirrors line the walls.

"Still, I wouldn't agree to it until Susan asked Jessica. I was like, 'If Jessica does it, I will.' And she was like, 'If Linda does it, I will.'"

Linda and Jessica now find themselves on the Greenup varsity. In mid-November, two weeks after homecoming and two weeks before UCA's Kentucky regionals, Coach Berry asked Linda and Jessica to move up to the big leagues.

"I think we're just gonna go to regionals with 'em," says Linda, still smiling at Jessica. "And then that's it. That's what they told us. 'Just do regionals and then you can go back on JV.' My mom thinks we got suckered again."

Jessica titters some more.

It all started when Berry told Aimee Lewis she had to call it quits. As the coach saw it, Aimee failed to put her heart into cheering. She took forever to recover from her knee injury in the spring. She's complained of all sorts of ailments that—Coach Peffer believes—"are mainly in her head." She didn't cheer at Kings Island. She hasn't once practiced full-out all year. And with regionals fast approaching, Aimee was still in no shape to cheer. Berry decided enough was enough.

Aimee's departure left Berry with eighteen girls going into regionals. UCA rules stipulate that only the girls who compete at regionals with a given team may compete with that team at nationals. And she likes to have at least nineteen girls for February's championships, twenty if possible. So Berry enlisted Linda and Jessica, girl number nineteen and girl number twenty. Now, if another cheerleader gets sick, injured, or Lord knows what else, Berry will still have plenty of bodies in Orlando.

Regionals take place in Lexington on Saturday, November 22. At the practice the previous Wednesday, the squad hits everything in the routine with pinpoint precision. The coaches carry on about how stiff and serious the varsity basketball players are when they pose for their team picture, and the girls joke between run-throughs about how senior cheerleader Libby Barber bought her boyfriend, Sam, a pet mouse for his birthday. Sam is terrified of mice.

The team's loose, easygoing air carries over into that night's tumbling practice here at Tammy Jo's. Only Linda and Jessica look tense. The two newest members of the varsity keep quiet, talking only to each other. They don't feel like part of the team. Not yet.

Linda says that only three people in the world make her feel "comfortable." Jessica's one of them. Then there's Shiritta Schaffer, whose family put up Linda when she and Shiritta cheered for Wurtland Middle School. And, of course, there's Melissa Morris, whose family gave Linda a place to stay during her ninth-grade year and hoped to provide for her indefinitely, till Mrs. Goble refused to let her move with them to Mason County.

This year, Jessica's family has picked up where the Morrises left off, carting Linda to and from cheerleading practice and letting her stay over most nights at their house.

"Me and Jessica, we've been friends since sixth grade," Linda mumbles, looking down at the dance floor and picking at the cuff of her "Greenup Cheerleader" sweatshirt. She raises her chin now and speaks up. "And when I was gonna move last year with Melissa and the Morrises, Jessica and Shiritta were the only ones that really cared. The other ones said they did, but that's just—"

Linda smiles.

"I think they wanted to cry."

Jessica throws back her head and laughs.

"At the banquet at the end of the year," Linda continues, "me and Melissa cried and then Jessica and Shiritta started to cry. And everybody was hugging us so everybody else started crying."

Laughing, Linda extends her arms toward Jessica, who's giggling uncontrollably. "Hug me!" Linda moans. "Hug me!"

As Mrs. Morris has said, Linda is a cutup. She loves to laugh, mostly because it's better than crying.

With Rachel Wills, for example, Linda laughs about the girls' shared poverty.

"We joke about it all the time," she says. "We say, 'Yeah, I'm poor.'"

Linda flashes a mischievous grin, which makes Jessica giggle again.

"'I don't got no money.'"

Linda and Jessica are both laughing now.

"We're just stupid about it."

Jessica and Linda giggle some more; then, slowly, the giggles subside till all that's left is silence. Linda looks down at the floor and picks at her sweatshirt cuff again.

"I don't like talking serious about it, 'cause I'll start crying," she says quietly.

More silence.

Linda's eyes fill with tears.

"Man. I'm gonna cry right now."

She mops her face with a swipe of her sleeve.

"But if we joke about it," she says, the corners of her mouth curling upward again, "I don't care."

Linda won't blame her parents for her troubles—neither her father, who recently got out of jail since his latest brush with the law, nor her mother, who still hasn't found a real job despite her family's poverty.

"Anytime you see me sad or anything," says Linda, "it's 'cause of money. But when I was with Melissa, that was confusing. I didn't know whether I wanted to go with them or stay here with my mom."

Linda pauses, then looks at Jessica with a grin.

"Eh, so I stayed here."

Linda laughs.

Unable to condemn her parents for the "confusing" situation she went through when the Morrises moved, Linda focuses all her bitterness and resentment on the evils of "money."

Cheerleading for Greenup County High School costs a lot of money. All cheerleaders, including those on the JV but especially those on the varsity, must sell all sorts of stuff—key chains or candy or calendars—to raise funds for the program. On top of that, each girl—or her family—has to pay for travel expenses and an endless cheerleading wardrobe including game uniforms, rain gear, sweatsuits, sweatshirts, letter jackets, ribbons, bows, shoes, pom-poms.

All that fund-raising, all those cheerleading costs, they stress Linda out.

Still, she loves to cheer. Linda says if the coaches held three two-hour practices every day after school instead of only one, it would be fine by her. She also recognizes that the program costs a lot of money, and that the money has to come from somewhere.

"But I'm fifteen," she says, "and I shouldn't be crying over money."

Linda says that the other girls on the varsity don't cry over money because—with the exception of Wills—their parents help them sell their stuff. Linda's parents don't help her. So Linda gets behind on her fundraising. Then Coach Peffer, who's in charge of the team's finances, will approach her and ask when she plans to turn in the money she's supposed to raise. Linda comes home to her parents crying, feeling helpless, poor, ashamed.

In turn, Linda's mom and dad become more and more bitter about Greenup cheerleading—particularly Coach Peffer—for putting this financial pressure on them and their daughter. Out of spite for the Greenup cheerleading program, Mr. and Mrs. Goble have now forbidden Linda to spend any of her family's money on cheerleading.

"I don't think Mr. Peffer means to look at me and say, 'You don't got no money.' But he makes me feel frustrated about money," Linda says. "And when I go home crying, I tell her it's Mr. Peffer, so my mom don't like him very much. . . .

"Anyway, I'm behind right now, I'm behind on selling candy. Jessica's mom helps her sell her candy and all this crap, and because my mom doesn't like them—I mean, she likes Candy, but she can't stand Mr. Peffer 'cause he's the one over money—she doesn't help me with money and stuff. I mean she'll give me money, but she'll say, 'Don't spend it on cheerleading.' And my dad'll give me money and say, 'Don't spend it on cheerleading.'"

When Berry and Peffer offered Linda a spot on the varsity, they told her that if she ever had any concern about money, she should simply ask them for help. Therefore, Linda has a hard time blaming the coaches or the program for pressuring her for money. And she can't blame her parents. They love her. Why else would they get so angry at Mr. Peffer when their daughter comes home from cheerleading practice crying about the fund-raising?

Ultimately, Linda places much of the blame for her monetary woes on her own slender shoulders.

"When they asked me back on the varsity, they said they'd help any way they can. And I guess I'm sort of shy and I won't go up to 'em and say, 'I need help.' I should, but I don't. It makes me feel guilty to ask. I don't like asking for help. Like Rachel Wills, she'll go up to Mr. Peffer and tell him, 'I can't do this,' or whatever. But I can't do that. I can't tell Mr. Peffer nothing. He's just like, he's not rude about it. If I tell him one day, 'I can't get the candy sold,' the next day, he'll ask me for the money. And I'm like, 'I told you yesterday I couldn't get it sold.' Sometimes I get it done, though. That's the only way to get happy I guess. . . .

"If I wasn't cheering, I'd have all the money I want."

Of course, if Linda wasn't cheering, she'd also have a lot less fun, feel a lot less productive, and as she puts it, she'd be awfully "bored."

Mrs. Morris and Melissa talk regularly with Linda and they, too, think it's good that Linda has managed to stay involved with Greenup cheerleading. They're especially glad that she's back on the varsity.

"Melissa's mom," says Linda, "she thought things for me were all bad 'cause of money and everything, and that I would've been better off staying with her and Melissa. But now that I'm back on the team, she's happy."

"Do you ever think about that, whether you would've been better off with the Morrises?"

"Yeah."

"What do you think?"

Linda looks down through her fidgeting hands with wide, glassy eyes. After a moment, she sighs.

"That I have no idea."

Linda sits there for a moment, picking at the cuff of her sweatshirt, then she tries to convince me and Jessica and herself that she's glad she stayed here in Greenup. She doesn't offer any reasons. She simply talks until there's enough distance between her and the thought of life with the Morris family. Then she's happy again.

"I'm glad I stayed here, though," she begins. " 'Cause, I mean, I came back from Mason County because Mrs. Morris asked my mom if I could go, and my mom said no, and Mrs. Morris couldn't take me out of school without my mom's permission. So Faye [Barber, a guidance counselor at Greenup High], helped Mrs. Morris get part-custody. That's why my mom really doesn't like Faye. The only reason my mom let me stay with the Morrises all that time was because of cheerleading, and she thought me and Melissa *needed* each other. 'Cause it's so boring at home. My sisters are always at work. And my brothers are always with their kids. So I'm like an only child."

Besides laughing and joking with her friends, the one thing that helps Linda forget what might have been is dancing. These days, it's her favorite part of cheerleading at Greenup High.

"When I first got into cheering," says Linda, "I liked the tumbling, but now I hate it."

"Why?"

"For JV tryouts [during the spring before her ninth grade year], all I had was a handspring back, and then, like a month into the season, I had my standing and was already doing alternates and bounders [two of the most difficult tumbling runs that high school cheerleaders do], and then I got my full [the hardest of all running tumbling, a pass that ends with a full-twist flip]. I did my full one time all by myself without nobody around me. And then I got tendonitis in both my knees. I could barely walk. It feels like arthritis, sort of. It's like behind your kneecap. I think it happened 'cause I went too fast with tumbling. That's what the doctor said. The coaches didn't push me to do it. I just did it all myself. 'Cause I liked it. Then after my knee started hurting, the coaches would expect me to do it. And I couldn't 'cause I was hurtin'. They didn't understand that. Then I started hatin' tumbling 'cause they were making me do it. Like right now, if they didn't *yell* at me, if they *believed* in me, then I could do anything. I could do my full, I know I could. But nobody ever believed in me. Tom [Pack, Greenup's gymnastics coach] believed in me sometimes, but then he'd be more concerned with Rachel Brown."

Linda wishes the Greenup coaches would be a little "nicer" in the way they push her to tumble. She says all they do is yell and be "mean."

Linda looks up from her lap with a glint in her eye that means she's about to exaggerate her point greatly.

"The coaches say, 'Come on! You can do it! Come on, you big PUSSY!'"

Jessica laughs, but Linda's bravado fades quickly and she looks down at her lap. "Oh," she says, genuinely feeling bad, "excuse my mouth." She looks me in the eye, as if to gauge my reaction, to see if I think less of her for using that word, then looks down again.

"Anyway," she says, "Candy and Mr. Peffer and them, they say stuff that makes you think, 'Oh, they believe in me because they told me to do it.' But I confuse myself, 'cause I couldn't do it if they didn't yell at me."

The only thing that makes Linda cry besides money, she says, is the tumbling. That's why she doesn't like it anymore.

Sometimes, Linda wishes she could be a flyer. She flew for the JV last year, but recently, she underwent a growth spurt and she can't "climb" anymore.

"At first when I was climbing, I was like, 'God! I hate this!' And now I want to do it. But I don't care too much 'bout that, though. I like being tall. I don't like being called short. I'd rather be tall and not a climber than short . . . Oh! And I don't base."

Linda smiles.

"I'm too weak to base, too tall to climb, so I hold signs."

In fact, Linda will be one of the varsity's four sign holders for the regional competition.

And she dances. And Linda loves the dancing. She hopes that one day she and Melissa Morris will both attend the University of Kentucky, share a dorm room, and dance on the UK dance team together. Other Greenup cheerleaders have gone on to join college dance teams, including Holly Gillum, a senior member of the 1997 Greenup national champions, who's now a freshman member of the UK dance team.

"I can't dance, if you haven't noticed," Linda says. "But I like it. I don't like real dancin'. It's too slow. I just like fast dancin'."

As for dancing with boys, Linda doesn't have much use for that, especially, she says, because she neither has a boyfriend nor expects to anytime soon. As Linda puts it, she's too "mean" to have a boyfriend.

"What do you mean when you say you're 'mean'?" I ask.

"Girls think they're in love with these guys," says Linda, "and so they have sex with 'em and let 'em do whatever they want, push 'em around, and yell at 'em, and tell 'em what to do, and tell 'em to *obey* them. One of my friends"—Linda glances sideways at Jessica—"had a boyfriend. And he told her what to wear and where she could sit in the morning and how to fix her hair."

Linda's smiling at Jessica right now, and Jessica's trying to contain her giggles by looking down at her lap and rubbing her fingers nervously.

"He wouldn't even let her wear fingernail polish, but"—Linda grins—"she's picking it off right now." Jessica stops fiddling and convulses with embarrassed laughter. Linda finishes.

"You know, *all* that crap. I told her not to do it, not to let *him* do it." Linda turns and smiles proudly at Jessica. "And she broke up with him."

"'Cause o' her," says Jessica dryly.

"But what do you mean when you say you're 'mean'?"

Linda thinks for a moment. "I wouldn't let him—"

"She don't put up with anyone's crap," Jessica puts in.

"If he told me not to wear fingernail polish," says Linda, "I would *cake* it on." She laughs. "And if he told me to wear my hair up, I'd wear it down."

"But you have a problem talking to Mr. Peffer about the fund-raising?"

"He's old!" Linda hollers. "Well, he's older. Like if an older guy, like a senior or something, if I got into a relationship with him, and thought I was in *love* with him, I'd probably be weak like Jessica was."

The Greenup coaches see a real change in Linda since her first stint with the varsity.

"The difference," says Susan Ray, "is she really wants to do it now. She's really doing it on her own. Before, she was sort of like, 'Well, I guess I want to do it.' Now, she knows she wants to do it, and she's willing to do what it takes—with her grades and the fund-raising and the transportation—to make it happen."

Linda doesn't feel as confident and powerful as Ray makes her out to be. She says she quit the varsity back in the summer because "the varsity girls didn't make me fit in" (again exonerating her parents of any responsibility they may have had). The difference now, Linda says, is she's got Jessica to stand beside her, and slowly she's beginning to feel more "comfortable" with the rest of the cheerleaders.

"I mean, I can stand the other varsity girls," Linda explains, smiling again. "But the JV, they made me feel fit right in, and the varsity weren't nice to me. Some of them were, I guess."

Linda pauses, thinks a bit.

"Of course, you might say that's the way I look at it 'cause I got a bad mental . . . attitude."

"What do you mean?"

Smiling, Linda says, "Oh, I've got low self-esteem or something like that." Linda motions toward Jessica. "That's what *she* says."

"I don't understand."

"Whenever someone looks at me," says Linda, "like Libby, she's mostly made me feel fit in this time, but the first time, she didn't know how to act around me because she didn't know if I'd bother her or not. So I guess that's why I thought, 'Oh well, she don't like me.' And just now [at tumbling practice here at Tammy Jo's], I don't know if Libby's in a bad mood or something, but I walked up to her—and I guess me and Jessica were too hyper for her—so we walked up to Libby and she was like . . ." Linda produces a dramatically scornful expression. Jessica giggles. "So I automatically thought, 'Oh, she don't like me.'

"The older girls just intimidate me," Linda adds. Then she chuckles. "Gosh! *That* was a big word."

All this self-consciousness has made it hard for Linda to let loose when she cheers. Coach Berry has tried to make her smile more. But Linda still can't muster a big, goofy, cheerleader smile. She just can't.

"I guess it's 'cause I don't fit in yet," says Linda. "I don't *feel* like I fit in yet. 'Cause I know how people talk about others. Like when Rachel Brown smiles, they're all like"—a sigh—"'Look at her. God. What is *she* doin'?' And I think people're gonna say that about me."

The last thing Linda wants is to give the other girls a reason to talk about her. She's seen how Rachel Brown has been ostracized by much of the team and she's terrified of being treated the same way. Often, her fear of what her varsity teammates think keeps her from following her instincts. And Linda has good instincts.

On the Wednesday before regionals, Miranda Elliott began to cry after a run-through in the school auditorium. Miranda crossed her arms over her chest, turned herself toward one of the side walls, and wept, but quietly.

April Creech tried to console her, rubbing her back.

The Greenup coaches didn't notice at first. Then, as Miranda began to walk back to the rest of the team, Coach Peffer saw her wiping tears from her face.

"What happened?" he asked.

"She got kicked in the titty," said April.

Miranda had helped catch April as April spiraled down out of the air after a basket toss. And April's feet whipped into Miranda's right breast.

"Oh, she got kicked in the titty," Peffer said, looking at Berry. The two coaches exchanged smirks.

Miranda tried to ignore the lingering pain and kept brushing away her tears.

Wanting to help somehow, Linda eyed her sympathetically but didn't say anything. Miranda noticed Linda watching her.

"I think I'm going to wear a padded bra," she whispered to Linda, and forced a smile.

Linda didn't know what to do. April had rubbed Miranda's back at first, but April had kicked Miranda in the first place. She was obligated.

Linda glanced from side to side. No one else had reached out to Miranda, nor were they going to. Neither would Linda.

She smiled weakly at Miranda, nodded, then turned away.

Thursday's practice goes much like those the day before. The girls and their coaches seem relaxed but focused. To begin, Berry has the team practice the various mount sequences here in the school's cramped auditorium. (The basketball team has the gym—again.) Berry's using four flyers this time around—the Kings Island trio of April Creech, Rachel Wills, and Kelena McClurg, plus Rachel Brown—though never more than three at once. At nationals, Berry must have four girls flying all at the same time to be competitive.

Only in the last couple of days has the regionals routine become so error free. Emma Hood came back to school only two weeks ago after her bout with bronchitis; at the same time, Linda Goble and Jessica Newell began the adjustment to life on the varsity. Meanwhile, Jennifer Stuart's recurring bad back, Brooke Meenach's ingrown toenail, and Aubrey Warnock's never-ending case of the flu have all made practice somewhat unproductive the past couple of weeks.

Now, the shakiest moment of the routine is hardly shaky at all. It comes at the beginning, when Rachel Brown, Wills, and April alight upon the hands of three teammates each, balance themselves on their right feet, then lean forward and pull their bent left legs up to their heads from behind. This move is called a Kerrigan because it resembles a pose that

figure skater Nancy Kerrigan struck as she glided across the ice en route to a silver medal at the 1994 Winter Olympics.

Wills falls during the first Kerrigan attempt, but April and Rachel hold theirs steady.

Kelena McClurg's grandmother, here to watch today's practice, walks into the auditorium.

Berry greets her and asks, "Have you slimmed down?"

"If I have, it's by accident."

"You look good."

"Well, I've lost my appetite recently."

Berry smiles. "I should be so lucky."

"Candy found it," Peffer jokes.

"Yeah." Berry laughs. "I found it."

Kelena's grandmother smiles and sits down on a small plastic chair on the stage beside the coaches.

The practice continues. The girls run through the second mount sequence, a group mount in which all the bases lift Kelena up in the middle of the formation, then lift Wills and April on either side. Suspended above the ground, Kelena bends over, holding a teammate's outstretched hands for support, while Wills and April each rest a foot on Kelena's back. The bases lower the three flyers a few feet and Wills and April step onto Kelena's back, switching over to the opposite sides of the formation. The team then re-creates the original pose, but with Wills and April on opposite sides of Kelena.

When Wills and April walk over her granddaughter's back, Kelena's granny grimaces and looks over with wild eyes at the coaches. Berry and Peffer don't notice. They order the girls to do the mount again.

The team pops the flyers back up into position. Wills and April step onto Kelena's back. Her grandma winces, looks frantically at the coaches. And the mount sequence ends as a mirror image of how it began.

This innovative move, called a tabletop walkover, is one of the few portions of Greenup's routine choreographed by Hank Light. Since the Kings Island competition in September, Light has been very busy with his all-star cheerleaders, and Berry, loath to beg him for help, turned over the choreography to outsiders, in particular Dave Marquez, a Californian she met through UCA. Marquez choreographed most of Greenup's regionals routine, including the dance segment, which the girls do *not* like.

"It's generic and stupid," Rachel Brown has said. "I don't know what you want to call it. It's just a stupid dance. It's a California-style-type dance—you know, 'cause the guy who taught it to us is from California. It's just like—oh, I don't know how to explain it. . . . Okay! What we do is flashy. What we like to do is the upbeat, street kinda dance. This is a look-what-they're-doin' kinda dance. Not so much flashy. It don't catch your eye. It looks like a third-grade dance. It's really easy."

And what makes a dance hard?

"The way you have to move your hips," Rachel explained, "and you know, stuff like that."

Translation: This dance isn't sexy enough for the Greenup girls. So they're not excited about performing it.

Light accepts his limited role in Greenup's regionals preparation in his typical "Que sera, sera" style. If Berry and Peffer want to use another choreographer, that's fine. Light has plenty to keep him busy, what with three all-star teams competing at the same regional competition, as well as that junior high squad from Pikeville, Kentucky, coached by his sister Lisa. Light still drives two hours to Pikeville and two hours back home at least once a week to offer her girls his expertise.

Light also has a new boyfriend. For the second time in his life, he's in love.

"All my friends think it's so funny," says Light. "Normally, I'm the Hard-Hearted Hannah, you know. And I haven't hardly gone out with anyone in almost a year."

It was eleven months ago that Light's first love jilted him. Since then, Light has kept a tight rein on his affections. But this new guy, he says, is "just exactly like me. I mean, we like the same movies, music, everything. It's amazing."

Light says he fell for his new beau in just two days. And in the past month, despite his busy schedule, hardly a day has gone by in which Light hasn't spoken with his boyfriend on the phone or seen him for lunch or had him over to his apartment for the night. The only strange thing, says Light, is that this guy has an ex for a roommate.

Light's not worried, though. He's too much in love to worry.

A few weeks ago, Light planned to take a week-long trip to Atlanta to hunt down a job there. But because he didn't want to take time away from his budding romance, he canceled. He now finds himself rethinking his desire to leave the Greenup area. He's that smitten.

Also, Light reasons, "The work at the gym [in West Virginia] has become very lucrative, *very* lucrative. I'd be stupid to leave. And with the money I'm making, I can travel wherever I want."

Suddenly, despite his avowed wanderlust, Light finds himself reclaiming Greenup as his home, and he's happy about it. He says he doesn't mind that Berry had someone else choreograph Greenup's regionals routine, but get him talking about it and he does seem to care a little. By hiring that guy from California, Berry chose to have her team perform a routine choreographed by someone other than Hank Light for the first time in seven years. Sure, Light's been awfully busy, what with the Pikeville squad and all his West Virginia all-star teams, but he would have made time for Greenup High. All Berry had to do was ask.

The Greenup girls continue to polish up their routine by going over the basket tosses at the end. After launching off their bases' hands, Rachel Brown, Kelena, and April fly up into the air, rotate their bodies with fists extended outward, then land in their teammates' waiting arms. Miranda grimaces in anticipation when she helps catch April, but this time no one gets hurt.

Susan Ray shows up with the new signs for the competition, and the team gathers around to look at them. Ray is supposed to have four signs, two that say "Go Big Green" and two that say "Beat Those Cats," all in green lettering on white boards. Berry had asked a local guy to paint the signs. And, as Susan points out with a smile—she's trying to find the humor in this—the guy painted two of the signs with a bright kelly green and the other two with a dark forest green.

"I can't believe it!" Berry raves. "How stupid do you have to be not to notice that they're different colors?"

"But he was so nice," Susan says. "He doesn't know nothing about cheerleading. He paints cars for a living."

"I can't believe it."

"He really had no idea," says Susan. "He handed them to me and he was on the phone, and I looked at them and you know my stomach dropped. I didn't know what to do. Then he put his hand on the phone and told me they were free. He really was so nice. So I just left."

"You didn't say anything?" Berry shrieks.

"No."

"I can't believe it."

"Once, at Russell," says a grinning April Creech, "we made signs with markers and glitter for Kings Island. It was baaad."

"Well, this isn't Russell," Berry snaps.

"Oh, I know," says April, taken aback.

After looking the signs over and trying to evaluate just how *awful* they'll look, Berry, Peffer, and Ray decide they should scrap them and find someone to make new ones. They need the signs done on the double, however. The Greenup squad is leaving school the next day, Friday, at one in the afternoon.

Peffer suggests Greenup's art teacher, and that sounds good to Berry. Peffer trots out of the auditorium to call the art teacher at home. Meanwhile, Berry tells the girls to take a break till he returns.

April walks up to Greg, who's been here watching the practice from the stage.

"Do you have any change?" she asks him.

"Nope. No change."

"Then give me a dollar."

With a melodramatic sigh, Greg digs into one of his jeans pockets and comes up with a dollar bill.

"You gonna stick around till the end?" April asks.

"No, I'm goin' home."

"Just stay and you can go home with me."

"That's not till five-thirty. I'm not stayin' here a whole hour. I been here long enough already."

April and Greg keep bantering as they walk out of the auditorium to buy April a soda.

Meanwhile, Candace Adkins and Aubrey Warnock tease their coach by telling her some dirty jokes they've found on the Internet.

"If your left leg is Easter and your right leg is Christmas," Candace says, "can I come up between the holidays?"

"Oh, Candace!" says Berry, laughing.

"Do you like chicken?" Aubrey asks.

"What?" Berry says, trying not to be taken in.

"Do you *like* chicken? Say yes."

"Yes."

"Well, if I can have a breast, you can have a wing."

"Oh, girls, that's awful!" says Berry, laughing some more. She glances over at Kelena's grandmother. "You-all are terrible."

"Candace," says Rachel Brown, "tell her the one about flossing."

Berry throws up her hands, still laughing. "No! I don't want to hear it. I don't want to hear it. You girls are awful."

Candace doesn't tell Berry the one about flossing, but she does tell her how she's managed to miss almost half a day of school—with Berry's help.

"I told my mom," Candace explains, "that 'Candy says I have to get my hair done before regionals so I have to.' Now I've got a hair appointment tomorrow morning in Huntington. It's gonna take two and a half hours!"

"Well, I did say I'd like you to do something about those roots," Berry says, citing the one part of Candace's shoulder-length hair that isn't bleached blond. "I'll give you that."

"Anytime I say, 'Candy says,'" Candace continues, "my mom, she'll do it. She won't do it if I don't say, 'Candy says.'"

"Next thing she's gonna say," Wills adds, "is 'Candy says I have to have this outfit. I just have to 'cause Candy says.'"

The rest of the girls all come up with their own "Candy says" jokes.

"Candy says I can't come home till four in the morning."

"Candy says I have to have these earrings."

"Candy says I have to have my own car."

"All right, all right," says Berry, laughing along. "Come on, let's get back to work."

Berry adores this group of Greenup cheerleaders, even if they are a little young, a bit immature, a tad irreverent, and even if they don't always treat each other as nicely as they could. But Berry feels frustrated by the girls' stubborn refusal to do as she says. The Greenup cheerleaders joke about the power that "Candy says" has over their parents, but the girls don't feel the strength of the coach's wisdom themselves. Despite her constant nudging, the cheerleaders won't ditch their loser boyfriends when they cheat, don't put a premium on female friendship, rarely practice as hard as they can, and refuse to believe in themselves.

April and Greg walk back into the auditorium with Coach Peffer. Greg has decided to stick around till the end of practice. Peffer tells Berry that the school art teacher has agreed to make the signs.

As Berry barks orders at the girls, Greg and Peffer sit down near Susan Ray.

"Hey," says Greg, "where are these regionals gonna be?"

"At UK," Peffer answers. "At Memorial Coliseum."

"I never heard of Memorial Coliseum," Greg says, confused.

"It's the one that came before Rupp Arena," Peffer explains. "It's where the boys' team practices now, and where the girls' team has games."

Greg chuckles.

"Boy," he says, "the girls get screwed every time, don't they?"

"Yes," says Peffer, turning away from Greg to watch the Greenup cheerleaders practice their routine. "Yes, they do."

At Memorial Coliseum the following Saturday morning, Rachel Brown practices a liberty amid a swarm of cheerleaders from all over Kentucky. Jennifer Morgan watches intently.

"Rachel's good during practice," Shmorg says to Sarah Dickison. "But in front of people, she tries too hard."

Somehow, Shmorg can't see that all Rachel needs is the support and acceptance of her teammates. If Rachel had that, she'd have no reason to try "too hard."

It's ten-thirty on Saturday morning, and the Greenup team has been here for over an hour, warming up, getting ready. Girls in brightly colored uniforms cover the basketball court where the UK Lady Wildcats play their games. As Peffer told Greg, it's an outdated stadium, with only two decks of bleachers on either side of the court, starting down on the floor and rising to the dimly lit rafters. Banners line the walls, paying homage to the national championship boys' teams that played here in the forties and fifties. The vision of hundreds of cheerleaders, crammed skirt to skirt, practicing the important, worrisome portions of their competitive routines, clashes somehow with the antique boys' basketball banners.

Hank Light is here, but he's not with the Greenup varsity. He's working with his junior and senior all-star squads, making sure everything is just so. Berry and Peffer are off fussing with the team's music—there's an issue over its speed—so the Greenup girls are left to their own devices. Diligently, they work on everything they can think of.

Linda Goble, who's not involved with any of the mounts, paces back and forth, arms folded, and watches her teammates practice. Every so often, she stops pacing to chew on her fingernails.

Rachel Brown has her bases hoist her up into that liberty again, then spins down into her teammates' arms.

"That looks good," says Wills, watching from the floor.

But Rachel doesn't seem to hear her. After months of enduring her teammates' criticisms, wanting desperately to turn them into compliments, Rachel now cheers in an isolated world, where none of the other cheerleaders may enter—even if, like Wills, they simply want to tell her something nice.

Wills turns away from Rachel. Then, with her nostrils flared, her teeth bared, she stands on the gym floor and practices her Kerrigan pose.

Jessica Newell walks up to Wills and grabs her face, trying to force her lips into a smile. Wills lets the Kerrigan pose go and laughs, revealing her shiny metal braces.

Most of the girls believe that Rachel Brown is too self-conscious, maybe self-absorbed, and that Wills is not self-conscious enough, maybe clumsy.

"Boy," says Sarah Dickison, "Wills is so skinny. And *bony*."

"Have you seen her mother?" Susan Ray says. "Her mother's really small. She's really, you know, petite."

"Isn't something wrong with her?"

"I'm not for sure."

At that moment, Berry and Peffer return from the Memorial Coliseum sound booth, audiotape in hand.

"Let's go, girls," says Berry. "Come with me."

The twenty uniformed girls follow Berry up the bleachers to a deserted hallway behind the stands. Light, having taken a break from his work with the all-stars, follows them.

"All right, girls," says Peffer crisply, "come listen to the music. There's no speed controls on the system they've got here, so if it's too fast or too slow, you've just got to do it the way it is. Okay?"

Peffer slides the tape into a small boom box and hits Play. The girls stare at the little tape player and listen to the music pound away. Some of them do the routine's dance moves along with the music, trying to get a feel for the tape's speed. Eventually, the music ends and the girls look blankly at one another.

"Line up," says Berry. "Let's do it."

The cheerleaders practice their dance there in the hallway of UK's Memorial Coliseum. It has no pelvic thrusts, no hip rotations, just sharp, asexual arm and leg movements.

"This has got to be clean," says Berry. "Keep it clean."

"I hope you know I did *not* choreograph this dance," Light whispers to me, his arms crossed tightly over his chest.

"I know."

Light smiles. "Good."

"I think the music's too slow," says Jennifer Stuart.

"No," says Berry. "It is what it is. If it's slow, you've just got to dance slow."

Inside the arena, the competition has started. The all-star teams will perform first, then the high school squads, with the all-girls large varsity—that's Greenup's category—slated for the very end.

The Greenup cheerleaders want to go inside and watch. Before letting them go, however, Berry gathers her girls together so she can say a little something to keep them focused.

"This past Wednesday," Berry begins, "during tumbling at Tammy Jo's, I overheard some woman telling someone that the varsity Greenup cheerleaders aren't as good this year as they are most years. 'They're sloppier,' she said. 'They make more mistakes.' That's what some people think about you-all."

"Who was it?" Wills asks bitterly.

"Oh, I don't know," says Berry.

"That makes me so mad," Miranda says.

The rest of the girls talk among themselves, angry and hurt that someone would say such a thing. Rachel Brown stands alone with her hands on her hips and the muscles in her cheeks flexing. Only Linda and Jessica seem unconcerned.

Light leans over to me and whispers, "Candy might just be making that up."

The Greenup girls, perfectly pissed now, walk back into the arena, where they meet up with Shawnda Bates.

Shawnda has come here with one of her cheerleading friends from the University of Louisville. The friend, Kristie, led cheers at a high school in Syracuse, New York, and she's always worshiped the amazing cheerleaders from Greenup County, so she and Shawnda drove an hour from Louisville to be here for regionals and to see Greenup perform in person.

After introducing Kristie to the team, Shawnda takes a seat among the good old Greenup entourage and watches the all-star competition.

Whenever one of Light's West Virginia teams takes the big blue mat placed in the middle of the basketball court, the Greenup girls stand and cheer loudly. The youth all-stars are on first, then the juniors.

Finally, it's time for Light's senior all-stars to do their thing. The announcer intones, "And now, from Hurricane, West Virginia, the Valley Senior All Stars, coached by Hank Light!"

Berry smiles.

"Did you hear that?" says Susan Ray. "They said his name."

Berry, smiling still, closes her eyes and nods.

Ray laughs. "They didn't do that for anyone else, did they?"

Wearing that wry smile, her eyes shut tight, Berry shakes her head.

As the high school portion of the competition nears, Berry tells the Greenup girls to put on their skirts. Standing up from the bleachers, the girls take off their white shorts and put on their skirts, leaving little balls of masking tape all over the floor.

Berry then herds the girls back up to the empty hallway behind the stands. There, she has the team go through the dance once more, as well as a few of the stunts. Together, April Creech and Rachel Brown practice their liberties. Rachel teeters a bit and has to dismount early.

Back on the ground, she talks nervously with her bases about what exactly went wrong.

"I got to pee like a racehorse," blurts Brooke Meenach.

"That's nice," Berry says.

Brooke skips down the hall to a bathroom.

The large varsity category is almost up now. There are only five teams, with Greenup scheduled last. When Brooke returns from the restroom, Berry leads the cheerleaders back into the coliseum and on down the bleachers to the gym floor. Standing beside the regulation mat, the girls will watch their competition perform.

The cheerleaders from Henry Clay High School go first. Based here in Lexington, Henry Clay won third place at last year's nationals with one of the few clean routines of the finals.

"I'm so nervous," says Megan West, her left leg bending and straightening and bending and straightening, "that I can hardly stand still."

As Henry Clay performs, the Greenup girls watch, their hard faces immobile.

Henry Clay looks tough. They have no noticeable errors and their hometown fans go nuts throughout the entire routine.

The Greenup girls look at each other, purse their lips, and raise their eyebrows. They've got their work cut out for them.

A mediocre squad from Pleasure Ridge Park High School performs next. They're easier for the Greenup girls to watch. The Musketeers even applaud Pleasure Ridge Park and cheer along during the call-and-response portion of the routine.

Next comes Paul Lawrence Dunbar, another Lexington school. Dunbar won nationals three years ago and placed second behind Greenup at this year's Kings Island competition. Tension winds up tight within each of the Greenup girls as the Dunbar team prances onto the mat.

Dunbar puts on an interesting, exciting routine. During the opening tumbling, four girls twice turn tumbling passes that end with full-twist flips. Thus they appear to have eight full twists. Greenup has five girls who will attempt full twists, but they'll only do it once each. Later, the Dunbar squad lifts three girls up into heel stretches, then lowers them and raises three more girls into heel stretches. That's six different girls with heel stretches. Impressive.

Dunbar's hometown fans cheer nonstop, raising their voices to ear-piercing crescendos after every one of the squad's showstopping tricks.

All the while, the Greenup girls hold their collective breath. They don't move. They don't blink.

At the end of Dunbar's routine, one girl drops down out of a stunt a beat early. A few of the Greenup girls breathe easy. Some smile at the slight bobble.

There's one more team—from Lafayette High School—before Greenup finishes things up.

The Greenup girls get into a huddle and say the Lord's Prayer, their arms wrapped around one another, their heads bowed. They appear to go through this team ritual rather automatically, however, without feeling the sense of unity that the huddle and the prayer have meant in the past. When they break the huddle, they turn away from one another, each thinking about the upcoming performance on her own. While Lafayette performs, the Musketeer cheerleaders pace back and forth, some with their hands on their hips, some shaking their arms in the air, trying to get their bodies—and their minds—loosened up.

Lafayette finishes.

Tom Pack raises his hand to high-five Rachel Brown. Rachel, her eyes unfocused, doesn't notice at first; then she dispassionately raises her own hand for Pack to slap.

Wills forces a big metal-mouth smile.

Linda Goble grips her "Go Big Green" sign.

April Creech smiles happily.

The announcer makes his introductions, and the Greenup girls spring onto the mat. Rachel Brown hits both of her standing back tucks. Wills's Kerrigan wobbles ever so slightly, but she holds on. The tabletop walkover draws oohs and aahs from the crowd. And the dance is sufficiently crisp.

The only misstep is slight: after her second standing, Miranda stumbles a hair.

There's zero energy, however. Rachel Brown flashes an over-the-top grin, but no one else does. April Creech's smile fades as soon as the routine begins, and Linda Goble looks almost unhappy out there. The rest of the team cheer as though they're back at the Greenup High auditorium, like it's just another boring run-through. Meanwhile, the paltry collection of Greenup boosters make precious little noise, even though they drove two and half hours from Greenup County to be here.

After the girls skip off the mat, Berry doesn't wait for them to catch their breath. She quickly leads the squad up the bleachers to the hallway behind the stands.

There, away from the crowds, away from the judges tabulating the scores, the Greenup girls gather around their coach. With tired, confused faces, they look to her for an explanation of what just happened. They are now ready to hear what Candy says.

Berry breathes in.

"Girls, I thought it was sluggish. It was very clean. You hit everything right on. But it didn't have the excitement. So I don't think you're going to win."

The cheerleaders look at one another silently, with wide, forlorn eyes. Tears roll down Sarah Dickison's cheeks, and occasionally she sniffles.

"I think Dunbar's going to win," Berry continues, "and you're going to get second or third."

Libby's eyes are watering now.

Rachel Brown shows no emotion whatsoever. Wills has moved over so she can rub Sarah's back. April has an arm around Libby. Linda Goble stands with her arms folded and chews at the inside of her lower lip.

"But that's okay," Berry continues. "Four years ago, Shawnda's freshman year, we got fifth at regionals and then won nationals. You hit *everything*. But you really didn't, you just didn't show . . . You've got to take *pride* in what you do, and *show* that, *show* that pride. And you know, our fans weren't as loud as I'd have liked. I mean, when Dunbar hit those stretches, their parents went crazy. When you-all hit your mounts, our parents were like, 'yaaay . . .'

"But look, we can come back from this! I've told everyone all year: this year's group has as much ability as last year's. You just haven't shown that inner drive. You've *got* to take it to the next level. *Now*. You've got to demand as much from yourself as you can give. I'm sure some of you think you've been doing as much as you can. But you haven't. You *haven't*. Not *one* of you has given as much to this team as you can. From *now* on, there can't be any more of these aches and pains, these runny noses. I *won't* take it. Not anymore. If you're sick, if you're hurt, you're going to have to suck it up. And if you miss a practice, you're off the team. I don't care if you're *dying*, you better make it to practice."

The girls listen to Berry intently. With every word she utters, their faces become more drawn, and their eyes turn a deeper shade of red.

"But you've got nothing to be ashamed of. We've just got to take it to that next level. And girls, you're going to have to get those heel stretches. Wills, you've got to start stretching out your hamstrings every chance you get, before you go to bed, when you shower, when you get up in the morning. You saw Dunbar's stretches. We've *got* to have those for nationals."

As Berry thought they might, the Greenup cheerleaders took third at regionals, behind first-place Dunbar and second-place Henry Clay. All of Light's all-star squads won first place in their respective divisions.

During the awards ceremony, Light and Berry sat together on the Memorial Coliseum bleachers and watched the Greenup girls await the worst.

"It's such a shame we're losing April Creech," Berry commented. "We could really use her come nationals."

"What?" said Light.

"Susan didn't tell you?" Berry said, turning toward him.

"No. What?"

"April's pregnant. She just found out this week."

Hank stared at Berry in stunned silence.

"Yeah," said Berry, "so now she's quitting the team to have the baby."

Nationals 'Ninety-Eight

Chapter Fifteen

Because . . .
I Don't Know Why

On a Monday, with regionals less than a week away, April's doctor told her that conception probably occurred in late October, around the time of homecoming weekend.

The day before, April and her mom drove to the only pharmacy in the town of Greenup—the only pharmacy within twenty miles of their home—and bought a home pregnancy test. April's mom was worried. Her daughter's period was nearly a month late at that point, and April had been experiencing severe nausea and exhaustion for over two weeks. April's mom knew that Greg and her daughter had begun having sex the previous summer, and she'd always meant to take April to a doctor to get her a prescription for birth control pills, but somehow she and April never got around to it.

April, meanwhile, wasn't all that concerned. She thought her mother was being overprotective. "I was late once before, and I never had any problems after that. Till this time. And we didn't really worry about it, really, 'cause we thought maybe I was just . . ."

April's thoughts drift. It's now mid-January 1998, and April's been off the cheerleading team for over a month and a half. She's sitting in the middle of the big old yellow-and-brown plaid sofa that rests along the wood-paneled wall of her family's den. Greg's lying down on the sofa with his head propped up at one end and his legs draped over April's lap. A small black-and-white TV attached to a VCR mutters softly from across

the room. Greg's watching a tape of *Weekend at Bernie's*. An ironing board
stands next to the sofa behind his head.

"I had been really, really sick a lot before regionals and my tumbling was
really, really bad," April continues. "Yeah, it was *really* bad. I had even fallen
on a roundoff–back handspring. But, I mean, I didn't freak out. I was sick
and thought there was something wrong, but I thought, maybe, you know,
I was just getting sick or something. I had been late before when I was
cheerin' and the doctor had said it was normal for an athlete like I was. He
said there were times when I could miss a whole month or two because I
was practicing so much and my body was worn down and stuff. So I
thought maybe that was it, for a little bit, but then . . . I guess not."

April laughs.

To take the pregnancy test that Sunday before regionals, April first had
to pee into a plastic cup. Then, using the dropper from the kit, her mom
applied a few droplets of April's urine to the little plastic tester. Mother
and daughter waited. Immediately, a thin blue line appeared on the white
rectangle. That was normal. The appearance of a single blue line meant
the test was working properly. But after a couple of minutes passed, a second blue line began to surface.

"Watching it turn to positive was just weird," says April, talking low. "I
was just really nervous. My mom was right there with me, too. And I was
going, 'Mom, it's positive.' And she's going like, 'Time's not up yet. Time's
not up yet. It could change.' And I was like, 'No, Mom.' And when the
timer went off, she just . . . cried. The whole first week she cried a lot. And
was upset. I thought she'd kill me. I thought my stepdad—well, he's gonna
be my stepdad finally, they're gettin' married this coming Valentine's—I
thought he would kill me, too. But he was just like, 'I'm sorry it happened
so soon, 'cause you're so young.' They were both really supportive about it.
And now, my mom's real excited about it. I guess."

"Did you cry, too?"

"Yeah. I guess it was not because I was upset though. It was just *shock*.
'Cause I wasn't expecting it. And, well, we're happy now, I guess. It was
just a shock at first."

While her mom cried, April wiped her own tears aside. She felt that
she had to get the news to Greg right away, so she phoned him at Giovanni's, where he was delivering pizzas that afternoon. April told Greg
right then and there over the phone.

"I was just surprised," Greg mumbles, his eyes on *Weekend at Bernie's*.

April laughs through her nose.

"I called him at work and I told him," she says, smiling wide, "and he was like, 'Really?'" April laughs at her droll impression of her boyfriend. "That was all he said. 'Really?'"

Neither Greg nor April nor either of their mothers ever seriously considered abortion. One of the only people who mentioned the idea to April was Candy Berry.

Berry knows firsthand how a high school pregnancy can limit a girl's life.

"Candy was really . . ." April stutters. "She tried . . . She told me I had an option. She told me I would be missed and everything. But I didn't want to get rid of it. Candy was real helpful. She told me that if I needed anything, I could come to her. And she said it's great to have a kid but it's also hard. It was like she *understood* what I was going through. . . .

"My grandma, on my dad's side, she was not very supportive at first . . . 'cause she was worried about my health and me going through a pregnancy and stuff like that. And she really wanted me to cheer. But nobody else said anything like that. I don't see my dad ever." April chuckles. "So it's not like he said anything about it."

Asked whether she misses cheerleading, April has trouble answering. Looking down at Greg's knees resting in her lap, she speaks haltingly, in a hushed tone, hardly audible over the TV. She wants to feel hopeful about her life now—with Greg, with a baby due in six months, without cheerleading. But she's got to be honest with herself. When she and her family moved from Russell to Greenup last summer, this wasn't how she planned to finish high school.

"Sometimes . . . I miss cheerin'," she says. "I been cheerin' so long that I think I was getting tired of it. I was just going to finish up my senior year, but . . . And I was going to . . . consider cheerin' in college. But . . . I don't think so now. There's . . . I might still . . . maybe just a little bit. But I don't think I will . . . be able to."

"Have you thought much about the team now that nationals are coming up?"

"A little bit . . . I think it'll be worse if they win. . . . I think I'll be upset then. . . . But . . . but I hope they do win."

"I hope they bomb," Greg mutters without moving anything but his lips.

April smiles. She seems to find his harsh honesty endearing.

"Whenever I'm not with him, I'm with my mom," she says, looking up, "so between the two of them, they keep me busy. And we got to hear the baby's heartbeat last Thursday, and that was really neat. But I haven't been able to feel anything, it moving or anything, yet. . . .

"They told me I could be active, but I'm not."

April raises her arms like a game show model, to better display the sofa, her sitting on it, and Greg lounging on top of her.

"This is all I do."

April has all the credits she needs to graduate, so she's not taking any real classes this semester. Instead, she shuffles papers a few hours a day as a teacher's aide and an office aide.

The only friend April has made off of the cheerleading team—apart from Greg—is Amanda Dean, who had to quit the Greenup varsity cheer team in the middle of the competitive season back in the fall of 1996, Amanda's junior year. She's offered to go walking with April once the weather warms up.

"That'll help," says April with a sigh. "Meanwhile, I just sit around the house. . . ."

She thinks a bit. "I always had a set schedule. I knew what I was going to do, every day, at about three-thirty. Now, I'm just like, 'I don't know what I want to do.' Sometimes, I set in my house so much that I'm just like, 'Oh God! I have to do something. I hate this!' My mom, usually— when Greg's at work—me and her will go do things. We go shopping and go looking for baby stuff. Tomorrow, we're gonna go looking for a prom dress and tonight, we're gonna look for baby stuff. And I go to my grandma's a lot just to get out of *this* house."

For the first time, Greg turns away from his movie and looks up at me.

"I was mad when her grandmother said something," he says emphatically. "I was mad when Candy said something, too."

Greg wants to return the conversation to the topic of abortion.

"What exactly made you mad?"

"The fact of it," Greg growls. "It [having an abortion] wouldn't go over really good with my family."

"My family, too," says April, adjusting quickly to the new subject. "My mom doesn't believe in it. She probably would have supported both of us if that was our choice, but—"

"My mom would have been against it," Greg interrupts.

April waits a moment to make sure Greg is finished. "Even if we weren't ready for the baby," she says, "I would have still had it, and given it up for adoption or something. I would never have killed it. But we're both happy, so . . ."

April looks down at Greg, who has returned his gaze to *Weekend at Bernie's.*

"So we're gonna keep it."

April and Greg first had sex out at his house on Route 7, a two-lane road that wanders around the hilly north-central expanse of the county. That was back in late July, not long after Greg proposed to April and gave her that diamond engagement ring.

"He was my first," says April.

Greg's mom immediately figured out what was going on and told April's mom. April's mom didn't get angry with her daughter. Rather, she sat April and Greg down and talked with them about the importance of being "careful." And she promised to take April to a doctor for birth control pills.

"I just kept puttin' it off and puttin' it off because . . ." April shrugs and laughs nervously. "I don't know why."

The first few times, April says, Greg wore a condom, but then he just stopped.

I ask why.

April looks at Greg watching the movie, but he says nothing. Greg isn't ignoring the question. He doesn't have an answer.

"Do you think condoms are sort of a pain to deal with?" I ask.

April looks hard at Greg's face. He takes a deep breath.

"Not really," he mumbles, barely audible.

April turns her gaze up toward the ironing board behind Greg's head.

"Not really," she echoes.

From August through November, nearly four months, Greg and April had regular, unprotected sex.

"That's not very long," says April, pleadingly. "It was just a little accident, I guess."

April's not the only girl at Greenup County High School carrying a child. Aimee Lewis, a onetime varsity cheerleader who won a national championship with the 1997 squad, got pregnant in December, within a month of leaving the team. Aimee's fifteen years old; she's due in August.

Then there's Greg's sister, Tiffany, a seventeen year-old senior, and Greg's stepsister Jama, nineteen, who are also both due this summer, around the same time as April.

Greg and April say they know at least eight pregnant girls at the high school. They also know another three who, like Amanda Dean, have already had a baby.

"It's in the water," Greg says.

"It really is," April says, nodding. "So I guess it's just a normal thing now." She says a number of girls on the varsity cheerleading team have had scares—late periods and so forth. "Their parents really don't know [they're having sex], so they can't get on birth control."

"Their parents would go crazy," says Greg.

"What happened to me, it'll probably happen eventually to some of them, too," April concludes.

April insists that's not such a bad thing. She says she's looking forward to being a mother. She'd planned on it happening at some point, anyway. This is a little sooner than expected. That's all.

Greg, meanwhile, is very excited about becoming a dad.

"He wants a boy really, really bad," says April. "At Christmas time, he put on all the packages, 'From Greg and his son.' So he really wants a boy. But I don't care either way, just as long as it's healthy."

In the second week of February, three months into her pregnancy, April will have a routine ultrasound examination. At that time, she and Greg can learn the baby's sex. The Greenup varsity will have just finished competing in the national cheerleading championships in Orlando, and will be enjoying a day of fun at Disney World's Magic Kingdom while April lies back in her obstetrician's exam room, has a nurse rub petroleum jelly on her abdomen, and then watches as the child growing inside her appears on a nearby video monitor.

"Greg sorta wants to be surprised," says April. "But I want to find out [whether it's a boy or a girl]. Because my mom, after we find out, she's gonna do the baby room and stuff. I have the whole upstairs to myself and there's an extra room, and it used to be my brother's room—he called it the drawing room because he loves to draw—it's gonna be the baby room. So my mom is lookin' for stuff for it. She's gonna decorate it. She's real excited about that."

If the baby is a boy, Greg and April plan to name it Zachary Austin, and if it's a girl, Katelyn Melissa.

"How would you spell 'Katelyn'?" I ask.

"We're not sure yet," says April, smiling.

"Probably the normal way," Greg says. He spells out his version of the normal way.

"Yeah," April says, "probably the normal way. Because I thought if we spell it different, then later on, if she couldn't find something with her name on it, you know, that'd be bad, so . . ."

"How'd you think of the names?"

"He picked out the boy name," says April, "and, well, he basically picked out the names and I was just like, 'Okay.'"

"They're just names that nobody else in the family's got," Greg says.

Greg and April were planning a summer wedding to take place shortly after high school graduation. But since learning of April's pregnancy, they've put all that on hold. They don't have the resources to start their own home and support a newborn child. So they plan to keep living at their respective parents' houses after the baby's born while they both attend college near Greenup.

April, who'd hoped to attend the University of Kentucky in Lexington, cheer for the national champion UK cheerleaders, and train for a career as a physical therapist, now says she wants to get college "over with" and has limited her career plans to the job of pharmacist. There's a school over in Ironton, Ohio, an extension of Ohio State University, that has a three-year pharmacy program. That, she says, would be perfect.

April also thought she might live in a bigger city one day. She'd gotten a taste of big-city life when she spent her middle school years in Lexington, and she'd always looked forward to going back.

"We had talked about going to Lexington," April concedes, "but not now that we've got the baby and stuff."

"I told her I don't want to leave Greenup," Greg says.

"Yeah," says April with a sigh, "he don't want to leave."

"I don't know why," Greg says. "I just been here so long."

"I used to live in Lexington," April reminds me—and maybe Greg. "So it wouldn't be that big of a deal for me."

Not to be outdone, Greg says, "We went to live in Lexington for five months once, but we came back."

"So it'll probably be some place around here," April says. "'Cause all our family lives around here, so . . ."

"Yeah," says Greg, "my grandparents offered me some land up in Boyd

County. So I wanna build a house up there. It's way out there, out in the country."

April's not terribly excited about that. "It's *real* far out," she says.

Greg and April say it wasn't that hard dating while she was on the cheerleading team. Despite all the time and energy she put into the squad, she still had plenty left over for Greg.

One thing irked Greg, however: "It didn't bother me how much she practiced," he says, "*unless* she whined when she got home."

April laughs uncomfortably.

"Every day, she'd have something to say about practice. It got aggravating after a while. She'd be whining about how tired she was and how much Candy yelled at her. It'd just be every day."

"What about that was aggravating?"

"Just listening to it. It was just every day. All day long."

"It was not," says April softly, looking down.

Greg went to most of April's cheerleading practices at the high school, and to most of the football and basketball games she cheered at, except for a few of the away games.

"Those times, I'd stay here and go and shoot pool," he says.

"It was frustrating," says April, talking about the times Greg didn't come to her practices or her performances, "because I was there and I didn't know what he was doing. He coulda been doing anything and I wouldn't know about it. He knew exactly where I was, he knew I'd be cheering, but he coulda been doing anything."

"What could he be doing?"

Silence. April looks at Greg.

"Just getting into trouble," Greg says.

"What sort of trouble?"

"Just certain people that I used to hang out with used to get me in trouble."

"Yeah," April says, now that Greg's opened up the subject, "they're not very nice people to hang out with."

"It's not that they're not nice people. It's that certain things they'd do would get me in trouble."

"Yeah," says April. "But I stopped that, so . . ."

"What sort of things would you do with them?" I ask Greg.

"Gettin' high, drinkin' . . . chasin' girls. That's about it. That's how I always got into trouble. Since my freshman year."

"He hung out with mean people," April says. "They just, they just don't have any respect for girls at all."

"Some of 'em did."

"They just didn't care how they treated girls. They'd cheat on 'em, they'd yell at 'em. It was baaad. So he'd be like, 'I'm going out with these people,' and I'd be like, 'Oh, God.' "

"They're all right with me," Greg says. "I don't care."

"Do you think you're like them?" I ask.

Greg thinks a moment.

"No," he says. "Not anymore."

"He used to," April says, "before we were together."

Greg's no dummy. It didn't take much for him to put April ahead of his shiftless buddies. But it took April getting pregnant for her to put Greg ahead of cheerleading.

"I told her a few times," says Greg, "I wished she'd quit. Man, I mean I was there [at cheerleading practices and performances] as much as she was."

"What did you say to that?" I ask April.

"I was just like, 'I can't quit.' "

"I thought it would make it easier to have her off the team," Greg says. "But it hasn't." Greg smiles slyly at April. "I still do as much running for her now as I ever did."

April giggles.

"He would pick me up and take me to games and everything," she says. "I'd call him early in the morning and make him take me to Saturday practices. Now, he's got to take me to the doctor's and over to my grandma's and every other thing."

April's pregnancy hasn't changed Greg's life much at all.

Chapter Sixteen

Psychological Warfare

It's early afternoon on Thursday, January 15, twenty-three days before the start of UCA's 1998 national high school cheerleading championships in Orlando, Florida.

April Creech's pregnancy is old, depressing news now, and the Greenup girls don't want to dwell on it. They've got too much else to think about if they're going to win another national title. Without April, Candy Berry has had to find a fourth flyer to join Kelena McClurg, Rachel Wills, and Rachel Brown. So she's decided to add sophomore Sarah Dickison.

Sarah has never been a flyer before, not in competitions or games or anything. She's got the perfect build for it—short, light, strong. At cheer camp back in the summer, she won a push-up competition against sixty-some other girls from throughout Kentucky, by doing fifty-four push-ups in a minute. She's probably the second-best tumbler on this year's team, next to senior Libby Barber. But she's always resisted flying because it scares her. Berry tried to get her to fly last year, when Sarah was one of just two freshmen on the varsity. When Sarah refused, Berry let it go. After the coach learned of April's pregnancy, though, she told Sarah that she had to overcome her fear of flying once and for all.

Here in the Greenup High auditorium, Sarah's three bases hoist her up over their heads while the rest of the Greenup team watches. The Greenup girls stand all around Sarah, their hands stretched up and out toward her, ready to catch her if she falls. During these crucial practices three weeks before nationals, Sarah and the other flyers will fall and fall and fall while they and their bases learn to hold the team's stunts upright. The previous day, Amanda Kitchen, one of the squad's strongest bases, fell backward after Kelena crashed down onto her. Amanda felt a sharp pain in her lower back after that, so today she's at the doctor's office, getting herself checked out.

Hank Light stands in for Amanda now, helping lift the petrified Sarah up into the air. Candy Berry appreciates his help, but she doesn't want to keep him in the routine for too long. If Berry loses Amanda for a protracted period of practice time, or even for the competition itself, then Greenup's whole nationals program might fall apart. As Susan Ray says, "Candy's stressed."

The routine's opening tumbling poses another problem. It's been sluggish, inconsistent. Linda Goble, one of the team's strongest tumblers, still isn't hitting her bounders tumbling run with much consistency. Five other girls are slated to turn bounders in the nationals routine, and a few of them scare Berry with their inability to hit the treacherous front handspring to a whip-back to a back tuck. Brooke Meenach still has pain in that big toe with the ingrown nail. Often, the toe happens to hit the floor awkwardly, causing pain to shoot up through her leg, and she'll pull up in the middle of a run. And again, there's Amanda Kitchen. Assuming she can compete at nationals, will her back be healthy enough for her to hit her bounders?

Rachel Wills, no matter how hard she tries, can't get herself limber enough to do a decent heel-stretch. She's working on it here in the auditorium. Her three bases hold her aloft while Coach Light and the rest of the team brace themselves all around her in case she falls. Wills balances on her bases' hands with her right foot, then struggles to lift her left foot up over her head. She sticks her tongue out through a scowling mouth and pulls on her left toe, desperately forcing her tight hamstring muscles to loosen. But she can't get her left foot up above her waist without bending forward.

"Stand up straight," yells Light. "Bring your foot to you, not you to your foot."

Wills teeters to her right, then falls lightly into her teammates' hands.

Ever since school started back in September, Wills has spent a half-hour every night before she goes to bed and a half-hour before she showers in the morning stretching out her hamstrings, the muscles in the back of her thighs that must be loose if she's to perform a heel stretch.

"It doesn't help," says Wills. "It wasn't that hard for me until, I think, I overstretched it. Now, it's to where I can't even do a toe touch without it hurting. I pulled it—probably in half." Wills laughs stiffly. "It feels like I did. Nothing helps. It seems like it gets worse as it goes on."

Still, Wills is a fighter. She might not look as polished as the other girls, but Berry trusts her to get the heel stretch good enough for the competition.

Rachel Brown is another story. Her heel stretch looks beautiful. But Berry can't trust her to keep it beautiful. At this point, Berry's having a hard time trusting Rachel with anything.

In mid-December, Rachel fell during a stunt and her back slammed onto Amanda Kitchen's knee. Amanda was okay, but Rachel was not: her back had folded over Amanda's knee.

While Rachel lay face-up, motionless on the carpeted auditorium floor, she opened and closed her eyelids, trying to get the tears out of her eyes, and gasped desperately for breath. Coach Randy Peffer called an ambulance and then Rachel's parents. As the Greenup team bent over her quietly, watching her still body, Rachel worried that she might be paralyzed. Between the pain in her back and her inability to breathe, she *felt* paralyzed.

When Mrs. Brown got the call from Coach Peffer that her daughter had taken a bad fall at cheer practice, she immediately rang up her husband on his car phone. As it happened, Mr. Brown was driving down Route 23, so he could quickly turn off and go to the high school.

"I stopped in and we put her on a piece of plywood," Mr. Brown says, "just rolled her over on it, took her to the emergency room that way. But her pain was just really bad. They gave her Demerol and stuff like that to block the pain. She could move her hands and feet so I wasn't worried about spinal problems. But she was having a lot of pain. You could see her back just knotting up."

"My body was swelling up and stuff," Rachel adds. "It really hurt."

Ever since that fall, Rachel has had a horrible time with her standing back tuck. During the November regionals, she hit her standing twice without any problems. But after that fall, she says, "the thought of going backward was scaring me."

Rachel couldn't bring herself to throw anything as simple as a back

handspring. Sometimes she couldn't turn a round-off to a back handspring. "Just stupid stuff," says Rachel. At a December basketball tournament down in Ashland, "Candy told me if I didn't do it that night, if I didn't do it with the squad—'cause I wouldn't even do it with the squad, I mean I couldn't even throw a back handspring, and it was really hard on me because all the girls were getting all mad and frustrated, but I could not make myself do it. I don't know, it was really hard." Rachel's words are tumbling over one another. "Finally, I threw a standing with Candy spotting me. She said if I didn't do it, she was gonna take me out of the [nationals] routine. But I did it and she left me in."

Rachel doesn't think her standing back tuck "mental block" happened because of that bad fall onto Amanda Kitchen's knee. Rather, she sees it as a problem that has built up within her ever-churning brain all year.

"I've been under a lot of pressure," Rachel says.

Even when the other girls held her good looks and her flirtatiousness against her, Rachel thought she would feel like a legitimate member of the team so long as she hit her standing. She could endure the nasty comments behind her back *if* she could land that standing. But without it, the pressure and the dread and the worry about not belonging weighed so heavily on Rachel that she nearly quit the squad in late December.

"This standing has just been my biggest downfall. From the beginning of tryouts, I've known I have to do it, and I've made myself do it. But it just got to the point where I couldn't make myself do it anymore. I got so scared and so worried about *if* I couldn't do it that I *couldn't* do it anymore. I think now I'm having more fun. I mean, I wasn't having any fun. At all. I was dreading every practice I went to, every game. Everything that had to do with cheerleading, I was dreading, because I was afraid they were gonna make me throw a standing.

"This is just the way Greenup is," says Rachel. "The rules in the beginning said you have to have a standing back. Candy took me even though I didn't have one because she trusted me enough to know that I would get one. Which I did. And I still have it. I just can't do it now. I mean, I can, but I, I don't know. Anyway, Candy's really been nice to me about letting me cheer games and about letting me be in competitions when she's had doubts about whether I would do it. Because I know if I was the sponsor, if I was her, I probably wouldn't let me cheer. I said to my parents, if she would take me out, I would understand why. I would be upset. I mean, I would be *very* upset. But I would understand why she would have to do it. Because you just can't put somebody in there that you can't rely on.

"I wouldn't even, I mean Candy and Mr. Peffer *both* had to spot me—*at the same time*. And that's a first-grade thing. They would say, 'Okay, if you don't do this, we're flipping you over.' I would freak out, and if I stopped, they would throw me over. They would make me do it. So then I started doing them and I got the repetition going again and now I'm doing a lot better. If I keep working at this pace, I'll be a lot better."

"Do you think you'll ever have this down?"

"Oh, yeah, I'll get it eventually. I had it at regionals. I was this way with my standing handspring backs last year at JV nationals. Oh, that was way worse. It just took time. I would stop just like I'm doing on my standings. I'd be like, 'Uh, can't do it.' But then I'd work through it and they'd yell at me a couple times and I started doing it again."

Rachel also got along with her JV teammates back then, and they supported her as she worked through her tumbling difficulties. This time, she's on her own.

"Candy and Randy haven't gotten to the point now where they're yelling at me again because if they yell at me, I probably wouldn't do anything. Because I'm really too hard on myself a lot of the time when I think, 'They're gonna be mad at me if I don't do this. They're gonna think this if I don't do that.'

"I just need to not worry about it and do what I know I can do. Then everything will be fine. But I haven't gotten that through my head yet. I analyze everything. I just think about everything. When I tumble, I think to myself, 'Okay, if I take my arms up, I'm gonna go up this much off the ground.' I've always done that. I think, 'What *can* I do to myself if I fall?' I know what can happen, what I can tear, what I can break, and I just worry myself."

"But the flying, that doesn't scare you?"

"No. I'm not scared a bit to climb. Because I want to do it so bad. And I know if I make one wrong move that makes something fall, they're gonna jerk me out. And I do *not* want that to happen. Right now, if I wasn't a climber, in all the mounts and stuff, I know they'd take me out. I know they would. Because they wouldn't really have any use for me. I'm glad that they have to have me climbing 'cause I'd be gone."

"What's the difference between tumbling and climbing? Why does tumbling scare you and not climbing?"

"I don't think about climbing, I don't think. I just do it. If I fall, I know they're gonna catch me, even if they just catch my arm. I know they're gonna catch something. And even if it does hurt, I know they'll dive under me 'cause otherwise they'll get in trouble."

"Do you think you worry more about the standing back tuck because with it, you're completely on your own?"

"Yeah, I guess. I really don't know. . . ."

Rachel abruptly changes the subject.

"Mr. Peffer and Candy have really helped me a lot through this. I thought they would be really upset and mad, but they understand what I'm going through. You know, it just takes time and a lot of work. I couldn't do it if they were being mean to me or if they were really pushing me. So they've been giving me a lot of help to get through this, spotting me and letting me do what I need to do, and not making me do it when I was really scared. That's really helped.

"But I've got to do it. At the Boyd game, I've got to do it then. They said if I didn't do it, if I just did a back handspring, that wasn't a big deal. But they *want* me to do it. And I *want* to do what they want me to do. So *I'm* going to do it. Whether I fall on my face or not, I'm going to do it."

"Y'all need to be working," Berry hollers from her plush armchair on the school's stage. "This standing around is ridiculous." Ten short days after this practice, on Tuesday, January 27, Berry expects her girls to perform their entire nationals routine after a home basketball game against Boyd County High School. But Berry's not going to let them go out and embarrass themselves, their coach, and the whole Greenup program by falling all over the place.

Rachel Brown asks Berry if she and her bases should add chanting to their heel-stretch stunt sequence.

"Y'all got to learn the stunt first, honey," Berry says with a huff. "You don't know the stunt well enough to add words."

Rachel tries the stunt again, without the words. Her bases pop her up over their heads, where Rachel is supposed to hold a K-stand, a pose in which she should balance on one foot and hold her body in the shape of a K. Rachel doesn't hit the K-stand quite right—she can't seem to hold her arms and legs in the proper positions. Her bases then drop her feet down to their shoulders and pop her back up to a heel stretch, but Rachel, her rhythm off from the muffed K-stand, falls while pulling her left leg up over her head.

"Geez-o-Pete!" says Berry. "I don't know anyone who makes things as hard as you. Just do it. Don't think about it."

Hank Light, meanwhile, lectures Wills about her heel stretch.

"Your body's got to stay in a straight line," says Light. "Your body's got to stay straight or it's impossible for the bases to control it."

"But don't you see?" Wills pleads. "I can't keep my leg up if I don't lean over, you know?"

With the whole team spotting her, including Rachel Brown, Wills pops up over her bases to the K-stand. That goes fine. Then she pops down and up to the heel stretch. She bends over and holds on desperately to her left toes with her left hand, then falls backward and lands on Rachel Brown's chest and face.

"I'm sorry, Rachel," says Wills, checking to make sure her teammate is okay. Rachel shakes it off, walking away with her hands on her hips.

"She was doing it great yesterday," Berry says of Wills. "Then she missed it once and got frustrated. So now she can't do it."

Rachel Brown, recovered, tells Wills that it looks like her body's not stiff and straight enough when Wills goes up to the heel stretch. As if Wills hasn't heard that a hundred times. Without looking at Rachel, Wills nods.

Kelena, practicing another stunt called a switch liberty, starts to bail to her left. Jessica Garthee and Shmorg run and catch her just before she hits the floor headfirst.

"Good catch, you guys," says Berry, her eyes wide.

The switch liberty only looks easy. With her left foot, the flyer steps onto three bases' hands. As the bases hoist her up into the air, the flyer balances on her left foot and then, at the apex of the lift, she yanks her left foot up, out of her bases' hands, and steps down with her *right* foot. The bases, meanwhile, must let go of the flyer's left foot at precisely the correct moment and grab her *right* foot before it comes crashing to the ground. That's the "switch." The "liberty" comes at the end, when the flyer holds a liberty pose—the flamingo stance—balancing with her right leg straight and her left leg bent beside it.

Amanda Kitchen walks into the auditorium with her mother. She's returned from her doctor's appointment, and apparently there's nothing wrong with the muscles in her back. An ovarian cyst is poking into her back muscles and causing the pain. According to Amanda's doctor, such cysts are common among teenage girls and shouldn't keep her from cheerleading, except, of course, for the fact that it hurts a great deal when she stands, walks, and—one would imagine—when she runs, jumps, or lifts anything heavy.

Amanda lies facedown on the stage's parquet floor, her head propped up on her hands, while her mom places a big bag of ice cubes on her lower back.

"So you'll be able to practice on Sunday?" says Berry.

"Yeah, I guess," Amanda mumbles from the floor.

"Good. You'll rest up today and tomorrow—you don't need to cheer at the Russell game tomorrow night—and the whole squad has Saturday off. So you'll be all rested for Sunday. Okay?"

"Okay," says Amanda, unenthused.

Linda Goble fills in for Amanda now by helping base Sarah Dickison. Linda doesn't normally base, but she does a fine job. Sarah hits her K-stand, then her heel stretch, and dismounts under control. Still, she looks terrified before, during, and after the stunt.

"She's scared of me," Linda declares.

"No, I'm not," says Sarah.

"You are."

"No . . ."

"You don't like me basin' you."

"Well . . ."

"See? You're scared of me."

Soon, it's time to practice the dance portion of the routine. Hank Light choreographed this new dance and the girls like it much better than that asexual dance from regionals.

Light says that at a cheer practice back in December, Berry and Peffer happened to leave the auditorium together. Suddenly, all of the cheerleaders crowded around Light.

"We're *not* doing that regionals dance at nationals," said Shmorg. "We hate it. You have to make us another dance."

The rest of the girls all nodded their heads solemnly.

"Okay," said Light, taken aback. "I'll talk to Candy."

When Berry returned to the practice, Light casually pointed out that the dance used at regionals was probably too long to fit into the new nationals routine. So would Berry like Light to create a new dance for nationals?

"Sure," said Berry.

And that was that.

The girls all love Light's new dance. They love the music, which features a man yelling "WORK THAT SUCKER TO DEATH! WORK THAT SUCKER TO DEATH! WORK THAT SUCKER TO DEATH!" The girls especially love the part at the end when they bend over like they're riding a racehorse, then slap their own butts four times like they're *whipping* a racehorse. They think that's "cute."

The only problem with the dance is that it calls for half the team to get down and thrust from their knees, and the carpet on the auditorium floor tends to scrape the girls up. Some thought to wear knee pads to practice, but not until they'd already shredded their knees over a month of dancing. Now, the pads can't keep the young scabs from ripping off.

"They started bleeding during school today," Shmorg says to Berry as she pulls on her knee pads, "and it soaked clear through my jeans."

"Hey," says Light, after the girls' third dance run-through, "Kelena needs to stay off her knees 'cause she's bleeding through the knee pad."

"That's fine," says Berry. "Kelena, why don't you just tell me?"

Kelena says nothing.

"She was afraid to," says Light.

"Well," Berry says, "I'm glad that I'm such a bitch that you-all are afraid to tell me these things. I mean, I would much rather you cut your knees all to pieces than have you stay off 'em for a while."

"I didn't say I was afraid to tell you," Kelena says, looking sideways at Light.

"Then why didn't you tell me?" asks Berry. "I hate it when you guys are so afraid to tell me stuff. I really hate that."

"She's a really nice girl," Rachel Brown says of April Creech. "She's really sweet. She never says anything bad about anybody. I think that's probably why a lot of people like her. It's just too bad."

Rachel pauses for a moment. She's talking slowly right now, choosing her words carefully, a rarity for her.

"The sad thing is, she's not like that. I mean I could understand if she was really promiscuous. But she isn't. She's always been real quiet. She's a real nice girl."

Rachel rubs her hands together and thinks about it all, sex, boys, cheerleading, pregnancy.

"April told us a couple days after regionals. And we were all like, 'No, you're not.' And she was like, 'Yes, I am.' We were all really surprised just because of it. Then we were like, 'Oh well.' It's not rare anymore. Right off-hand, I can probably name five people who are that I know. I don't know if it's a lot of peer pressure or what. I don't know. I don't think a lot of people see anything wrong with it anymore. It's just something you do. It's tough. Because a lot of them are our best friends that you see it happen to."

Cheerleading, Rachel says, keeps a lot of the girls from getting into the sort of "trouble" April now finds herself in.

"I think that's what has kept a lot of girls out of trouble," she says. "I think that if four or five of our girls weren't on the squad, they'd end up the same way April is. Or worse."

Rachel believes that April made a mistake not by having unprotected sex, but by having sex at all. And Rachel agrees with April's decision to keep the baby. The Brown family doesn't believe in abortion. If you're mature enough to have sex, Rachel and her parents feel, you should be mature enough to have a baby.

"Candy always warns us," says Rachel. "She says, 'You guys have a set image and people think a lot of you.' She always tells us to keep our heads up and our hands to ourselves. She warns us, she tells us not to do things.

"But it's just like kissing now. It's that bad. People just don't think about it anymore. Nobody has any morals or anything. It's really sad."

Rachel believes that having sex outside of marriage is wrong and that a girl who does it hasn't "any morals." After a year in which her dream of becoming a Greenup cheerleader came true, only to be marred by her own teenage escapades, Rachel's learned her lesson. She's not a rebellious teenager. She simply wants be liked. So a part of her believes that what she did with Kelena's boyfriend must be wrong, maybe immoral, if it makes so many of her teammates dislike her.

Rachel Wills has an entirely different perspective on teenage sex.

"What do you think April's mistake was?" I ask Wills.

"Not protecting herself," Wills says quickly. "That's stupid, I think."

She stares past me. "It was kinda hard because me and April were good friends," she says. "It was kinda hard to accept that. I guess I kinda knew it was gonna happen, kinda figured it would. It seems like it always does, you know. And then there was Aimee [Lewis]. . . ."

Shiritta Schaffer, who has overheard Wills talking here at the dance studio in Tammy Jo's gym, says, "I think Greg felt like he had to prove something. Because he actually bragged about the whole thing. At first he did. But I can tell he really cares about April—sometimes. It's not exactly that he wanted to have a kid, it's just he wanted to prove something to the guys and to everybody else because people used to talk about him. He just felt he had to prove something."

"How did people talk about him?"

"They make fun of him," says Wills.

"They call him a big butt," adds Shiritta.

"My boyfriend [Jesse Stapleton] gets along with him real well," Wills says.

"And April really likes him, right?" I ask.

There's a pause. Wills and Shiritta look at each other.

"I think she does," says Wills. "Well, I know she does."

Wills seems to dislike Greg so much that it's hard for her to imagine that April actually likes him, maybe even loves him.

"I feel so bad for her," says Wills, "because she had all these dreams and expectations for herself. That was hard for me, because I knew how she felt, I knew what she wanted. I knew she *wanted* to cheer in college. I felt so sorry for her. But there was nothing I could do about it. I didn't want to talk with her. I didn't want to tell her what I thought she should do because that's not my place. But I know it's hard on her."

"Would you have had an abortion under the same circumstances?"

"I don't know," says Wills. "I know where April's coming from. But you've got to think about your whole life. Your whole life is ahead of you. I guess, you know, if you did make that mistake, it's your fault and you have to live with it. You *should* live with it. But I don't know. . . ."

Wills does know she would never get engaged while still in high school.

"I mean, I care about Jesse," she says, "but I don't want to rush into anything. He feels the same way. If things last, you know, they last. If he cares that much about me, he's gonna wait on me. If Jesse wants to marry me, he can wait until I'm out of school and out of college. Because I've got so much other stuff that I want to do with my life. I mean, I'm not condemning Greg and April for it. If they feel that way, that's fine. I'll be behind them no matter what. It's just not how I feel. I don't want to rush into something like that. That's a lifetime decision, you know? I feel that way. I feel like if you decide to marry somebody, it should be forever. You should feel like you *want* to be married to him."

"Do you ever worry about getting pressured by boys into doing something you don't want to do, getting engaged, having sex, stuff like that?"

"Jesse, he does anything I ask him to do for me," Wills says with a snort. "He's waiting outside in the parking lot right now to drive me home."

Shiritta laughs at that.

"But Pat [Heineman, Wills's foster mother], she's real strict on us. Me and Jesse have been going out for two years and three months and there's probably been one time when we've been by ourselves. One night, after a ball game, Pat told us to go on home alone. So me and Jesse went to my home together, and then Pat was there right afterward. We were alone for maybe five minutes. And we just set and watched TV." Wills smiles. "And ate Cheez-Its."

Linda Goble tends to agree with Wills. April's mistake wasn't having sex, she says; it was having unprotected sex. Linda's heard Greg and a few other kids at Greenup High say that April and all these other Greenup girls have gotten pregnant because "it's in the water," and that makes Linda laugh.

Smiling mischievously, she says, "I don't drink that water."

On Sunday, practice begins at nine in the morning at the high school gym. The girls arrive a few at a time, looking bleary-eyed. Linda spent Saturday night with the Schaffers, and now she's wearing a sweatshirt with "Shiritta" embroidered on the collar.

While the girls stretch, Coach Peffer asks Berry and Susan Ray to help him list Greenup High's athletic accomplishments for a UCA questionnaire.

"Well," says Berry, "the basketball team went to the Elite Eight, the baseball team was state runner-up, the football team won districts for the second year in a row—"

"There's the great dance team, don't forget," says Ray, sarcastically.

While Ray giggles at her own joke, Peffer smirks and Berry rolls her eyes. Greenup's dance team is not that good, largely because the best dancers at the school lead cheers.

"Did you see the dance team at that ball game last week?" says Berry. "The way they were rubbing their boobies and all that? I was just wondering, 'Where's the pole?' I mean gosh! They were all—" Berry, sitting on a bleacher, rubs herself all over with both hands, from her chest to her thighs and back up again. Then she stares wide-eyed at her assistant coaches. "No wonder kids are so sexually active!"

As the Greenup girls stretch out their tired bodies, Berry begins to get angry. Amanda Kitchen isn't here. It's past nine-fifteen and Amanda Kitchen isn't here.

"I swear," says Berry, "that girl don't care one whit about this team."

Berry tells the girls who are here to practice their stunts, the K-stands to the heel stretches, then the switch liberties.

"Sarah's group," Berry says, "you-all can't practice yours 'cause Kitchen's not here. That's too bad. She said she was gonna be here. But she's not, so you-all can't do your work. You need the work, too. You need the work. Nationals is in three weeks."

Berry's frustration with the Greenup squad has reached the breaking point. She's sick of nudging and nudging and nudging the cheerleaders without them making any progress. Berry feels ignored, distrusted. The girls won't follow her directions, they won't tell her about their problems. They won't let Berry coach them.

The time for nudging is over. Now, it's time to push. One way or another, Berry's girls will do as their coach commands.

Rachel Brown tries to hold her heel stretch up but she leans to the right. Slowly, the lean becomes a fall and she lands on Megan West, hitting her in the nose.

"Rachel," says Berry, "you didn't fight to keep it up that time. You gotta fight."

Rachel gives it another go. This time she drifts, and ultimately falls, to the left.

"I was fightin' for it that time," she says to Berry.

The coach, hands on her hips, sighs and looks away from Rachel.

"Worry about these stunts, y'all," says Berry, as she overhears a few of the cheerleaders talking quietly. "Don't worry about everything else in the world. If you're going to worry about something other than these mounts, worry about world hunger or drug abuse, but don't you dare worry about boyfriends."

After the stunt work, Berry tells the girls to practice their standing tumbling and running tumbling. In a little while, the coach says, they will perform the routine's first forty-five seconds, which consist entirely of tumbling.

"Miranda," says Berry, "you need to work at this harder."

Confused, Miranda looks at Berry. The tumbling practice hasn't started yet, and Berry already wants her to work harder?

"Don't look at me like you don't know what I'm talking about," Berry bellows. "You know darn well you haven't hit a standing back in the last two ball games."

Miranda turns away from Berry with tears in her eyes.

"I mean, for gosh sakes," Berry says, "accept your faults! That's the problem with kids today. They can't accept that anything's wrong with them."

At Berry's request, Peffer leaves the gym to call Amanda Kitchen's home and her doctor's office. He returns a few minutes later having gotten no answer at her house and an answering machine at the doctor's office.

Meanwhile, the girls tumble on their own. Some talk and giggle among themselves while doing so.

"Quit talking!" Berry hollers. "You're upsetting your coach. Do you realize that in three weeks you're being judged for the national championship? Do you honestly believe you have time to talk? It's all about commitment, girls!"

Rachel Brown decides to practice her standing back handspring to a back tuck. That move is easier than the standing back tuck, but Rachel still has trouble. On her first few attempts, she only turns a back handspring, stopping before the back tuck.

"Don't start that shit," Berry growls to herself, then yells: "You throw it, Rachel! I don't care how bad it feels. You throw it!"

On her next attempt, Rachel stops again after the handspring. Then she gives it another go and turns the back handspring straight into a back tuck.

"I am mad as hell that Kitchen isn't here," says Berry, ignoring Rachel's triumph.

Rachel decides to practice her standing back tuck with Tom Pack spotting her.

"Rachel," says Berry, "get a little pride in yourself and do that by yourself."

Rachel ignores Berry and goes on practicing with Pack.

Soon, it's time to run through the first forty-five seconds of the routine.

"I've got a comment," says Berry. "Most of you have just stood around and haven't done anything. You should be ashamed of yourselves. If you fall, it's your fault."

On the first tumbling run-through, the Greenup girls look awful. Rachel Brown falls on her knees after her standing back. Linda Goble hits her bounders, but she looks slow and awkward doing so. Wills falls at the end of her bounders run, and Brooke Meenach and Jessica Newell don't even do their bounders—they pull up after the whip-back and before the tuck. Shiritta stumbles and falls at the end of her full-twist flip.

If the girls look closely, they can see smoke coming out of their coach's ears.

"You're going to come back at four-thirty today and practice your mounts for another hour and a half," Berry announces. "I don't care if you've got something planned. I've got things to do, too. If you're going to win nationals or even have a hope of winning nationals, then you've got to get this right."

Brooke tears up. Her parents are counting on her to look after her younger siblings throughout the afternoon, and Brooke doesn't know how she's going to attend this new four-thirty practice and baby-sit at the same time.

"You guys, there's no excuse for this," says Susan Ray, addressing the team's lackluster tumbling. "You girls are so talented. You can do better. All of you and your parents put the blame on Candy for not winning regionals because you didn't have a good enough routine. You didn't have enough tumbling. Well, now you've got a good routine with lots of elite tumbling, and what are you doing with it?"

There's a long pause as the exhausted girls sit silently on the gym floor, still panting for breath. Brooke is crying quietly.

"Okay," says Berry. "A moment ago, Miranda looked at me like I'm crazy when I got on her about her back tuck. Now, Brooke's losing it because I'm telling you-all to come back at four-thirty. This program is about being your best. You set high goals and you *work* toward 'em. You don't just set your goals up on a shelf and *look* at 'em!"

With that, Berry tells the squad to go take a break and get some water. Slowly, quietly, the girls walk out of the gym toward the hallway where the bathroom and water fountain are.

"Wouldn't you like to be a mouse in the wall out there?" says Ray with a smile.

"No!" says Berry. "And you know, the ones that come back last are bitching the most."

Once the girls all file back into the gym, Berry orders them to run through the opening tumbling again.

Rachel Brown misses her standing back. She turns it into a back hand-spring. Wills hits her bounders this time, as does Linda Goble. But Brooke pulls up early on hers and starts crying. Her ingrown toenail is bothering her again, and she's still worried and upset over the prospect of cheerleading practice this afternoon. Sarah Dickison lands her full-twist flip, but she starts crying afterward and lies down on the floor while gripping her right ankle. Sarah's had a lot of problems with that ankle. It's been sore for three weeks now.

"No wonder it hurts, if you land that low," Berry says to Sarah.

A few girls tend to Sarah, bending over her, rubbing her back, asking gently if she's okay.

"You-all aren't doctors," says Berry. "You can't help her any. I told her to wrap that ankle. If she doesn't wrap it, no one can help her."

Berry orders the girls to practice their heel stretches. Linda Goble again fills in for Amanda Kitchen and helps lift Sarah up into the air. Sarah cries throughout the stunt. Her right ankle is killing her.

None of the flyers fall on their heel stretches, but they don't look crisp in going up and coming down.

"Bad," says Berry. "That's bad."

The coach sighs.

"All right," she says. "Take a break and then we'll practice the dance once. Then you can go home. I may be a bitch, but I'm not an ogre."

During the break, Berry talks with Brooke Meenach about why she's so upset about the new afternoon practice. Through more tears, Brooke tells Berry about her baby-sitting commitment.

"Look, I'll call your mom," says Berry. "And if she wants, the kids can come to practice with you and we'll look after them."

Looking relieved, Brooke goes off to get some water.

After the dance run-through, all the girls leave the gym and head home, except for Rachel Brown, who continues to practice her standing back tuck with Tom Pack spotting.

Berry watches.

Rachel's having trouble throwing it even with Pack's protective hand under her back.

"Rachel Brown," says Berry, her voice echoing in the near-empty gym. "I have never been as disappointed in someone as I am disappointed in you. That you won't even throw it with a spotter!"

Without looking at Berry, Rachel nods.

"You nod, but you have no idea," says Berry.

Tom Pack places his hand on Rachel's back once more and Rachel gets ready to try again, but Berry interjects.

"Tom, let her alone," the coach orders. "She's got to do it by herself."

Pack backs away from Rachel, leaving her all alone in the middle of the gym floor.

Rachel crouches as if to jump up into a back tuck, then she straightens her legs.

"I can't throw it," she says, grimacing.

"If you can't throw it by this afternoon, you're not going to be in the routine!"

"I'm mad," says Rachel. "I'm mad at myself."

"Oh, man!" Berry says, throwing her hands up in disgust. "This is psychological warfare."

"We're a good squad," Rachel Brown insists. "We're just immature. We're really petty. We have a lot of talent but everybody's worried about everybody else and whose boyfriend's who and if they went out with their— It's really petty. And when we go to practice, the big topic is, 'What did you do last night? Did you talk to my boyfriend? Did my boyfriend call you?' You know? It's stupid!"

Rachel says she's not the sort of person who makes a habit of stealing other girls' boyfriends, and she hopes that the other cheerleaders have come to trust her more as the season's progressed. If they haven't, then they're being "petty" and "stupid." Rachel still hopes to maintain her "good cheerleader" image, however, and even as she rebukes her teammates, she tries to be nice. She never separates herself from the rest of the team. By using the royal "we," she lumps herself in with all of the other girls.

"Since the beginning of the year, we've become a lot better friends—I think," Rachel says wishfully. "At the beginning of the year, we had all our little cliques. This clique would tumble together, and that clique would tumble together, and they did *not* mix. But now, you just tumble with whoever whenever. I mean, we're all much better friends than we used to be. At the beginning of the year, we all made fun of each other. We back-stabbed everybody.

"What still affects us is the . . ." Rachel gropes for the right word. "The hatred—well, not so much the hatred—the bad attitudes toward each other. I mean, it's like, if somebody walks in and their hair is really big, then somebody'll be like, 'Did you see her hair today?' I mean stupid stuff, real petty."

Berry hasn't known all the details of who's fooled around with whose boyfriend, but she's sensed tension within the team since the summer. Back then, she told the girls to let their assorted jealousies go, and she assumed that eventually the cheerleaders would all learn to value each other at least as much as they value their boyfriends. In her twenty years coaching cheerleaders at Greenup High, Berry has come across many rifts between girls over boyfriends. But in her experience, the girls always manage to iron them out and put the boy troubles behind them. Yet here it is, January, with only a month to go before nationals, and many of the Greenup cheerleaders still hold grudges.

At a cheer practice during the first week of January, Coach Berry gave the girls an important talking-to, her one last effort to set them straight.

"This is the worst squad I've ever had, attitude-wise," she told them. "The way you guys talk about each other and try to hurt each other. I've never had to deal with a team like this. You guys need to think about what you're doing. You know, it's in the Bible."

Berry pulled out a Bible she'd brought from home with a bookmark in it, and read a selected passage out loud. The passage dealt with the golden rule, the importance of being nice and good to others.

"God really isn't going to like this too much. He *doesn't* like it," Berry continued. "Last night, I stayed up really late thinking about all this, thinking about what you girls keep doing to each other. I was worried about all your souls. And I've never done that with a team before. I mean I'm not that religious of a person. But I'm scared for how you guys are going to turn out."

Says Rachel of Berry's speech, "I think that scared a lot of people. That really made 'em think. And ever since then, there really hasn't been a negative comment about anything. But it was bad. It was really bad for a while. . . .

"I think that's gonna be the main factor of winning or not—if we can all get along."

Candy Berry tracked down Amanda Kitchen to make sure she came to the four-thirty practice. And Amanda participates with the rest of the girls in the team's stunt work, lifting Sarah Dickison up over her head while grimacing from the pain of the ovarian cyst pressing into the muscles in her back.

Berry also managed to drag Hank Light to the afternoon practice so he can choreograph the stunt at the end of the routine. He missed the Sunday morning practice because of a previously scheduled workout with one of his all-star squads at the gym in West Virginia. He works with the Greenup varsity only once a week these days, on Thursday afternoons. The rest of the time, he works with his all-star squads and the junior high team over in Pikeville, Kentucky.

Now, while Light teaches the Greenup girls how to perform the end stunt he's devised—it involves Wills and Kelena leapfrogging over one of their bases into mounts on either side of a raised Rachel Brown—Berry asks him if he can attend Greenup's practice on the upcoming Tuesday afternoon.

No, Light says matter-of-factly. He'll be working with the Pikeville team that day.

Berry gets annoyed.

"You're just like the girls," she says to him, in front of the cheerleaders and the handful of parents watching the practice. "When they want to come, they come. But when they don't, they don't. We haven't had a full squad all year. And we haven't had a full-time choreographer all year."

Light ignores Berry's jab and continues his work with the girls.

Later, after that afternoon practice has ended, Light predicts that Berry will temper her tough, vinegar-based Sunday attitude with sugar and spice throughout the rest of the week.

He's right: during the following after-school practices in the Greenup High auditorium, Berry jokes and chats with the girls as if she's just another high-schooler.

At the beginning of the Tuesday practice, Berry discovers a copy of *Glamour* lying open on the auditorium stage.

"Whose magazine is this?" she asks.

"It's Megan's," says Brooke, looking up from her stretching.

"I came over here and I pick it up and it's open to this awful article," Berry says mysteriously, with a slight smile.

"What article?" says Brooke.

"What's it about?" Sarah demands.

"Oh, it's just awful," Berry says, heightening the intrigue.

"What does it say?" says Wills.

"Oh, you know," says Berry, acting embarrassed, "'Does Size Really Matter?'"

The Greenup girls all giggle.

Berry turns to Megan. "I hope you're not worried about that," the coach says to her, continuing the joke.

"I'm not," Megan says, blushing, but enjoying the fun as well. "It was just the first article in the magazine."

"Oh, sure," says Rachel Brown, tittering, pushing her way into the team's fun. "Sure!"

"It was," Megan insists.

"At the school my mom works at, there's a seventh-grader who's pregnant," Jennifer Stuart announces.

"No!" says Berry. "No way!"

"Yes," Stu says. "It's true."

"There's a sixth-grader who's pregnant in Huntington [West Virginia]," Shmorg offers. "And you know who got her pregnant? Her brother!"

All the girls make faces, and some laugh at the thought of such a lurid story.

"That's gross," says Berry, still playing along. "That's just sick."

Berry knows what she's doing. Her harsh criticism of the girls the previous Sunday, followed by her mellow joshing throughout the week, has somehow produced an intense work ethic among the cheerleaders. The week's worth of practice goes very well, and Berry begins to believe that these girls, immature or not, sinful or not, mean-spirited or not, just might be able to win a national championship.

Amanda Kitchen has begun taking anti-inflammatory pills which, she's discovered, numb the throbbing in her back better than the pain pills her doctor first prescribed for her. At the Wednesday practice, Amanda wears a T-shirt that says, "Pain Is Temporary, Pride Is Forever." She's determined now to do whatever it takes to win a national championship.

Wills starts holding her heel stretches. Linda Goble regularly hits her bounders with speed and grace. And at Thursday's practice, Rachel Brown lands a standing back tuck without anyone spotting her.

The Greenup cheerleaders have all become possessed by an extreme sense of urgency.

"We're only national champions for two more weeks," says Brooke during a break in practice on Friday. Brooke means that statement as a call to arms, that it's time to put up or shut up.

But Berry doesn't like it: "That's a terrible thing to say."

"Well, you know what I mean," Brooke returns.

"No. That's a terrible thing to say!"

"You know," Brooke says. "We're 1997 champions for only two more weeks."

"You all *are* national champions," Berry declares, "until someone takes it away from you. Or you give it away."

By the end of the week, the girls have begun to get the message—and Rachel Brown couldn't be happier. With the entire team focused on winning nationals, Rachel feels more supported and accepted than ever. The girls need her to do well if they are to win, and on Friday, she and the other flyers hit all of their nationals mounts with stunning precision.

The girls still haven't performed the entire routine at once, however. On Saturday, January 24—just three days before their first public performance, at the Boyd County basketball game—Berry holds practice at Tammy Jo's gym and orders the girls to run through the whole nationals routine without stopping.

On a rectangular, two-inch-thick mat identical to the one they will perform on in Orlando, the Greenup girls fall, fall, fall, fall, fall.

The first go-around is the worst. Rachel Brown misses her opening standing back. Jennifer Stuart falls on her knees on her standing back and pushes through the rest of the routine with tears in her eyes. Kelena drops to the floor on the first mount after the tumbling and also cries the rest of the way. Wills doesn't even try her switch liberty, the timing's so off by that point. Miranda falls forward on her standing back handspring to back tuck. And Rachel Brown falls in the middle of her heel stretch, with Wills crumpling after her. During the dance, the girls look exhausted, not excited. And upon attempting the final mount, Kelena collapses to the floor, followed by Wills.

The girls sprawl across the royal blue mat, immersed in a confused stupor. Many fight back tears.

"And you guys think you don't need to practice," Berry jokes. "That's why it's good you're practicing on the mat, so you don't kill yourself when you fall."

"I hate this floor," says Miranda, stating what many of the girls feel. "I'd much rather be in the gym." Even though the mat makes landings softer, the girls simply aren't used to it.

"Well, too bad," says Berry, "'cause this is what you're performing on."

"I'm not complaining. I just—"

"Yes, you are," says Berry.

The Greenup girls keep at it. During the fifth run-through, they have only two falls. But Berry gets on them for not making it showy enough.

"Candace," the coach yells at one point, "don't flare your nose holes! SMILE!"

Physically, the routine takes a lot out of the girls, especially Sarah Dickison with her sore ankle, and Stu with her sore back, and Brooke with her ingrown toenail, and Shiritta, whose knee is bothering her, and, of course, Amanda Kitchen with her ovarian cyst.

"Y'all are crying and whining like babies," Coach Berry bellows. "At least when you're hurt, you could smile. There are six or seven of you that are hurt and you can't be crying about it. You've got to smile. Now! You've got to make the judges love you. They've got to like you better than everybody else."

The day before the Boyd County basketball game, the cheerleaders perform okay but show nothing spectacular, and Berry considers canceling the team's exhibition the following evening. Berry asks the squad's seniors if they want to stick to the plan and perform the full nationals routine after the Boyd game. The five seniors confer for a moment, then tell their coach that they still want to go for it. Berry decides to trust them.

During the opening introductions of the Greenup High basketballers the night of the big Boyd game, Sarah Dickison falls while throwing a running tumbling run across the gym floor. She lands hard on her tailbone and can't cheer the entire game because of the pain and swelling.

"She'll be okay," Susan Ray says during halftime. "It just hurts like hell, that's all."

Sarah rejoins the squad after the game, and—miraculously—the Greenup cheerleaders nail every bit of their routine in front of their screaming hometown fans. Rachel Brown hits her standing back tuck. The opening tumbling is great—Linda Goble and Wills both land their bounders beautifully, as does Amanda Kitchen, and they all manage to smile broadly the whole way through. No one—not Berry, not Light, not the girls themselves—expected such a flawless and exciting performance.

"You see what we do when we're in front of a crowd," Miranda says, smiling.

"What did you think?" I ask Wills.

"Pretty good," she says with a shrug.

"Do you think you-all can win nationals if you perform like that?"

"Yeah," she says dryly, keeping a tight lid on her hope. "Maybe."

"Did you see Rachel Brown?" Light exclaims. "She beamed!" Light sped here from Pikeville to see this performance.

I ask him whether the Greenup girls will win the national championship if they put on an equally good show in Orlando.

Standing on the gym floor, amid the swarm of jubilant Greenup fans who have all come down from the bleachers to congratulate the cheerleaders on their fantastic performance, he thinks a moment. "You never know, but it'll take a darn good team to beat us."

"I feel like we have a chance," says Wills, ever cautious, prepared for disappointment. "I mean, I know we do. Because every one of us, individually, we're strong. But together, it's hard for us to put aside everything and work together. You know, blaming each other for our own personal problems and stuff. Everybody brings it to practice. I know there's a lot of times when somebody'll come in and something'll be bothering them and they'll take it out on you. And you just have an awful practice. . . .

"We could win, and we couldn't. I just don't know. If we pull together as a group, instead of just working for ourselves, if we work for each other, I think we could. I *know* we could. Of course, I haven't seen the other schools' routines, so I don't know. . . .

"It'll be a letdown if we don't," Wills continues. " 'Cause we've put so

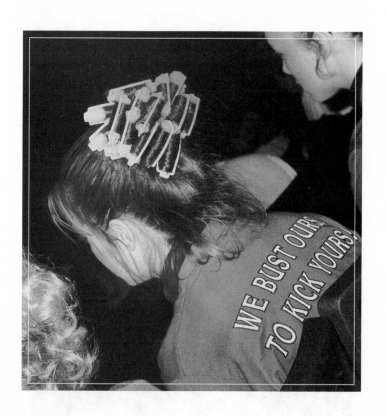

much effort and hard work into everything. I know I have. I mean I work my butt off."

Wills has begun to emerge as an especially important member of the Greenup team. She has slowly but surely won a great deal of respect because she takes it upon herself to support any cheerleader who can use her help, particularly Linda Goble and Rachel Brown. Despite her natural leadership ability, however, Wills still finds herself held back by the unnecessary criticism of some of the more experienced cheerleaders on the squad.

"It kinda makes me mad," she says. "It hurts my feelings when some of the girls yell at me, people in my partner stunts will yell at me like, 'You're not doing this right. You're not doing that right.' And I feel like I'm trying the best I can. I'm like, 'Maybe it's something *you're* doing wrong.' But it's always me because I'm the person on top. It's a lot of pressure."

Wills has plenty to prove as a cheerleader, but she knows she can't prove anything on her own. That's why she spends so much time and energy helping the other girls along.

"I remember last year, when we [the JV cheerleaders] came home from Florida, it was like, 'Oh, the varsity did this and the varsity did that,' you know? And we tried just as hard as the varsity. It was just that one squad was better than us. It was kind of a letdown for us. Everyone was all, 'The varsity was so good. You should have seen them.' And we were like, 'Thanks.'

"People talk bad about our team this year. They say we're weak. We've had people at school say there's no way we can win nationals."

As determined as Wills is, she refuses to get her hopes up. Disappointment, she has learned, is an inescapable part of life. Her father, with his boozing and his abuse, and her mother, by moving away from Greenup and leaving her only child to fend for herself, taught Wills that.

"If we win, that's good," she says. "But if we don't, I know it'll be a letdown, but it's something that I went through before, you know?"

She thinks a moment, then says softly, "It would be nice if we won this year."

Asked how important it is for her and the rest of the Greenup varsity to win nationals, Linda Goble chuckles and says, "It's important. It's real important."

After the loss at regionals, Linda says, she didn't cry. Because regionals didn't matter that much to her.

"But this time," she says, "if we don't win, I'll probably cry."

Linda tries to imagine what she'll feel if she and the rest of the varsity don't win in Orlando. After moving from Greenup County to Mason County, then back to Greenup; after living with the Schaffers, then the Morrises, then her mom, then the Garthees and sometimes the Schaffers; after finally getting a chance to cheer for the varsity; after all the pressure-filled fund-raising—what if Linda doesn't win a piece of the national cheerleading championship?

"I *know* I'll cry if we don't win," says Linda.

"It's everything," Rachel Brown says of the national championship. "I mean, after all the stuff I've gone through this year, with everybody, all my tumbling, all my injuries, it wouldn't mean anything if we didn't win nationals. That's the whole reason why I cheer, not for the pep rallies, not for the ball games, not anything else. It would all be a waste if we don't win nationals."

"In the beginning," says Mr. Brown, "I didn't want Rachel to be on the team, because of the money, the time, and everything else."

Now, Mr. Brown says he wants his daughter to buck up and fight through her fears—of the standing back tuck, of falling, of hurting herself, of embarrassing herself, of upsetting her teammates.

"After going through it with her," Mr. Brown says, "I want her to go all the way. I want her to clear this one last hurdle. She's come this far. She can finish it."

Chapter Seventeen

The Best Team in the Land

Greenup County High School canceled classes for the remainder of the week following the Tuesday night basketball game against Boyd County because of a flu epidemic. According to Randy Peffer, 340 kids in the Greenup County school system missed school that Tuesday, January 27, with the flu.

"This happens at least once a year," Rachel Brown says, unimpressed.

In a small community like Greenup, with only a handful of schools serving the entire population, the flu can often run rampant. When that happens, the school system's administrators like to close school for a few days to let the sick kids recover.

The Greenup cheerleaders use the extra time to practice and get a head start on the school work they're going to miss when they head down to Florida. Many varsity members have caught the flu, however, and throughout the week, they cough and hack up phlegm during workouts at Tammy Jo's.

"Y'all need to spit that out," Berry instructs the girls during one practice. The coach has also come down with the virus, so she speaks in a hoarse rasp. "My doctor told me that we girls always swallow that stuff and don't spit, and that only makes you sicker. Don't worry about being ladylike. Just spit it out."

Rachel Brown is one of the worst coughers in the bunch.

"I think I've got TB," Rachel says melodramatically.

"You don't have TB," says Berry.

"Well, it's getting there," Rachel insists with a smirk.

Some of the other girls giggle at Rachel's joke, and smile at her. Ever since Berry pushed the squad to work harder toward nationals, the Greenup cheerleaders have begun to warm up to Rachel. Their common goal has made them forget their long-held grudge.

The coughing among the cheerleaders continues. When it becomes deafening, Berry halts practice and tells the girls to go drink some water.

"My lan'," the coach says, "it sounds like an infirmary in here with all this crouping."

Greenup High basketball sticks to its schedule throughout the week despite the cancellation of classes, and the cheerleaders perform their nationals routine in front of the crowds assembled at each game. On Thursday and then again on Saturday, they do their thing on their home court. But they can't seem to execute the routine with the same excitement and polish that they brought to the night of the Boyd game.

During the Thursday night performance, Rachel Brown and Miranda don't land their standing back tucks. Libby doesn't land her full-twist flip. Sarah falls during her heel stretch, and Rachel Brown falls during her switch liberty.

After the game Saturday night, the girls do better. All of their mounts stay up. But Rachel and Miranda miss their standing backs again, and Rachel misses the handspring–to–standing back that comes late in the routine.

"You guys are not going to win if you don't all do the standing tumbling," Berry tells them afterward. "I'm sorry, but that's just the way it is."

Rachel tears up.

"It may seem like a lot of pressure," says Berry. "But you-all have *got* to do it so the rest of the squad has a chance."

Shawnda Bates drove over from Louisville to attend the game that Saturday night. With just a week before nationals, she wanted to wish her former teammates good luck, and she wanted to see how the new routine looked.

The following Sunday morning, she sits in on a practice at Tammy Jo's. At Berry's urging, she tells the Greenup cheerleaders what she thinks of their routine.

"I think it's good," she says. "All you gotta do is smooth out those stunts and make it more exciting. It's awfully difficult, harder than any I've ever done."

Shawnda loves being back with the Greenup cheerleaders, but it's odd for her now that she's no longer one of them.

"I miss Greenup," she says. "I miss cheering for Greenup. It's different from Louisville because everybody here was so close on the squad. My senior year, we were all so close. In college, everybody's older and the older people have their friends and the younger people have their friends. It's not a family. In high school, we were always all together. But in college, it's so big that you don't have all the same friends like we did in high school. That's the thing I think I miss the most."

Shawnda's kept in touch with her friends on this year's squad, Greenup seniors Kelena, Shmorg, and Libby, and they've told her about the team boyfriend drama, how this year's team is not one big, happy family.

"That's something that holds you back," Shawnda says. "They need to get that stuff out in the open. Last year, we would have just told each other. They've got a lot of potential. But it's a young team, a very young team. They haven't really established who their real friends are yet. Friends are gonna last longer than boyfriends. But they still think boys are their lives. They'll learn. They'll learn that boys aren't always going to be there when you need them. But your friends are."

There's a part of Shawnda that would love to be back on the Greenup squad so she could set this new team straight.

"When I watched them [at Kings Island]," she recalls, "I wanted to be up there—even though I wanted to be with the Louisville squad, too. But it was fun, it was exciting to have all my Greenup friends watch me and them know that I cheer at a college. But I don't know. I still miss Greenup."

Shawnda recalls the pep talk she gave the Greenup girls before they performed at Kings Island.

"I told 'em that there was nobody there that could beat them. Which I don't think there is. I don't think there's anybody better than Greenup. Even if there is, I'll still never think that."

That's why it was extremely difficult to watch the Greenup squad lose at regionals.

"That was disappointing," Shawnda says. "I always want 'em to win. I always want 'em to be better than everybody. I brought a friend, too. And I wanted to show her how good Greenup was. My best friend, Kristie, she's a cheerleader at Louisville, and she's from Syracuse, New York. Her high school squad knew of Greenup County. They watched 'em every year, they followed 'em. And I thought that was so cool, so I was like, 'Hey, you wanna go watch Greenup County?' And she just thought that was the greatest thing. Then I took her and they lost."

As a member of Louisville's coed JV, Shawnda hasn't yet performed in a competition. The Louisville cheerleaders compete only once a year, at the National Cheerleading Association's college national championships in May.

"I miss the competitions," she says. "That was my favorite thing, being competitive. It's just different in college. I mean, I'm glad I have time to study and everything. But I do miss competing."

Still, Shawnda's very happy at Louisville. She loves the city and she's having a great time meeting new people and experiencing new things.

"I switched my major," she says. "From dentistry to nursing. I want to be a trauma room nurse now. Because I don't want to go to school for a long time. I still have to go to school for a while with nursing, but not as long. And it's still something working with people. Also, I want to work in a big city. I like Louisville a lot. My mom doesn't like that—she wants me to stay in Greenup, but I don't think I'm going to. I like the city. I love it. Compared to Greenup, it's very exciting. People who live there don't think it is, but to me, it is. There's lots more to do, places to go. There's always something, something going on. The city, the buildings, it excites me. Me and a couple of friends are going to get an apartment or a house this summer. Then we'll see if I *really* like it. . . .

"I always think about what would have happened if I had gone to ACC or Morehead. Because ACC's a community college, and Morehead's such a small, little school. I just wonder if anything would be different. In Louisville, there's always places like clubs to go dancing, and restaurants, and a lot of times, there's concerts, just a lot of stuff to do. There's like six or seven malls. I never went out in high school. The only place I went out, really, was the movies. There's just nowhere to go in Greenup. There's like two places.

"I think before your life is settled and you decide exactly what you want, you need to go out and experience new places, just get an idea of the world. There's a thing at Louisville where you could go for a semester at a college anywhere in the United States. I was thinking maybe New York, you know, go to a real city. It's just an idea. I don't know if it'll ever go through. I mean, I love where I am. I love all my friends."

Shawnda's heard about April Creech's pregnancy and thinks it tragic that April's permanently lost her chance to explore the world outside of Greenup.

"It surprises me a lot," Shawnda says of April's pregnancy, "because I don't understand how she had all this free time. We never did. We had time to go on dates and stuff. But I guess I had more important things on my mind. Cheerleading was my life. It still is, sort of. . . . But I think it's devastating to think that that could happen to such a young girl. I think it's horrible."

Shawnda's also heard about the other girls who've gotten pregnant. I tell her that, with all the other pregnant girls at Greenup High, April says she doesn't feel that "horrible." But Shawnda doesn't buy it.

"It's like the 'everybody's-doing-it' scenario," she says. "Well, *I* would feel weird. Just being so young. I'm still *extremely* young. I would still feel *very* weird. I don't care if there's *thirty* other girls. I would still feel out of place."

Shawnda broke up with her boyfriend, Nick Warnock, during the summer after her senior year because she was a UCA camp counselor and was always away. Currently, she's single.

"Are guys in college different from guys in Greenup?" I ask.

"No." Shawnda laughs. "I don't think guys really change."

The Greenup squad finishes a run-through of their nationals routine here on the mat in Tammy Jo's gym.

"Tell 'em what you think, Shawnda," says Berry. "I know you've got stuff to say."

"It's still not exciting," Shawnda says. "And the stunts. The stunts were bad that time, especially Rachel Brown's." Shawnda shrugs, as if to acknowledge how blunt she is. "Sorry," she says.

"Linda Goble," says Berry, "think of the cockiest cheerleader you've ever seen, and you play that part. You've got to be like, 'Yeah! Woo!' and smile and jump up and down and point, you know?"

Linda chews on her fingernails and feels the rest of the squad staring at her. Then, all of a sudden, Linda smiles a huge, ridiculous smile, jumps, points at an imaginary crowd, pumps her fist in the air.

"Yeah! Go Linda!" Rachel Brown hoots.

The girls all laugh.

"Am I being showy enough?" asks Rachel, serious now. "I'm sticking my tongue out."

"I think we'll all be more showy when we get down there," says Wills.

"Yeah," Sarah Dickison puts in. "We do better with a crowd."

"I don't know about that," says Berry. "In my experience, you perform ninety percent the way you practice."

The cheerleaders and their eighty-some-person entourage of coaches, parents, and siblings plan to travel from Greenup County to Orlando on February 4, the Wednesday before nationals weekend. Starting at one P.M., they'll drive the 150 miles to the Louisville airport in a caravan of sixteen cars and vans. The drive shouldn't take them more than three hours, they figure. Therefore, the Greenup troupe should arrive in Louisville around four P.M., giving them plenty of time to park in the long-term lot and check in for their five-thirty P.M. flight direct to Orlando.

On the night before their scheduled departure, Greenup County receives a light dusting of snow. The local weather man says that some areas of eastern Kentucky might have two to three inches of accumulation, but nothing major.

When the Greenup girls awaken Wednesday morning, there's already a half-foot on the ground, and the snow is still coming down hard. School's canceled throughout the county, and the Greenup coaches move their departure time up a couple hours, to eleven A.M.

April Creech hoped to go to the high school, where the Greenup cheerleading contingent will meet and pack up their cars before heading out. She wants to wish her former teammates good luck at nationals. She'll be thinking of them. But April's mom and Greg don't want her driving on the snowy roads. So April stays home.

The first thirty-some miles down Route 23 are treacherous. But that's to be expected. Route 23 isn't a main highway. Once the Greenup crew gets to Interstate 64, they should encounter nothing but clear, smooth highway as they head west to Louisville.

The incessant surprise snowfall has covered I-64 with ice and snow, however. Bumper-to-bumper along the one-automobile-wide portion of packed snow, the Greenup cars can't drive more than thirty-five miles an hour without the risk of skidding out of control and ending up stuck in the loose powder on either side of the roadway. Over the hundred-mile leg to Lexington—the first two-thirds of the way to Louisville—the Greenup caravan encounters more than thirty cars stuck on the side of the road.

It's nearly three P.M. when the Greenup crew reaches Lexington, and the local radio stations report that almost a foot of snow has fallen on the city. According to satellite pictures, the massive storm dumping snow over the eastern half of the state is going nowhere fast.

As the Greenup troupe makes its way around Lexington's outer loop toward Louisville, the string of cars moseying through the snow ahead of them suddenly stops: a jackknifed truck is blocking the road a few miles ahead. The cheerleaders and their families have to park in the middle of snowy, cold I-64. They're definitely going to miss their five-thirty flight now, and Lord knows when they'll finally make it to Louisville or whether planes will even be able to take off in this horrid weather. The radio says that the snow will continue to fall all day, then into the night, maybe into the next day and the day after that.

Waiting and waiting on the snowy Kentucky highway, the girls get a bit desperate. They know they haven't always worked as hard as they should. They know they've gossiped and picked fights with their teammates. Maybe Coach Berry was right when she said that God could see what they were doing. And maybe He didn't like it. Maybe God sent this storm to punish them, to keep them from leaving Kentucky, to deny them their chance to redeem themselves, their chance to pull together and win the national cheerleading championship.

The Greenup girls sit there in their immobilized cars for more than three hours. Then, slowly, the traffic in front of them finally begins to move. Carefully, but with some urgency, the Greenup team and their fans push on to Louisville. At ten P.M., eleven hours after leaving Greenup High, they finally arrive at the Louisville airport. They've obviously missed their flight to Orlando, which took off on time because Louisville wasn't hit as hard by the storm as Lexington and points east. The Greenup cheerleaders were lucky they hadn't booked their flight out of Lexington. If they had, they'd be more stuck than they already are.

After a couple of frantic hours at the Louisville airport, the Greenup coaches finagle themselves and the cheerleaders onto a flight to Chicago that night. But there's not enough room for all the parents and siblings.

The coaches and the girls spend the night in Chicago while their families sleep in Louisville. The next day, Thursday, assistant coach Randy Peffer, the team's all-purpose problem-solver, books the cheerleaders onto a flight that touches down in Orlando at four P.M. The girls' parents fly in from Louisville that night.

Friday, the girls try to put their adventure behind them. Back home, the governor has declared a state of emergency throughout eastern Kentucky. In all, a foot and a half of snow has fallen over two days and two nights. Many thousands of people lack heat, electricity, and operable phone lines. A handful have died in the forbidding cold.

But here in Orlando, it's sunny and comfortably cool; the Disney grass is bright green and the Disney palm trees blow gently in the wind. To the Greenup cheerleaders, this looks and feels like the promised land.

They practice Friday morning at a gym in downtown Orlando, then return to their hotel, the Disney All Star Sports Resort, where they hang out by the big, shiny-blue pool and schmooze with the hundreds of cheerleaders from throughout the country who have come to compete for the national championship.

The cheerleaders go to bed early that evening, then wake up at five-thirty A.M., before the approaching dawn. The girls shower, dress, and pack their green-and-gold duffle bags with their taped skirts and their bright white competition shoes.

At six-forty-five on a cold, bright Orlando morning, the girls stride through the turnstiles that lead into the Disney/MGM Studios. Wearing their gold Greenup Cheerleader sweatsuits trimmed with green, they all chant in unison:

> *We are the girls from Greenup County that you've heard so much about.*
> *We jump and shout and flip about and knock the people out.*
> *Oh, as we go marching—and the band begins to P–L–A–Y,*
> *You can hear us shouting:*
> *The girls from Greenup County are on their way!*
> *He-ey!*

The Greenup cheerleaders performed with uninspired stiffness during the preliminary round.

Beforehand, with all the other varsity eyes trained anxiously upon her as she practiced her standing back again and again, Rachel Brown became nervous, extremely so. She even took some pills her father had given her to calm her down. Wills made a concerted effort to support Rachel during the preperformance warm-ups, telling her how good she'd been doing of late, and how pretty and strong she was. Then, during the performance,

Rachel somehow landed all of her standing tumbling, including her standing back.

Neither Brooke Meenach nor Amanda Kitchen landed their bounders tumbling runs, however. Instead of ending the run with back tucks, they finished with weak back handsprings. Of the six girls slated to throw bounders, only Wills and Linda Goble hit them and hit them well. Jennifer Stuart, still bothered by a sore back, was the only girl on the squad who didn't land the opening standing back. She did a back handspring instead. Libby Barber, the team's strongest tumbler, put her hands down on the mat at the end of her super-difficult tumbling run.

Except for Rachel Brown, the girls seemed confident before they bounded out in front of crowd at the Indiana Jones theater. After they chanted the Lord's Prayer together, they huddled up and yelled, "BACK TO BACK!"—a reference to their status as defending cheer champions.

But the girls' upbeat attitude evaporated when they took the mat. Those Greenup girls who "love to jump and shout and flip about and knock the people out" were nowhere to be found.

"That was absolutely ridiculous!" Coach Berry fumed afterward, standing in the middle of an MGM walkway outside the theater. The cheerleaders huddled around her. Most had their heads downturned in shame. Brooke and Libby cried softly. Passersby couldn't help but look at the apoplectic coach as she raved.

"There was no excitement! No voice! Stu, you didn't even *try* your standing, and it stuck out like a sore—" Berry jabbed her right thumb up into the air. "I will not let you go out there tomorrow and look like that— *if* you make it to the finals. Your tumbling was awful. Olive's group"— Berry searched out the face of Rachel Wills—"good save on that heel stretch. I thought it was going to come down. And the signs, the signs weren't held up when they were supposed to."

Light had come up with the idea of buying hundreds of signs with "Greenup County" printed on them and distributing them among the Greenup fans. In the middle of the routine, when the cheerleaders holler, "Hey, all you Greenup fans! Out, in the crowd! Hold up your signs and yell it loud!" Berry wanted the throng of Greenup parents to hold up the signs and scream, "Greenup! County! Greenup! County!" During the preliminary performance, however, the girls' parents somehow missed their cue.

"So we lost *those* points for crowd participation," said Berry. "You know, that's why we spent a hundred dollars on the damn signs!"

She took a breath.

"I don't understand *you*, and *you*, and *you*, and *you*," she continued, pointing at Brooke, then Amanda, then Libby, then Stu. "You-all didn't attack it. You looked tired. You need to be a whole lot louder and a whole lot more excited. You didn't get the crowd behind you."

Hank Light wasn't as upset as Berry. While the head coach railed at the girls, Light conferred quietly with Tom Pack and Susan Ray.

"You-all, it wasn't that bad," he said, reminding the other assistant coaches how cold it was that Saturday morning, and how—because of a new UCA rule forbidding tumbling on the parking lot asphalt or anyplace else without a mat—the Greenup girls didn't practice their tumbling as much as they should have before going out in front of the judges and the crowd.

"I know," said Ray. "They need more time to warm up, especially in cold weather like this. They should have the parents sign a waiver saying it's okay for their kids to tumble on the concrete. Or they should have mats all over the parking lot."

"Yeah," Pack said, sighing, "but they can still do better. If they're gonna win, they gotta do a lot better."

The Greenup cheerleaders look tough during practice Saturday afternoon. At the Academy of Elite Gymnastics in downtown Orlando, the girls appear happy, confident, and strong. Berry's ranting has finally sunk in, maybe. Or Light was right about the girls' only problem being the early-morning cold.

Whatever the reason, the stiffness is gone, the confidence has returned. Sure, the Greenup girls didn't perform terribly well in the prelims, but they still made the finals. Now, they simply need to nail everything in the finals.

"Already, it don't look like the same bunch of kids as this morning," Light says to Berry after the third straight successful run-through.

Berry and Light spent much of the morning watching the forty-two other all-girl large varsity squads perform in the preliminary round. And they have conferred with friends who coach teams not competing in Greenup's division.

"Michelle said it. Scott said it," Light tells the Greenup cheerleaders, citing two small varsity coaches, one from California's Los Alamitos High

School, the other from Tennessee's Boaz High. "You guys look like the best out there."

If, of course, they perform with near perfection. And after this practice, they seem capable of that. Amanda and Brooke are hitting their bounders now. Rachel Brown and Stu are landing most of their back tucks. The team has also added a little attitude to the routine—during the butt-slapping part of the dance, they now grunt with each whack.

Also, the flyers have shined. Even Rachel Wills is smiling energetically.

"Olive," says Berry at one point, "that was good. You were very person-able that time."

The following morning, Sunday, the Greenup girls return to the gym and spend another two hours practicing hard and well. By the grace of God, they feel that they've got a good chance to win this thing.

The cheerleaders kill time the following afternoon by wandering around MGM Studios, watching other teams perform, cheering on those they know. As they mingle with the thousands of cheerleaders swarming throughout the amusement park, the girls wear—at Berry's request—tight cutoff jeans ("Daisy Dukes," some call them) and white long-sleeved T-shirts with "Greenup County" printed on the front, and on the back:

LOVED by few,
HATED by many,
RESPECTED by ALL!
GREENUP COUNTY CHEERLEADERS

Sunday night, the Greenup cheerleaders report to the cold, dark MGM parking lot. It's eight o'clock. The finals will begin at nine, and the Greenup girls will be the second of seventeen teams to perform.

The girls' parents staked out their seats in the Indiana Jones theater hours ago, *after* Coach Berry repeated her strict instructions on how and when to lift up their "Greenup County" signs. Phil Brown, Rachel's father, has taken it upon himself to distribute the extra signs to friends of the Greenup program from Los Alamitos High, Boaz High, Pikeville Junior High, Florida's Merritt Island High, and others. To each group of fans, Mr. Brown carefully and seriously explains how and when everybody should hold up their "Greenup County" signs—over 300 in all.

When the Greenup girls arrive at the MGM parking lot, they're wear-ing their gold nylon sweatsuits over their brand-new green-and-gold

zigzag-patterned finals uniforms. With the lights of the Indiana Jones
theater glowing a few hundred yards away, the girls huddle up in the dark,
outside the big white UCA warm-up tent.

For a few moments, the nineteen girls push their heads together, wrap
their arms tightly around one another, and talk quietly. Then they decide
to pick out a star to wish upon.

Their arms still resting on their teammates' backs, the girls turn their
faces toward the night sky.

"Which one?"

"The brightest one. Over there."

"Which one?"

"That one."

"Make a wish, on three."

"Close your eyes."

Each of the girls finds the chosen star in the night sky; then they all
close their eyes, and they whisper together, "One, two, three."

It's time to get down to business. First things first: the four flyers—
Rachel Brown, Wills, Sarah Dickison, and Kelena—all stretch out their
hamstrings. Wills lifts her right leg up onto Stu's shoulder. Standing and
facing Wills, Stu helps force Wills's legs as wide apart as possible, pulling
Wills's waist toward her, straightening Wills's upturned right leg until it
points straight up in the air.

Berry then hustles her cheerleaders inside the tent. The Greenup girls
can use the tent's mats for just four minutes, and not until it's officially their
turn, but they can stretch and warm up on the asphalt inside until then.

While the girls file into the tent, Light exchanges high-fives with each
one. Rachel Brown is the last to come through. Light high-fives her, then
gives her a bear hug.

UCA has positioned space heaters throughout the tent, so the girls can
do without their sweatsuits. After they take their gold jackets and pants
off, Berry has them put on their new skirts.

"Aubrey," says Berry, "roll the top of your socks down like you're supposed to."

Finished stretching, the girls start turning walkovers on the pavement
inside the tent.

The UCA officials watch them closely. Berry knows UCA will probably let the girls turn tame tricks like walkovers and cartwheels on the
hardtop, but not much else.

"Sarah," Berry says, "those walkovers will help your ankle as much as anything. Let's go!"

Wills finishes a walkover, then frantically retraces her path. Finding what she dropped, she exhales heavily and smiles big.

"My good luck bracelet fell off and I was like, 'Man!'" Wills says to Berry. "I found it now."

"Yeah," Berry says with a tight smile.

"But that's good," says Wills. "Because if your good luck bracelet falls off, that's good luck."

Berry orders Rachel Brown and Coach Light over to a far corner of the warm-up tent. Then Berry tells the rest of the Greenup cheerleaders to clump together near them, so that the UCA officials can't see Rachel or Light. Now, Rachel can practice her standing back and the UCA officials won't notice.

Flanked by the wall of Greenup girls, Light puts his hand on Rachel's lower back, then glances quickly over his shoulder to make sure the UCA people aren't paying attention.

"Okay," he whispers.

Rachel makes two fists, bends her knees, then stops. She makes two fists again, bends her knees, and explodes upward. Pivoting around Light's hand, Rachel spins her tucked body backward and lands squarely on her feet.

"Yes!" she says, her teeth clenched.

Berry tells the girls to stay clumped by this corner of the tent.

"One at a time," says Berry, "you girls come over here and do a standing back."

While Wills waits, she turns to Jessica Newell.

"See how my stretch is, okay?" says Wills.

Wills bends her knees then straightens them, and shoots her right leg up into the air until she catches her right toe with her right hand.

"You're still bending over before it comes all the way up," Jessica says.

Wills tries again.

"How's that?" she asks.

It looks just like her first attempt.

"Good," says Jessica.

"Rachel Brown!" Berry whispers urgently. "Come on and do it again."

Rachel goes back behind the clump of cheerleaders and throws her standing back, this time with Coach Pack spotting. Again, she gets good height and lands well.

Excited, Rachel claps her hands together and sings under her breath, "We are the girls from Greenup County that you've heard so much about . . ."

Over the tent's P.A. system, a UCA official announces that it's time for the first four teams competing tonight to warm up on the mats.

"Okay, girls," says Berry as the Greenup cheerleaders prepare to take their mat. "I want to see the partner stunts first."

"You may begin," the UCA voice intones.

"Go, go," says Berry.

The four flyers rise up on their bases' hands to perfect K-stands. In exquisite synchronicity, they pop down, then up to heel stretches. Beautiful. Wills's awkward stretch is nicely camouflaged when she's flanked by the other three flyers. The girls then spin down into their bases' hands.

"Okay, switch libs," says Berry.

The girls execute the four switch liberties precisely. No wobbles. Excellent.

"It's too good," Light mumbles anxiously, "I'm afraid the judges aren't gonna see the switch." Nothing he can do about it now.

"Now, tumbling. Go!" barks Berry.

Rachel Brown hits a standing handspring to a back tuck and sighs.

Rachel Wills and Linda Goble count to three, then run and turn their bounders in time with each other—run-run-run-run, round-off, whip back, back tuck. They land perfectly, three feet apart and at the exact same time. The two girls turn toward each other, give high tens. Linda hoots happily.

"Woo!"

Shiritta stumbles and falls at the end of her full-twist flip.

Rachel Brown tries a standing back without a spotter—the rest of the girls suddenly stop what they're doing and watch—and she lands it. Then she jumps up and yells, "Yeah! Omigod!"

As Rachel bounds over to Wills and gives her a big hug, Light pumps his fist in the air and bites his lower lip.

"You should have seen us yesterday," Light says to a UCA staff member. "We were rolling all over the floor."

"Okay, do the dance," Berry orders.

The girls assemble themselves in formation. Coach Peffer hits Play on the team's boom box. And the girls are off, thrusting and writhing and smiling, their curled ponytails bobbing all over the place. Then comes the part where the girls bend over and slap themselves like they're whipping a horse.

"HUAH! HUAH! HUAH! HUAH!"

Psyched, the cheerleaders high-step out of the tent and over to the theater, clapping and chanting.

"We are the girls from Greenup County . . ."

When the team stops outside the theater, Linda Goble dances by herself to the music booming inside. With her eyes closed, a big happy smile on her face, she wiggles in front of a space heater warming up the cold Disney driveway.

Jessica Garthee sees Linda dancing, and she runs over and hugs her.

Arm in arm, Linda and Jessica ask Berry to put some extra lipstick on them.

While Berry applies the makeup to the two girls, Sarah Dickison walks up to the coach and asks a question.

"Do you think we can win?" Sarah asks.

"I just want you to do what you can do," Berry says.

The team and all four of their coaches huddle up and say the Lord's Prayer together. There's then some discussion about what to yell "on three." Someone suggests "teamwork."

"Yeah, that's good."

" 'Teamwork' on three."

"One, two, three—TEAMWORK!"

"Y'all, rush the floor," hollers Light above the roar of the crowd. "Rush!"

Light peeks in at the arena full of fans waiting anxiously for the finals. The hordes of Greenup cheerleading friends and family are holding up their "Greenup County" signs all over the theater.

"Look at all those signs," says Light. "All those signs. All for you."

The girls crane to see. Once they catch a glimpse, their nervous energy grows.

"This is our last chance," says Amanda Kitchen.

"This is our last chance," Rachel Brown echoes.

"We gotta all smile big, guys," Wills says. "We gotta be like, 'Yeah! Yeah!' "

"We are not scared," says Shiritta.

"We are not scared," Linda Goble mumbles.

"AND NOW, LAST YEAR'S NATIONAL CHAMPIONS, AND WINNERS OF EIGHT VARSITY NATIONAL CHAMPION-SHIPS . . . GREENUP COUNTY HIGH SCHOOL!"

The Greenup girls attack the crowd, yelling, pumping their fists, demanding every bit of everyone's attention. Eventually, they settle into their opening formation.

The music starts, the girls take a step, and they all turn standing back tucks.

Rachel Brown puts her hands down when she lands.

Bounders come next. Wills, Linda, Amanda Kitchen, Jessica Newell, Kelena, Brooke—they all nail them. Amazing.

Berry, Light, and Pack jump out of their coaches' seats in the front row, yelling and shouting. Coach Peffer has left the theater. He can't watch.

The girls go into the group mount. Rachel Brown and Kelena ascend on either side of a raised and bent-over Wills. At the top of the mount, Rachel and Kelena brace themselves, each with one foot on Wills's back. Then, disaster. Rachel begins the next bit a beat early. She lifts her right foot off Wills's back and shifts her weight before her bases are ready. She slips through her bases' hands and almost hits the ground. Her bases keep hold of her and still manage to push her back up into position at the end of the sequence. Because of the near fall, however, Rachel is a hair late getting to that final pose.

The Greenup girls keep fighting. The K-stand–to–heel stretch sequence goes well, and when the team's chant calls for everyone in the audience to "hold up their signs and yell it loud," the entire theater rocks with the words, "GREENUP! COUNTY! GREENUP! COUNTY!"

The switch liberties also go well, but again, Rachel starts her dismount slightly ahead of the other flyers.

The crowd doesn't care. They hoot and holler and yell their approval of everything the Greenup girls do. During the dance, the hundreds of girls in attendance squeal with delight when the Greenup cheerleaders slap and grunt suggestively.

The team hits the final mount, yells, "YEAH!" and that's it.

Breathing hard, their heads spinning, the Greenup girls must now smile into an ESPN camera just offstage. A technician gives Shmorg a microphone, then backs away. A blindingly bright light shines on the squad huddled before the camera.

"Greenup County cheerleading has won so many national championships over the years," the technician says to Shmorg. "To what do you attribute your team's long-term success?"

Gulping air between words, Shmorg rambles on about the "strong tradition," the "great coaching," the "good tumbling instructors." When she stops talking, the ESPN techie mercifully turns off the light and relieves her of the microphone.

Rachel Brown had been holding it in. Now she cries.

Standing among the rest of the squad, in a dark driveway beside the theater, Wills consoles her.

"It's okay, it's okay," Wills says.

Wills didn't see Rachel's early dismounts, particularly the rather obvious one at the beginning of the routine when she almost fell to the floor. As it turns out, however, Rachel's not crying about that.

"I put my hands down on my standing," Rachel says through her tears.

"Don't worry," says Wills, rubbing Rachel's back. "No one saw that. You're fine."

Rachel continues to cry.

Some of Rachel's bases are now talking with the other girls about how Rachel almost fell during that opening mount sequence. Tension and worry spread through the team.

Light appears and gathers the girls together. Berry has chosen him to soothe their tender spirits right now, because she doesn't feel up for it. Not yet.

The girls are all very confused about what happened during their routine. Can they win the championship?

Rachel tries not to cry while Light talks.

"Everything between yesterday and today was like six million times better," he says. "The beginning tumbling was so good. My gosh. And the crowd loved you."

As the girls pelt Light with questions, he's compelled to add, "Rachel Brown's side had a slight bobble during that first mount, but they saved it and got it up. I'm not giving up. It depends on what everybody else does. You gotta just go on. It happens. You guys should be proud, 'cause whether or not you hit it, you really accomplished a lot tonight. That's what it's about."

"Whatever happens," Wills states loudly, trying to protect Rachel Brown from the inevitable onslaught of blame, "we tried our hardest. We're *all* winners."

Linda Goble has her arms folded tightly over her chest and she cranes her head down so she can chew her fingernails. Linda's horribly worried.

The Greenup cheerleaders walk together over to the warm-up tent to retrieve their sweatsuits.

"We are the girls from Greenup County that you hear so much about," Wills sings.

Rachel Brown sniffles, then joins in softly.

". . . and the band begins to P-L-A-Y . . ."

Back by the theater, Susan Ray says to Light, "It's the sort of thing that happens, and most squads let it fall, so I don't know."

Light's not so hopeful.

"If everybody else hits everything, we'll be lucky to get fifth," he says angrily. "Rachel basically freaked out because she didn't do her standing. She let it get the best of her."

Wearing their sweatsuits now, the Greenup cheerleaders file back into the theater to watch the rest of the teams perform.

On the way, Shmorg tells her teammates about how badly she did answering that question in front of the ESPN camera. "You guys, you don't understand," she says, close to tears. "It didn't make any sense. I'm really gonna cry when I see it on TV."

"No, no," Wills assures her. "You did fine. I thought you did fine."

A few other girls join in and compliment Shmorg on her poise.

"Great job!" a cluster of cheerleaders holler at the passing Greenup girls. "You were so awesome!"

The Greenup cheerleaders politely thank them.

Inside the theater, the girls sit down on the floor in front of the performance mat. For an hour, they stay there, watching team after team compete. Many of the other squads look good. Too good. Germantown looks good. Dunbar looks good. Calallen High School from Corpus Christi, Texas, looks good.

As they sit and watch all these teams perform, the Greenup cheerleaders become more and more certain that they're not going to win the 1998 national cheerleading championship. Wills refuses to crack. She's masking any emotion she may be feeling right now. Rachel Brown looks like a zombie—her face drawn, streaked with tears; her eyes wide, unfocused. Linda Goble, who looked lost at first, unsure what to think or feel, now has tears tumbling quietly down her cheeks, as she picks fretfully at the cuffs of her sweatsuit jacket.

The Greenup parents appear similarly stunned.

Kelena's mom is bitter. "It's all money," she says. "I mean, how many teams did Germantown bring down here from Memphis? Six? They had a junior high, a freshman, a JV, a varsity . . ." And for each team the school paid a hefty entry fee. "UCA *has* to give them the championship!"

Jessica Garthee's father dreads the return home. "Last year, when the varsity won," he says, "there were two, three hundred people in the school gym to support 'em and stuff. The JV got first runner-up and they didn't get nothin'. If these girls don't win, they'll probably lock 'em out of the gym. That's just how it works in Greenup."

Throughout the rest of the competition, Diana Brown, Rachel's mom, stands silently with her jaw clenched, holding a "Greenup County" sign up over her head with one hand, as if she's trying to raise it as high as she can.

The coaches gather together in the driveway outside the theater, all except Hank Light. He says he'd rather not miss any of the other performances and he doesn't want the other coaches to know how upset he is.

Randy Peffer's eyes are red and moist. He didn't see what happened, but he knows just the same.

Susan Ray puts an arm around him.

"Are you okay, Randy?" she asks.

Peffer nods.

Berry's got to get herself together before she can talk with her cheerleaders. Right now, she's too disappointed. Berry wanted her girls to leave Orlando happy, confident, and, most important, united. She's afraid now, afraid of what the girls will take home to Greenup from this year's national championship.

Before the awards ceremony, she gathers the squad together in the dark outside the theater and talks to them for the first time since their finals performance.

"I still love you, and I'm proud of the way you pulled together," Berry says. "For better or worse, you're a team. Remember that. For better or worse, you're a team."

During the trophy presentations, Jeff Webb, the founding father of UCA, delivers a wide-ranging speech about everything from the history of cheerleading to the history of ESPN to sportsmanship. He ends with the words, "Winning's not always being first. If we teach them that, we've got a big problem. Winning is about participating with dignity and courage."

* * *

Greenup took seventh place. Germantown won the championship, the Memphis school's first varsity crown. After the awards ceremony, as I said my final good-byes to the Greenup coaches and cheerleaders, Berry told me that Wills had written a poem for her teammates and had given each of them a copy shortly before the squad left the hotel to participate in the 1998 national cheerleading championship.

"The girls thought, of all the stuff you've got about them in that book of yours, you ought to have this poem," said Berry.

None of the girls wanted to part with her copy of the poem. So Wills read it aloud to me. It's called "Together We Can."

> *The time has come once again*
> *To show what we can do,*
> *To work together as a team,*
> *Not just as one or two.*
> *Together we can do anything that our hearts desire.*
> *You know we have done it even though we are tired.*
> *So let's look to one another for comfort and cheer.*
> *Let's lean on one another as we cry our tears.*
> *Because together we have a goal that we all have set.*
> *And that's to be the best team the judges have seen yet.*
> *So let's go out on that floor as a winning team.*
> *Let's do what we do best and make that crowd scream.*
> *Because together we can do it.*
> *Together we can.*
> *Together we can be the best team in the land.*

Epilogue

After the '98 finals, Rachel Brown locked herself in her Disney World hotel room and cried all day. Her older sister, Sara—who'd stayed home in Greenup—told Rachel by phone that word had already spread through the county that Rachel was to blame for the Musketeers' defeat.

When Rachel returned to Greenup, she dreaded showing her face at school. She could feel the other students watching her, talking about her. She also avoided her private gymnastics lessons—anything that reminded her of nationals.

As spring tryouts drew near, most of the girls on the 1997–98 Greenup High cheerleading team decided to hang up their skirts. Rachel Wills and Linda Goble—as well as Jessica Garthee, Brooke Meenach, Megan West, Shiritta Schaffer, Amanda Kitchen, Miranda Elliott, and Jessica Newell—chose not to go out for the following year's squad. Candace Adkins transferred back to Russell High, and the five senior cheerleaders—Jennifer Morgan (Shmorg), Jennifer Stuart (Stu), Kelena McClurg, Libby Barber, and Emma Hood—graduated. So a total of fifteen girls left the team.

Rachel Wills decided that she wanted time and energy to prepare for college, to see Jesse, and to generally enjoy her senior year. Wills has plenty to do without cheerleading, and she doesn't think she'll miss it "that much."

Shiritta Schaffer and Amanda Kitchen persuaded Linda Goble to join an all-star team over in Willowsburg, Ohio. The girls wanted to stay in high-end competitive cheerleading without having to answer to Candy Berry. But Linda quit that squad after only a few months of practice when she found herself in great pain every time she tumbled. The tendonitis in her knees had gotten too bad to work through.

Linda then got a job at McDonald's in an effort to keep herself busy and make the money she's always missed. Serving burgers and fries, however, was almost as bad as turning back tucks and whip-backs on bum knees. So after a month of work, she quit McDonald's, too. Going into her junior year at Greenup, knowing she'll probably spend most of her time at home with her mother, Linda doesn't know what to do with herself. Most likely, she says, the year will be "awful boring."

April Creech and her boyfriend, Greg, graduated from high school in early June. A short time later, April gave birth—seven weeks prematurely—to a little girl that she and Greg named Katelyn Melissa McKenzie, just as they'd planned back in January. Because she was born so early, Katelyn Melissa had to spend the first two weeks of her life in the hospital before she could come home to April's parents' house. Greg has also moved into the Creech home to be closer to April and little Katelyn.

April says that at first Greg was "sort of" disappointed that his first child was a girl, but now he's "just real happy about everything." As of late July, April and Greg still haven't made any concrete plans to attend college in the fall.

Shawnda Bates's college plans are also up in the air. Back in the spring, she and the rest of the University of Louisville's JV cheerleading team did not attend the NCA nationals in Daytona Beach as they'd planned. Last-minute money problems kept the JV from making the trip. That didn't bother Shawnda too much, however. In general, she had a great first year at U of L.

"She really liked it," Mrs. Bates says of her daughter and Louisville. "But we didn't like it. It was just too far away for us. So we've kind of talked her into staying here for a year."

Mr. and Mrs. Bates have convinced Shawnda to spend her sophomore year of college at little Morehead State University in Morehead, Kentucky. It's not as big a school, isn't situated in nearly as big a city, doesn't have as diverse a student body, and doesn't have the same high-end reputation. But it is much closer to Greenup County.

"She can stay so much closer and get basically the same education," says her mother. "At least for a year."

Candy Berry and Hank Light have also missed Shawnda and loyal, hardworking cheerleaders like her. But now, maybe, their wait is over.

Since the spring exodus of cheerleaders from the Greenup High varsity, Berry, Light, and the rest of the Greenup coaches have begun to rebuild the program with inexperienced young cheerleaders who are eager to learn and grow. Some of them remind Berry of Shawnda when she was a freshman.

"I was extremely disappointed at tryout time," Berry recalls. "I could not believe that these kids that I'd given my heart and soul—I mean to some of these girls, I was a surrogate mother, so it really was a slap in the face. You know, for me, all this isn't about winning. It's about the camaraderie . . .

"I thought about quitting myself. It was like I'd built a beautiful house and someone was comin' and defacin' it. But I'm not going to let it stand that way. Those kids that quit have thrown paint on this program. So now we're givin' it a whitewash. For me, it's personal."

Berry took only twelve girls onto the varsity after tryouts. Many of them couldn't do standing back tucks at first, but they worked hard and by the middle of the summer, they could all hit them. One member of the new Greenup varsity worked closely with those young girls, supporting them as they tried to turn their standings again and again: Rachel Brown.

"Rachel's really doing great," says Hank Light. "She's like the strongest one. She's our best flyer and she's almost got her full-twist flip. She's not let up one bit."

Rachel says she thought of quitting the Greenup High cheerleading team. She thought maybe she'd go out for a local all-star team or maybe she'd try a new sport all together, like soccer or softball.

"I was like, 'Thank you, God, I'm done. I'm never cheerin' again.' But I mean, I love cheerin'," Rachel says. "And I really want to extend my career to UK. And I wanted to do it for Candy."

Only three other girls from the previous year's team also chose to stick around—Sarah Dickison, Aubrey Warnock, and Krista Dowdy. (The other eight varsity members are freshmen.) With only twelve girls on the squad, they know they won't be able to compete in UCA's large varsity category, as they have before. But Rachel says that she and the other varsity veterans don't mind being stuck on a small squad, as long as they give themselves a chance to win. Of course, at this point, they don't have a choice. But a small varsity national championship is still a national championship.

"After nationals, I felt like I let myself down and I felt like I let everyone else down," Rachel says. "But I wasn't the only reason we lost. I was part of the reason. But I wasn't the only reason. I've got to stop beating myself up about it. I still won't watch it on ESPN, though. I watched it once, but I won't watch it again, ever again . . .

"This year is nothin' like last year. This year, we're not at each other's throats. Everybody's behind everybody like one hundred-ten percent. Everybody's developing so quickly. Everybody's improving so quickly. It's getting back to the old way, I think. We're just like the old cheerleaders. We're friendly. We're nice . . .

"Me and Aubrey and Sarah and Krista, we called the new girls over after tryouts and said, 'If we do hear you-all bickering or anything behind each other's backs, then you're gonna get punished. We're gonna tell Candy.' I mean, stuff still happens. Girls say stuff like, 'Oh, you saw my boyfriend at the mall and talked with him.' But last year, it was like, 'You *slept* with my boyfriend!'"

"Those girls that didn't come to tryouts," says Hank Light, "they thought, 'Well, we'll quit and that'll be the end of Greenup County cheerleading.' But Candy, she's kinda like, 'I'll show 'em.'

"It's almost like you can't go up anymore so you've got to fall all the way to the bottom before you work back up. The twelve we've got on the varsity are very strong—nine of them have their full-twist flips. We only had six last year. And we've got sixteen girls now on the JV. The sixth and seventh graders coming up have a lot of talent." Light pauses, thinking.

Since deciding to stay in Greenup last year, he seems prepared to choreograph Greenup routines on into the indefinite future. His local all-star coaching is going great—in the spring, his senior and youth squads both finished fifth at nationals while his junior squad took third—and Light realizes that he cares too much about the future of Greenup cheerleading to step aside.

"It's almost like you can see it coming again," Light continues, talking about Greenup's renewed cheerleading talent—he could just as easily be talking about his own renewed commitment to the program. "It makes me feel kinda old," he concludes.

"You want to work with the kids that want to do it," Candy Berry says. "It's really neat to have the excitement level back. And the pride is coming back to the squad. I'm not saying that last year's girls weren't proud, but they could be real catty. These girls, this year, they genuinely like each other. For me, it's kinda like gettin' some fertilizer at my roots. It's fun."

As the summer comes to a close, with September and the new school year right around the corner, some of the girls who quit are having second thoughts. If those girls come back to Greenup cheerleading, Berry could field a complete large varsity squad. But the coach doesn't think that would be fair to the girls who've worked through the summer, and she doesn't want a repeat of the problems from the year before. So Berry won't take any of the defectors back.

Asked if Berry might budge on this, whether she might take pity on the girls who quit last spring, Light does not hesitate.

"No," he says. "And I agree with her. They didn't want to put forth the effort. They didn't want to work through the summer. And they figured if they all went together, then Candy would take 'em back. It doesn't work that way."

Rachel Brown, meanwhile, sympathizes with her former teammates, but she doesn't miss them.

"They're really regretting that they quit, because there's not really anything for them to do now," she says. "I mean, cheerleading was their life."

Rachel says she'll always remember how awful it was to fall at the '98 nationals. But she points out that Shawnda Bates also had a bad fall at nationals during her sophomore year with the Musketeers, and that during her senior year, Shawnda led Greenup to its eighth national championship.

"Falling was a bad experience," Rachel says, "but I think it was good for me, made me stronger. Now, when I'm workin' on something, I just think I've got to get it better than last year. We have a great chance this year in small varsity. And hopefully, by next year, we'll have a full squad. Maybe next year. I'm lookin' forward to it."

Acknowledgments

I'd like to thank many people for their contributions to this project. Peyton McElroy, my wife, got me interested in cheerleading in the first place, and she has supported me emotionally and sometimes financially over the two years I worked on this book. J. Allen Williams, a good friend and the photographer at *The Leader* newspaper in Charlotte, North Carolina, spent many hours over many days in a hot, cramped darkroom, developing my negatives into the photographic prints that appear here. Wade Baker, John Deem, and Tucker Mitchell—good friends all, and my former coworkers at *The Leader*—all offered crucial advice and help after I left my job there and started work on this book. I'd like to thank Tucker Mitchell, *The Leader*'s editor, as well as Sis and Stan Kaplan, the paper's co-owners, for taking a chance on me and providing a wonderful place to write.

Marshall and Diana Craig, my parents-in-law, opened up their home to me during my two trips to Florida for the national cheerleading championships, and encouraged me along every step of this long book-writing process. Sally McElroy, my mom—and a great writer—never doubted that I could do this, and her belief in me has always been contagious. Christina Baker-Kline offered some early advice, including telling me what a book proposal was. Joanna Swayze took the author photograph. Aman Chaudhary counseled me on how to juggle seven characters. Alex Starr and Will Georgantas both read early drafts and loaned their insight. (A special thanks, by the way, to the other members of T.A.N.K. for no particular reason.)

I owe a great deal—much more than I can say here—to Denise Roy, who, through her faultless editing, made sure that this book became all it could be, and to John Hodgman, my agent—and often my therapist-slash-confessor—for shepherding me through all the chutes and ladders of the publishing world.

Finally, and most importantly, I'd like to thank everyone I met from Greenup County, Kentucky, especially, of course, the wonderful GCHS cheerleaders and their fantastic coaches. For over a year of their lives, Candy Berry, Hank Light, Susan Ray, Randy Peffer, Tom Pack, and all the Greenup cheerleaders and their parents let me follow them around with a camera, a notepad, and a tape recorder. And they always treated me like another member of their extended Greenup family. I'll never forget the compassionate, loving Greenup County community, where the people truly live by the oft-maligned notion that "it takes a village to raise a child."

Photo Listing